MAN, MYTH,
AND MAGIC

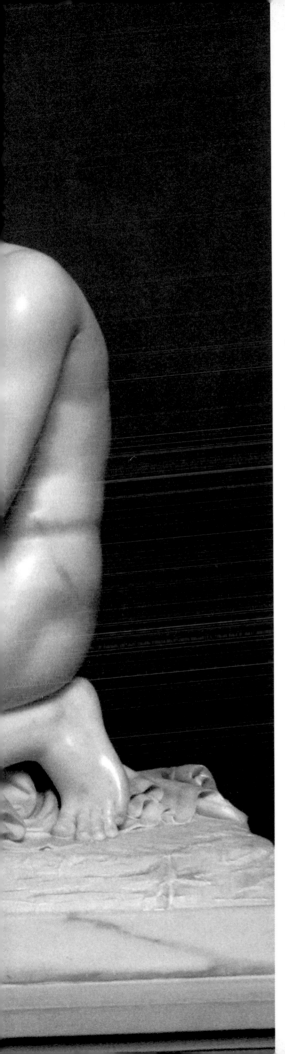

MAN, MYTH,
AND MAGIC

Animals and Animal Symbols in World Culture

Cavendish
Square

New York

Published in 2014 by Cavendish Square Publishing, LLC
303 Park Avenue South, Suite 1247, New York, NY 10010

Library of Congress Cataloging-in-Publication Data

Armstrong, Edward Allworthy.
  Animals and animal symbols in world culture / Rev. E.A. Armstrong.
    pages cm. — (Man, myth, and magic)
  ISBN 978-1-62712-575-8 (hardcover) ISBN 978-1-62712-576-5 (paperback) ISBN 978-1-62712-577-2 (ebook)
  1. Animals and civilization. 2. Animals—Symbolic aspects. 3. Animals—Mythology. 4. Animals—Folklore. I. Title.
  QL85.A76 2014
  590—dc23

                    2013037031

Editorial Director: Dean Miller
Editor: Fran Hatton
Art Director: Jeffrey Talbot
Designers: Jennifer Ryder-Talbot, Amy Greenan and Joseph Macri
Photo Researcher: Laurie Platt Winfrey, Carousel Research, Inc
Production Manager: Jennifer Ryder-Talbot
Production Editor: Andrew Coddington

Photo Credits: Cover photos by Raja Ravi Varma (1848–1906)/*Sri Shanmukaha Subramania Swami*/ C. Cunniah & co. Glass Merchants 248-249 Devaraja Mudaly Street Madras/*, Pieter Lastman (1583–1633)/*Jonah and the Whale*/Google Art Project/*, Utagawa Kuniyoshi, 1798–1861/Tenjiku Tokubei riding a giant toadn/*;- E. Michael Smith/cat EMS-96004-Rosecrucian Egyptian-Cat-Mummy/*, 1; Gunnar Bach Pedersen/Thorvaldsens Ganymedes/*, 2–3; Hieronymus Bosch/Bosch, Hieronymus - The Garden of Earthly Delights, central panel - Detail- Raven/*, 7; Wolfgang Sauber/Teotihuacán - Figur mit Federschilden/*, 5; Wolfgang Sauber/St.Jakob Kastelaz - Phantastische Lebewesen links 2/*, 9; Phó Nháy/Erawan/*, 11l; Claveyrolas Michel/Escorial 18/*, 11r; Pedro Berruguete/Birthofchristwithangelsberruguete/*, 13; Reinhardhauke/Kruft St. Dionysius und Sebastian 2212/*, 14; Konrad Witz/Konrad Witz - Fischzug Petri/*, 15; Jan van Eyck, Hubert van Eyck/Gand, san bavone, int., polittico dell'agnello mistico 03/sailko/Own work/*, 16–17; Hans Hillewaert/lonchophylla robusta (flight)/*, 18; Andreas Praefcke/Kwakiutl bear mask Museum Rietberg/Own work/*, 20; Gunawan Kartapranata/Garuda Brass Statue/*, 23; Vioncent Sellaer/Vincent Sellaer (circle) Leda und der Schwan/Dorotheum/*, 24–25; Wolfgang Sauber/Teotihuacán - Figur mit Federschilden/*, 26; MarcusObal/Madrid Bullfight/*, 30t; Leemage/UIG/Getty Images, 30b; George Groutas/Bull leaping, fresco from the Great Palace at Knossos, Crete, Heraklion Archaeological Museum/*, 33; E. Michael Smith/cat EMS-96004-Rosecrucian-Egyptian-Cat-Mummy/*, 35; Habib M'henni/Deux coqs II Neapolis/*, 37; Raimond Spekking/Der Hahn - Toni Stockheim (3318-20)/CC-BY-SA-3.0/*, 38; Published by James Wasserman/cow Hathor Mistress of the West/*, 39; Grace/Cows decorated for Diwali/*, 40; AlejandroLinaresGarcia/CoyoteHeadAnahuacalli/*, 41; Watanabe Shuseki/Cranes Watanabe Shuseki Hanging scroll color on silk/*, 42; Hedwig Storch/Kom Ombo, Sobek 0315/*, 43; AnemoneProjectors/Carrion Crow aka Corvus corone/*, 44; Andreas Praefcke/Ravensburg Gesellschaftskapelle Fenster 5 Wappen/*, 46; John Gould/Coccyzus Americanus by John Gould/*, 47; Utagawa Hiroshige/Utagawa Hiroshige - Cuckoo flying under a full moon - Google Art Project/*, 48; Jebulon/Herakles Cerberus Antonin Wagner Hofburg Vienna/*, 49; Reggaeman/Honjo Hachimangu 08/*, 51; Worcester Art Museum, Worcester, Massachusetts, USA/Pot-bellied Dog Figure, Mexico, State of Colima, 200 BC - 500 AD, ceramic, Pre-Columbian collection, Worcester Art Museum - IMG 7646/*, 52; Deror avi/Armon Knossos P1060073/*, 53; Gunnar Bach Pedersen/Thorvaldsens Ganymedes/*, 55; Campana Collection/Zeus Naucratis Painter Louvre E668/Bibi Saint-Pol/*, 56; Matteo Ianeselli/Trento-Cathedral of Saint Vigilius-relief of the Holy Roman Empire/CC-BY-SA-3.0 & GFDL/*, 57; Jan Kameníček/Easter eggs - straw decoration/* 59; Yann/Ganesh statue, Ahmedabad, India/*, 61; Buyenlarge/Getty Images, 62r; Joe Mabel/Seafair Indian Days Pow Wow 2010 - 052/*, 62l; IlSistemone/NaplesGalleryUmbertoIPesci/*, 63; Pieter Lastman - Jonah and the Whale - Google Art Project/*, 64; Infragmtion of New Orleans/Frog In Your Throat Box 1/*, 67t; Jastrow/Pygmy frog Louvre CA6022/*, 67b; Hans Grien/Wiedzmanamiotle p/*, 68; Francisco Goya/426px-GOYA - El aquelarre (Museo Lázaro Galdiano, Madrid, 1797-98)/Mirar abajo/*, 69; Hiart/Brahma on Hamsa, Tibet, 17th-18th century, gilt bronze and polychrome, HAA/*, 70; Wenceslas Hollar Digital Collection/Wenceslas Hollar - The hares and frogs 2/*, 73; SuperStock/Getty Images, 74; Tony Hisgett/Ferruginous Hawk (3863032876)/*, 75t; Dorothy Hardy/Loki and Svadilfari by Hardy/75b; Jastrow/South metope 30 Parthenon BM/*, 76t; JMW Turner/Joseph Mallord William Turner - Death on a pale horse - Google Art Project/*, 78–79; Pascal Radigue/Sagittaire naples/*, 80; Ji-Elle/Masque hyène Bwa-Musée barrois (3)/*, 81; Didier Descouens/Cerf-volant MHNT Dos/*, 83t; Paul Souders/Gettty Images, 83b; Thomas A. Flood/Swallowtail 05 06 07/*, 84–85; Siegfried Kramer/Getty Images, 86t; Barrett & MacKay/Getty Images, 86b; Wolfgang Sauber/Chichén Itzá - Tumba de Chac Mool 3 Jaguarkopf/*, 88l; DeAgostini/Getty Images, 88r; Charlie fong/Guardian lions outside Daci temple/*, 89; Xuan Che/Hochdorf bronze container, greek lion, detail/*, 90; Hugo van der Goes/Hugo van der Goes - The Fall of Man and The Lamentation - Google Art Project/*, 92; Arpingstone/Magpie arp/*, 93; Guardians of Day and Night, Han Dynasty/Robert Temple's The Genius of China/*, 95; David Tipling/Getty Images, 96; Bernard Gagnon/Mosaic of Byzantine Church of Petra 02/*, 97; Marie-Lan Nguyen/Tetradrachm Athens 450 reverse CdM Paris/CC-BY 2.5/*, 98; Raja Ravi Varma/Murugan by Raja Ravi Varma/*, 100; Google Art project/Pelican Feeding her Young - Google Art Project (6805760)/*, 102; 1927: sale of the collection of Dr Martin at Spink & Son Ltd/Aeneas Latium BM GR1927.12-12.1/*, 103; John Scofield/National Geographic/Getty Images, 104t; Andreas Praefcke/Sepik pig mask Berlin-Dahlem/*, 104b; George Catlin/Medicineman.Catlin/*, 105; Hieronymus Bosch/Bosch, Hieronymus - The Garden of Earthly Delights, central panel - Detail- Raven/*, 106; Keven Law/Flickr - law keven - Robin Redbreast - Lincoln Inn Fields Park - Holborn, London, England - Thursday December Thirteenth 2007/*, 107; Alex Spade/glasgow TGSA05045/*, 109; U.S. National Archives and Records Administration/Post card. Salmon leaping falls, Ketchikan, Alaska. - NARA - 297786/*, 110; Vassil/Cathédrale de Chartres 210209 07/111l; Rory Moore/Barcroft Media/Getty Images, 111b; Tim Graham/Getty Images, 112; Bengt Oberger/Sälskulptur Kvarnparken Nora Danderyd/*, 113; HTO/Namaroto spirits and the Rainbow Serpent Burlung/*, 114; AlejandroLinaresGarcia/DevMaskSerMAPDF/*, 115; A. Davey/Ethiopian Orthodox Religious Painting, Yeha, Ethiopia (3145483169)/Elitre/*, 116; Man vyi/Vèrrine églyise dé Saint Pièrre Jèrri 2/*, 118–119; Sailko/Ravenna, sant'apollinare in classe, mosaico (prima metà del VI secolo)/*, 120; Jebulon/Serpent Præter Vienne/*, 122; Thomas S. England/Time Life Pictures/Getty Images, 123; Utagawa Kuniyoshi/Warrior Minamoto Raiko and the Earth Spider LACMA M.2006.136.292a-c (1 of 2)/*, 125; sailko/Maiolica di casteldurante, piatto con perseo che libera andromeda, 1525-1530 circa/*, 126; Optimist on the run/Horn Dance, Blithfield Reservoir - 2006-09-11/CC-BY-SA-3.0 & GFDL-1.2/*, 127; Georg Schöbel/Georg Schöbel An Allegory of Destiny/Bonhams London/*, 128; Cygnis insignis/Frontispiece of Andersen's fairy tales (Robinson)/*, 129; Rolf Broberg/Televerket Gbg entremosaik/*, 131; FA2010/Leda mit dem Schwan Volkstedt KFM 08-105/*, 132; Durga/Durga Mahisasuramardini/*, 133; Bernard Gagnon/Dragon and Tiger Pagodas 04/*, 135; Petrusbarbygere/Tenjiku Tokubei riding a giant toadn/*, 135; Wolfgang Sauber/St.Zeno Reichenhall - Grab Skelett 3/*, 137; Wolfgang Sauber/Aquileia Basilica - Ausgrabungen Mosaik 10/*, 138; Reinhardhauke/Chartres Saint-Aignan804/*, 139; Andreas Praefcke/Tlingit amulet Museum Rietberg RNA 309/*, 140; Ralph Hammann/StPierreJeuneP244/*, 141; Eugenio Hansen, OFS/Igreja Santa Clara de Assis em Porto Alegre, Brasil5/*, 143; Carl Larsson/Carl Larsson - Little Red Riding Hood 1881/Bukowskis/*, 144–145; Andrei Stroe/RO B Carol Park green woodpecker/*, 147; George Pickow/Three Lions/Hulton Archive/Getty Images, 149; Universal Images Group/Getty Images, 150; Arnstein Rønning/Jynx torquilla (Ramsoy)/*, 152–153.   * Wikimedia Commons.

Cavendish Square would like to acknowledge the outstanding work, research, writing, and professionalism of Man, Myth, and Magic's original Editor-in-Chief Richard Cavendish, Executive Editor Brian Innes, Editorial Advisory Board Members and Consultants C.A. Burland, Glyn Daniel, E.R Dodds, Mircea Eliade, William Sargent, John Symonds, RJ. Zwi Werblowsky, and R.C. Zaechner, as well as the numerous authors, consultants, and contributors that shaped the original Man, Myth, and Magic that served as the basis and model for these new books.

Printed in the United States of America

Contents

A Reader's Guide to *Man, Myth, and Magic: Animals and Animal Symbols in World Culture*

Wherever cultures have grown up, there are common universal themes running through their religions, storytelling, and mythologies. Throughout our existence, humans have shared and competed with the birds, beasts, and insects of the world for land and resources. Through domestication animals have provided sustenance yet, increasingly, they are embraced as bastions of friendship and loyalty.

Human beings have always been fascinated by other living creatures on the planet. In an all-embracing urge to perceive magic in everything, we have included animals in our belief systems and folktales, and this has provided us with a precious mythological heritage. Animals throughout history have been part of wonderful stories—they can represent gods, bring you luck, protect you and your ancestors, and portend of coming events—and have shared in mankind's life and progress in every way.

Man, Myth, and Magic: Animals and Animal Symbols in World Culture is a work derived from a set of volumes with two decades of bestselling and award-winning history. It is a comprehensive guide to more than three millennia of history in which humans interact with the creatures of the earth, air, and water. This book in the *Man, Myth, and Magic* series provides an excellent perspective on mankind's complicated relationship with all creatures from the tiniest insects to the largest beasts.

Objectives of *Man, Myth, and Magic*

The guiding principle of the *Man, Myth, and Magic* series takes the stance of unbiased exploration. It shows the myriad ways in which different cultures have questioned and explained the mysterious nature of the world around them, and will lead teachers and students toward a broader understanding of both their own and other people's beliefs and customs.

> *The magical mimicry by which a man turns himself into a beast may also be the magic by which he transforms himself into a god.*

The Text

Within *Man, Myth, and Magic: Animals and Animal Symbols in World Culture*, expert international contributors have created articles—arranged alphabetically—the depth of coverage of which varies from major pieces of up to 10,000 words to concise, glossary-type definitive entries. From the alligator to the wryneck, key animals from every continent are profiled, with articles focusing on how different cultures viewed the creatures with which they shared land. Many of these they considered omens of things to come, some as gods and devils, comparing the beast that some societies viewed as good and virtuous and others as evil incarnate. In addition to the numerous articles on specific animals, there are also entries on the role of animals in Christian art, how shamans took the form and power of animals in key ceremonies, and how some cults worshipped and interacted with snakes. While there are generalized discussions of animals, birds, fish, and insects that serve as excellent overviews on the topic, most notable animals also have their own entries.

The work is highly illustrated, and subjects of major interest are provided with individual bibliographies of further reading on the subject at the end of each article.

What made it possible to create this work was the fact that the last century has seen a powerful revival of interest in these subjects at both the scholarly and the popular levels. The revival of scholarly interest has created the modern study of comparative religion and modern anthropology, both of which concern the investigation of so-called indigenous or first peoples and their beliefs and rituals (which have been found far more complex that originally believed). There has been a flourishing revival of interest in ancient civilizations, mythology, magic, and alternative paths to truth. This interest has shown no sign of diminishing in this century; on the contrary, it has grown stronger and has

The Garden of Earthly Delights (detail), Hieronymus Bosch (c. 1450–1516)

explored new pathways. At the same time, scholarly study and commentary regarding the subjects of this series have continued and much new light is thrown on some of our topics. The present edition of *Man, Myth, and Magic* takes account of both these developments. Articles have been updated to cover fresh discoveries and new theories since they first appeared.

With all this, *Man, Myth, and Magic* is not intended to convert you to or from any belief or set of beliefs and attitudes. The purpose of the articles is not to persuade or justify, but to describe what people have believed and trace the consequences of those beliefs in action. The editorial attitude is one of sympathetic neutrality. It is for the reader to decide where truth and value may lie. We hope that there is as much interest, pleasure, and satisfaction in reading these pages as all those involved took in creating them.

Illustrations

Since much of what we know about myth, folklore, and religion has been passed down over the centuries by word of mouth and recorded only comparatively recently, visual images are often the most powerful and vivid links we have with the past. The wealth of illustrations in *Man, Myth, and Magic: Animals and Animal Symbols in World Culture* in World Culture is invaluable, not only because of the diversity of sources, but also because of the superb quality of color reproduction. Dogs, cats, bears, wolves, eagles, and so many other beasts are all recorded here in infinite variety, including tomb and wall paintings, as well as artifacts in metal, pottery, and wood. Examples of animal artwork from all over the world are represented.

Back Matter

Near the end of the book is a glossary that defines words that are most likely new to students, edifying their comprehension of the material. The A–Z index provides immediate access to any specific item sought by the reader. This reference tool distinguishes the nature of the entry in terms of a main entry, supplementary subject entries, and illustrations.

Skill Development for Students

The books of the *Man, Myth, and Magic* series can be

consulted as the basic text for a subject or as a source of enrichment for students. It can act as a reference for a simple reading or writing assignment, or as the inspiration for a major research or term paper. The additional reading suggested at the end of many entries is a useful resource for students looking to further their studies on a specific topic. *Man, Myth, and Magic* offers an opportunity for students that is extremely valuable; twenty volumes that are both multi-disciplinary and inter-disciplinary; a wealth of fine illustrations; a research source well-suited to a variety of age levels that will provoke interest and encourage speculation in both teachers and students.

Scope

In addition to being a major asset to social studies teaching, the book provides students from a wide range of disciplines with a stimulating, accessible, and beautifully illustrated reference work.

The *Man, Myth, and Magic* series lends itself very easily to a multi-disciplinary approach to study. In *Man, Myth, and Magic: Animals and Animal Symbols in World Culture*, literature students will be interested in the symbolism and various anthropomorphic attributes of animals in myths, legends, and written works of prose and poetry from cultures all over the world. Students of art and architecture, whether as scholars or creators, will find the marvelous illustrations depicting the subjects particularly helpful; because the views and lore surrounding every animal varies from culture to culture, their representation significantly changes. Readers of history will see the importance that animals, both wild and domesticated, have played in civilizations on every continent: the eagle as a glorious symbol for so many armies and nations; the various cattle kept for survival, whether on a ranch in North or South America or, more sacredly, in an Indian village; the mighty tiger as the ancestor creature in myths from various Asian cultures.

When they delve into the book, students can fully appreciate how inextricable other living creatures are from mankind's story of survival, adventure, and pursuit of connecting with the divine. In addition to its relevance to study areas already mentioned, this volume provides strong background reference in anthropology, philosophy, and comparative religion.

Conceptual Themes

As students become involved in the work, they will gradually become sensitive to the major concepts emerging from research. They can begin to understand the roles that members of the animal kingdom have played, and still play, in the development of major themes and motifs underlying much of the world's belief systems. For example, the con-cept of how humans interact with animals—pragmatically, companionably, religiously—exists in all major civilizations and faiths, giving importance to when certain animals arrive on the scene or cross a person's path. The theme of animals as spirit guides or even hosts of deceased loved ones is prevalent in a great many myths, sometimes giving the characters an enlightened view, sometimes leading them to perdition.

Animals appear in fables, and as a result artwork, throughout the known world, with the moral-teaching creatures of Aesop, lucky crickets of Chinese lore, and the ubiquitous serpent of deception and evil. What similarities and differences exist in the concept of animals and their symbols among all cultures? Any personality trait a human has can be transferred onto a lowly insect or majestic quadruped. Migration, hibernation, and hatching eggs all suggest renewal and rebirth intrinsically bound to the greater forces of nature. In legends and in fact, these mute beasts aid us in explaining what we cannot control, within us and around us. Knowing this legacy can make for a keener understanding of the effects we have on those with whom we share our environment. All these areas are challenging ways for more advanced students to use both this individual volume and the other title selections in this set.

Alligator

Indian tribes of the tropical Americas have many gods in the form of alligators, native to those regions. In North America the Choctaws venerated the alligator and would not kill it; the Chickasaws devoted a major ceremonial dance to it; in the southern United States, alligator teeth were used to help a baby's teething, to cure snakebite, and to keep witches away; an old North Carolina superstition says that alligator gall helps sore eyes, and that the fat can cure cancer.

Animals

Africa is still sometimes troubled by outbreaks of the leopard men, who disguise themselves as claws, and part of whose body they eat. In India sacred cows wander the streets unmolested. Long ago an Egyptian mob murdered a Roman for killing a cat. The early Christians were accused of worshipping a donkey. Norse berserkers in the skins of bears or wolves were feared for their crazed ferocity in battle. Fionn mac Cumhaill, a great Irish hero of legend, could turn himself into a deer or a dog at will. His two faithful hounds were the sons of his sister, who had been magically transformed into a bitch. The Minotaur of ancient fable was a man with a bull's head who lurked in the Cretan labyrinth, offspring of Queen Pasiphae and a bull that came from the sea.

In folklore there are talking animals and animals which marry human husbands or wives. Some animals are said to sense the presence of ghosts. It is lucky to see a white horse. A black cat can be either a good luck charm or an omen of evil. The Devil frequently appeared in animal form to witches, who were also accused of suckling familiar spirits in animal shape. In South

Creature mixed out of man, bird, and fish, wearing a Phrygian cap

America sorcerers have jaguar familiars and African witches are believed to ride on hyenas at night.

Behind all this is an outlook which does not clearly differentiate between men, animals, spirits, and gods. Primitive man does not draw our accustomed distinction between human beings and animals at all. They share the world with him, on his own level, and he admires them, fears them, respects them, in a way which is

foreign to us in cities or in our long-domesticated countryside. They are creatures of the same kind as himself, though differently shaped and in some ways better equipped. So they can turn into men, and vice versa. If a man wants to acquire the speed of the deer, the strength of the bear, the cunning of the fox, the night sight of the cat, he imitates the animal. He dresses up in its skin, mimics its cries, dances out its movements. He ruts as a stag, as a leopard he sinks his fangs into flesh. By imagining himself as an animal, he can induce a state of mind in which he feels he has become it.

The line between man and animal is easily crossed, man being an animal himself. So is the line between animals and the spirit world, because in primitive thought everything that exists has a spirit as well as a body. Men have souls which survive death. So do animals, and like the ghosts of men their spirits may be good or evil. The gods, like the animals, have powers which surpass those of men. A god may be seen in an animal which shares some quality with him. The magical mimicry by which a man turns himself into a beast may also be the magic by which he transforms himself into a god.

Man-Wallaby

Totemism is a type of social organization in which groups of people associate themselves closely with an animal (or a plant or an object) as wolf-men, bear-men, or whatever it may be. They use the totem as a badge of identification, much as a feudal knight was identifiable by the emblems on his armour, and the system may have originated from resemblances between a man and a particular animal. But it was evidently not merely a matter of saying of someone, 'he looks or behaves like a bear' but of implying, 'he is a bear'. In Australia, 'even today, when an aborigine says he is, for example, wallaby, he means what he says. He and the wallaby species are "one flesh". . .' Except in special circumstances he does not kill or eat a wallaby, and he and his group are responsible for carrying out the rituals which ensure a plentiful supply of wallabies for everyone else. This is because he and the wallabies are descended from the same ancestor, a hero of long ago who was both a man and a wallaby.

Sacred Cat and Crocodile

Whether totemism lies behind the animal cults of Egypt is disputed, as there is no certain evidence of any totemic stage in Egyptian history, but the importance of animals in Egyptian religion astonished Greek, Roman, and early Christian authors and embarrasses Egyptologists. Most, though not all, of the Egyptian gods were portrayed as animals, or as human beings with animals' heads, or in other mixed human and animal shapes. The sky goddess Hathor could be shown as a cow or as a woman's face with the horns and ears of a cow. The goddess Taurt, 'the great one', had the head of a hippo, the back and tail of a crocodile, a woman's breasts, and the claws of a lioness.

Some animals were sacred in particular localities: the people of Bubastis in the Nile delta, home of the cat goddess Bast, would never kill a cat. In the Faiyum, where Sebek the crocodile god was worshipped, there was a pool of sacred crocodiles. Huge cemeteries have been discovered containing the mummified bodies of dogs, cats, crocodiles, falcons, and bulls. Recent excavations at Sakkara have found traces of a cemetery of mummified baboons, who were given names and apparently venerated as gods.

All cats were divine in Bubastis but in other instances only one animal of a species embodied a god. At Memphis the Apis bull lived in splendour as 'the herald of Ptah', a god who was not himself represented as a bull but always in human form. When the bull died, a calf with the special markings which identified it as the successor had to be found. For forty days the calf was attended by women, who at intervals displayed their sexual organs to him. Then he was brought by boat to Memphis, his cabin lined with gold.

The prominence of animals in Egyptian religion was not merely a tolerated survival from more primitive times. Their cults aroused genuine devotion and were costly of time, trouble, and money. In the late 4th century BC, the funeral of one Apis bull was so expensive that the funds set aside for it were used up and it was necessary to borrow an extra amount equivalent to $40,000 in modern money. Henri Frankfort has commented that 'there is something altogether peculiar about the meaning which animals possessed for the Egyptians. Elsewhere, in Africa or North America, for example, it seems that either the terror of animal strength or the strong bond, the mutual dependence of man and beast (in the case of cattle cults, for instance), explains animal worship. But in Egypt the animal as such, irrespective of its specific nature, seems to possess religious significance; and the significance was so great that even the mature spec-

The Front Rank of Nature

To primitive man nature is his living larder, to which—especially at the lowest stages of culture—he has to repair directly in order to gather, cook, and eat when hungry. The road from the wilderness to the savage's belly and consequently to his mind is very short, and for him the world is an indiscriminate background against which there stand out the useful, primarily the edible, species of animals or plants . . . A sentiment of social nature is built round each species, a sentiment which naturally finds its expression in folklore, belief, and ritual.

. . . the same type of impulse which makes small children delight in birds, take a keen interest in animals, and shrink from reptiles, places animals in the front rank of nature for primitive man. By their general affinity with man—they move, utter sounds, manifest emotions, have bodies and faces like him—and by their superior power—the birds fly in the open, the fishes swim under water, reptiles renew their skins and their life and can disappear in the earth—by all this the animal, the intermediate link between man and nature, often his superior in strength, agility, and cunning, usually his indispensable quarry, assumes an exceptional place in the savage's view of the world.

Bronislaw Malinowski

The majesty of animals has always inspired man, in all cultures.

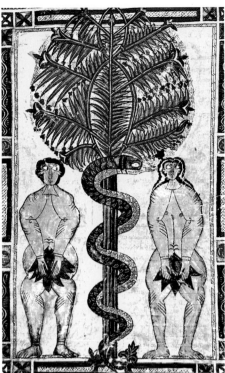

The snake is forever linked to the Fall of Man.

ulation of later times rarely dispensed with animal forms in plastic or literary images referring to the gods.'

Animal and God

One theory of animal gods is that the god is first worshipped as an animal and later acquires human characteristics. His human nature grows gradually more important until he becomes fully human, though the animal often retains a connection with him and is sacred to him. But in many cases no such evolutionary pattern can be demonstrated; for Egyptian deities, for instance, or for Celtic gods. For example, the Celtic god Cernunnos, 'the horned one', who was closely connected with the stag and also with a peculiar ram-horned serpent, appears as part stag or serpent and part human in both the earliest and the latest representations of him.

Magic, Science, and Religion

Again, although the symbolism of an animal and its connection with a particular god naturally tend to be based on its own most striking charac-teristics, the symbolism and the origin of the connection are not always clear. Wolves, as fierce predators, are associated with war gods, like the Roman Mars or the Teutonic Tyr, but also with the Greek god Apollo, who was not a war god. The inquisitive and chatter-ing baboon seems well suited to Thoth, the Egyptian god of intelligent inquiry who invented speech. But whether this is the correct explanation and whether, if it is, the ape was connected with the god because it embodied part of his nature or, the other way around, its connection with him for some other reason influenced later ideas of his nature, is uncertain.

Immortal Snake

One beast which has taken a firm grip on the human imagination is the serpent. It was thought to have found the secret of avoiding death, because it sloughs its old skin and appears rejuvenated in a new one, and so in myths, like the Babylonian epic of Gilgamesh, it steals the immortality which the gods had meant for man. This may have been its original role in the story of Adam and Eve. The Eden story later gave the serpent its connection with the Devil, a connection assisted by the snake's phallic shape which linked it with lust, and also with fertility.

Some snakes were seen to live in holes in the ground or to appear from crannies in rocks, which connected them with the earth, with fertili-ty again, and with the underworld and the dead. In Mesopotamia, the Sumerian and Babylonian goddesses of the underworld were identified as serpents. In Greece, sacred snakes were one of the marks of an under-ground god or spirit; honey-cakes were offered to them. The Fijian god Ndengei is a giant snake who lives in a cave and when he moves the earth quakes.

The cult of the house snake, offered milk and breadcrumbs, and addressed as 'master of the house', is not entirely dead in Greece even yet. There are many shrines of snake gods in India and python gods were common in Africa until this century. The plumed serpent appears in ancient Mexican religions and snakes, especially rattlesnakes, in the myths and rituals of North American Indians.

Bull and Boar

The bull is another important beast in the history of religions, impressive for its strength, its pawing hoof and fierce charge, and its formidable sexual powers. Enlil, the great Babylonian god of fertility and storm, was addressed as 'overpowering ox, exalted overpowering ox'. Gods of thunder, storm, and rain, which fertilizes the earth, were often pictured as bulls. In India the Aryan sky god Dyaus, the red bull who smiles through the clouds, 'bellows downward', which evidently means 'thunders', and later several Hindu gods have bull forms. Mithras, the Persian god of light whose cult rivalled Christianity in the early centuries AD, was connected with the bull. In Crete, the spectacular and lethal sport of bull leaping was a religious ritual. The first Minos, or bull king of Crete, was begotten by Zeus in the form of a bull, and the bull was also connected with the noise and destruction of earthquakes. The horns of the bull, as of other horned animals like the stag, were widely regarded as peculiarly sacred and powerful.

Celtic mythology abounds with sacred boars, magic pigs which reappear whole after being killed and eaten, and fearsome supernatural boars which are hunted by heroes. In Welsh legend, King Arthur and his men hunted Twrch Trwyth, a king who had been turned into a boar, for treasures—a comb and shears—which he carried between his ears. Pork was the meat on which chieftains feasted in northern Europe, as did warriors after death in Valhalla, and the Celts buried pigs' bones and joints of pork with the dead. But elsewhere, as among Jews and Mohammedans, pig's flesh has been considered 'unclean' and forbidden.

Sun Chariot

The horse-taming nomads of southern Russia, who spread into northern Europe, Greece, the Middle East, and India in successive waves over a period of hundreds of years after c. 2000 BC, connected their swift and powerful stallions with the sun, and imagined the sun crossing the sky in a horse-drawn chariot. The Celtic war god was closely associated with horses, perhaps because of the use of horse chariots in battle, and in France and Britain the Celtic goddess Epona, 'divine horse', was popular with the cavalrymen of Roman armies. Freyr, the fertility god of the Vikings, was linked with both the boar and the horse.

The Animal in Man

The sacred horses of Freyr illustrate one of the reasons for sacrificing an animal to a god, which is simply to give him a good meal. In the 10th century AD a Christian king of Norway, Olaf Tryggvasoh, went to Thrandheim and seized a stallion which was about to be sacrificed 'for Freyr to eat'. But there is another and deeper motive, for the slaughtered animal may be believed to embody the god and the worshipper

In magic an animal is used for its own inherent occult qualities or because of its links with supernatural forces.

who eats its flesh eats the god—if only temporarily and partially—he becomes the god.

In the savagely orgiastic worship of Dionysus the lines between animal, man, and god were spectacularly crossed. Dionysus was described as 'mad' and 'raving'. His worshippers, who were predominantly women, went out to the mountainside dressed in the skins of fawns, some of them

suckling young animals at the breast, baby deer perhaps, or wolf cubs. As they sang and danced they felt a strange excitement. They began to run, finding in themselves superhuman energy and strength, until in frenzy they hunted down animals, wild or tame, and tore them to pieces alive, gnawing at the raw flesh. They behaved, in fact, as if they were animals in animals' skins, suckling their young or tearing their prey. In the release of fierce animal passion their god possessed them. It seems that the animals they hunted embodied Dionysus himself so that, torn and devoured, he became one with his worshippers.

The same principle, that by imitating an animal and giving free rein to the animal elements in his nature, a man can reach a state of frenzied intoxication which breaks the chains that bind him to his human condition and makes him a sharer in the divine, appears in many other parts of the world. It lies behind the pagan European customs of dancing in animal costumes and masks which the Church tried to suppress and which have been preserved or revived in existing folk ceremonies. The *Liber Poenitentialis* of Theodore, Archbishop of Canterbury in the seventh century, forbids people to dress up as stags or bulls or to put on the heads of beasts on the first day of January.

All Creatures Great and Small

Medieval Christianity had its animal symbolism too. The lamb and the fish stood for Christ, the dove for the Holy Ghost, the sheep for the righteous, the goats for the wicked. Animals were carved in profusion in churches, not only as pleasing decorations but because God made them all and in each of them could be seen something of the mind of the Creator. The man, the lion, the ox, and the eagle, which stood for the authors of the four gospels, also showed that the complete Christian must be a man for reason, a lion for courage, an ox for sacrifice, and an eagle for contemplation.

In the bestiaries fables of animals taken from pagan authors were given Christian interpretations, like the fable of the male elephant, an animal in its sagacity so totally uninterested in sex that he would mate only when the female gave him the aphrodisiac mandrake plant to eat. The elephants were interpreted as Adam and Eve in Eden, the mandrake as the forbidden fruit. Not until Eve gave Adam the fruit did he know sexual desire and the result was the expulsion from paradise. In the habits of the elephant God had painted the lesson of the Fall for men to see and understand.

Astrology and Magic

The European magical tradition, also seeing the universe as a logical design and interested in the underlying links connecting it together, makes much play with animal symbolism. Most of the signs of the zodiac are named for animals and traditional popular astrological lore is interestingly totemistic, in the sense that people are supposed to have the characteristics of their zodiac animal. Those born under Capricorn, the Goat, are told that they butt away obstacles and leap over difficulties like goats bounding from crag to crag. Those born under Leo, the Lion, are commanding and powerful like the king of beasts, and have fine heads of hair (manes), and large handwriting (paw marks).

In magic an animal is used for its own inherent occult qualities or because of its links with supernatural forces. 'If we would call any evil Spirit to the Circle', says the Fourth Book, added to Agrippa's Occult Philosophy but probably not written by him, 'it first behoveth us to consider and to know his nature, to which of the planets it agreeth . . .' It describes the

forms in which the spirits may show themselves, including a she-goat, camel, and dove for spirits connected with Venus, a horse or a stag for those of Mars, a cow or a goose for spirits of the moon. Other magical textbooks give similar descriptions, following the tradition which goes back to ancient Mesopotamia that demons appear in animal forms.

The purpose is to help the magician to understand the nature of the spirit or demon which he attempts to summon up and master. Its animal symbols and characteristics contribute to a vivid mental picture of it, on which the magician concentrates during the ceremony in which it is conjured up. Behind this is the old magical belief that to imagine supernatural power, in its appropriate animal or other form, is to be possessed by it, to become it, to control it.

FURTHER READING: There is much interesting material in J. G. Frazer, The Golden Bough *(St. Martin's Press, 1980) though not all Frazer's conclusions are now accepted; also in Mircea Eliade,* Patterns in Comparative Religion *(New American Library). For the Celts see Anne Ross,* Pagan Celtic Britain *(Columbia University Press, 1967); for Egypt, Henri Frankfort,* Ancient Egyptian Religion *(Harper Row, 1961); for the bull, J. R. Conrad,* The Horn and the Sword *(Greenwood, 1973).*

Animals in Christian Art

Animals are frequently represented in Christian art from its simple beginnings in the Roman world to its great flowering in the medieval period. Whether incised on sarcophagi, decorating the interiors of churches, carved into pew ends and misericords in choirs, appearing in Renaissance paintings or found in the pages of psalters

Angels and animals in attendance at *The Birth of Christ* by Pedro Berruguete (1450–1504)

and devotional books, a wide range of animals, including birds, fish, and insects have a special place in Christian art. Animals are used as symbols, in depictions of biblical narrative and in the stories of the saints. They are integral to the religious landscape.

The largest earliest surviving group of Christian paintings is found in the catacombs in Rome—the hidden art of a semisecret group who decorated the burial places of their dead in traditional style. The paintings depict animals such as the peacock, an ancient symbol of immortality whose flesh was believed not to decay, and a lamb being carried on the shoulders of a shepherd, which could be viewed as a popular pastoral scene, but which to the initiated would clearly indicate Christ the Good Shepherd rescuing the lost. The image of the Good Shepherd was important in early Christian art and also appears in a third century fresco in the remains of a house church in Dura Europas in Syria. The symbol of the fish is also found in the catacombs —the Greek word for fish—'icthus'—being an acronym for 'Jesus Christ Son of God Saviour'. The cult of Christianity spread along the

Roman imperial highways and remarkable evidence of its early existence on the outposts of the empire has been uncovered in a villa in southeastern England, one room of which was used for Christian worship as shown by the fourth-century frescoes decorating its walls in which is a bird, possibly a dove signifying the Holy Spirit.

After Christianity received official approval under the Emperor Constantine in 313, worship ceased to be a covert matter and could be publicly conducted in large buildings whose interiors offered rich scope for mosaic and fresco decoration. Lambs became one of the most commonly used animal symbols in Christian art, although their significance shifted and developed over time. The beautiful fifth century mausoleum of Galla Placidia in Ravenna has an exquisitely decorated mosaic interior that includes a pastoral scene of Christ the shepherd, seated, surrounded by six white lambs, secure and poised, in a rich meadow landscape. One of the animals is standing close to Christ and lifting its head toward his outstretched hand. The sixth century Basilica of Sant'Apollinare in Classe, near Ravenna, continues the theme with lambs representing both the twelve apostles and faithful Christians. Again the lambs are shown as stately, dignified creatures. The lamb also symbolizes the person of Christ, the last Passover or Pascal sacrifice, as shown in the fifteenth century Flemish altarpiece by Jan Van Eyck. Sant'Apollinare includes other important animal symbolism relating to three of the four Gospel writers where the animals are all shown with wings: the lion (St. Mark) reflecting the kingship and resurrection of Christ; the eagle (St. John) representing the divinity of Christ as the eagle soars upward to the heavens; the ox (St. Luke) standing for the sacrifice and the priesthood of Christ (St. Matthew is represented by a winged man).

The ox, with its attributes of forbearance and physical strength, and the ass or donkey—a humble beast of burden and the antithesis of temporal power and kingship—are typically shown in depictions of the nativity, standing behind or to one side of the Holy Family. The ass also occurs in the beginning of the passion narrative as Christ enters Jerusalem.

As the Germanic tribes moved into areas previously under Roman control they brought with them a very different decorative style where the natural world provided the inspiration for lively, often fantastic, representations of birds and animals. In Britain, this Germanic influence fused with the Celtic art of the Irish monastic tradition, resulting in a unique and distinctive expression that was important for later medieval religious art across Europe. The seventh century *Book of Durrow*, containing the four gospels, is illustrated with intertwined animals in highly complex patterns, as is the Lindisfarne Gospels produced around 715 where birds and dogs feature in the interlaced designs. The carved stone crosses that can be found in Britain reflect the use of lively animal motif. The Anglo-Saxons were renowned throughout Europe as expert metal workers and brought their skills to bear on the sacred as well as the secular. The Alfred Jewel is a tiny masterpiece some 2 ½ inches long, with a cloisonné enamel depiction of a saint mounted in filigree gold that terminates in the head of a dragonlike beast and is believed to be

The eternal Christian image of a dove. Here, in stained glass at the church of St. Dionysius and St. Sebastian in Kruft, Germany.

From the miracle of 500 loaves and fishes to making the apostles fishers of men, the figure of Christ is forever associated with fish imagery.

the head of a pointer used in reading a Gospel book. The inscription indicates that it was commissioned by King Alfred in the ninth century. Animal forms are also seen in the external decoration of the twelfth century church at Kilpeck on the English/Welsh border, where snakes swallowing their tails writhe their way up the pillars of a door above which are mythical creatures including the manticore and basilik (qv.). Elsewhere on the building are more prosaic representations of other animals such as a hare, a hound, a ram, and a lion.

As Christianity became integrated within society so the canon of the Bible and the lives of the saints provided material for artists. Particular saints came to be associated with animals. For example, St. Jerome (born c. 341) spent a number of years as a hermit in the Syrian desert before returning to his life as a scholar. His life was to provide rich inspiration for a great number of European artists who included animals with particular religious significance in their paintings. Amongst these are deer—the stag, the adult male red deer, was symbolic of

the human soul in its quest for salvation—and the goldfinch, popularly associated with the passion of Christ and often used in religious art; the red feathers on its head were believed to originate from its attempts to remove thorns from the brow of Christ. More than any other animal, Jerome is linked with the lion that came to his monastery in order that his wounded paw could be treated and healed. Jerome is often shown hard at work on his books while the lion lies contentedly at his feet like an over-large domestic cat.

At a more intimate level, a very large number of devotional and other books were produced in the later medieval period, including calendars and books of canon law, as aids to Christian piety. These include depictions of animals in both a domestic and natural context and give scope for a wide variety of illustration and detail not possible in a single work such as a painting. One such is the early fourteenth century Luttrell Psalter, where the birds and beasts that would have been familiar to everyone in most of Europe at the time are minutely observed, whether the yoked oxen drawing the plough, the hen with her chicks, or the snail in motion with horns fully extended. *The Bedford Book of Hours*, a lavishly illustrated manuscript produced in the fifteenth century to celebrate the marriage of Anne of Burgundy to the Duke of Bedford, includes a depiction of the animals leaving the ark (an improbable looking craft) with a woman, presumably Noah's wife, helpfully loading the birds onto the gangplank. These manuscripts also gave the opportunity to express wry humour. The highly important decretals of Pope Gregory IX, a key source for church law, include in one version made in France at the end of the thirteenth century a wide range of marginal illustration among which is a large rabbit sitting composedly on a stool with one leg crossed over the other, a man being threatened by a giant snail which he is trying to repel with a slingshot, and a group of geese hanging a fox, no doubt for crimes against poultry.

The central panel from the Jan van Eyck painting, *Adoration of the Mystic Lamb*, portraying numerous pilgrims showing their devotion to the Lamb of God. Some consider the work the first great oil painting, and it influenced subsequent works for centuries.

Ass

Often a symbol of stupidity, and sometimes of lust; in Christian symbolism it stands for humble patience and courage: some classical writers accused the Jews and the early Christians of worshipping as an idol.

Barnacle Goose

For centuries the Irish ate the barnacle goose during Lent, convinced that it was a species of fish; its then unknown breeding habits and association with the sea prompted mythical explanations of its origins; it was variously thought to hatch from shellfish, from barnacle-covered driftwood, or from a fruit like a melon.

Bat

The bat is an animal with leatherlike wings and hideous appearance, a creature of the shadows. One species, the vampire bat, is a notorious drinker of blood. The bat's physical characteristics and its apparently supernatural ability to hunt its prey in total darkness have been largely responsible for the frightening reputation it has acquired over the ages as a creature of occult power.

The bat has taken on some of the significance of both the bird (symbol of the soul) and the demon (dweller in darkness), and has been represented in folklore as witch and familiar, ghost and devil, and occasionally as a tribal god.

Shakespeare refers to the bat as an ingredient in the hellbrew of the weird sisters in Macbeth.

Eye of newt and toe of frog,
Wool of bat and tongue of dog.

The Chinese, taking a kindlier view of the creature, maintain that the bat flies head downward because of the weight of its brains. Aesop ascribed its night-flying habits to attempts at evading its creditors. But in most parts of the world the bat is a mysterious

The bat inspires feelings of fear and apprehension.

and terrifying creature of the night, a death symbol to the Irish, a ghost to the natives of British Columbia, and an embodiment of the dead among Ivory Coast natives. In Europe, Asia, and America the sudden entry of a bat into a house foreshadows the death of the occupant. In China, however, the bat symbolizes a long and successful life.

It was an established principle in medieval times that the Devil often assumed the shape of a bat and, because of this, Sicilian peasants even today burn bats alive or nail them with wings outstretched to their doors.

Macabre Burdens

Evil spirits in the shape of bats were believed to enter the bodies of human beings, from which they could only be evicted by skilled exorcists. Nigerian witch doctors, who are particularly adept at this art, skillfully extract bats and frogs from the mouths of patients who happen to be afflicted in this particular way. In some parts of the Southern United States, evil spirits are conjured out of human beings into the bodies of bats, which then obligingly flit away into the darkness with their macabre burdens.

In the *Remaines* of Denis Granville, published by the Surtees Society, there is an anecdote describing how a Frenchman, suffering from melancholia, was attended by a physician, a surgeon, and a priest who brought with them a bat in a bag. While the priest prayed, the surgeon made a small incision in the sick man's side, and at the same time the physician suddenly released the bat, which began to flutter about the room. Convinced that the evil spirit had now left his body, the patient made an instant recovery.

La Voisin, the abortioner and sorceress of seventeenth century France, made use of bats' blood in the Black Mass. Something often found in gruesome rites of this nature was the body of a bat that had been drowned in blood, since this served as an agent for the release of psychic energy. And bats' blood was often an ingredient of witches' flying ointment, because it was supposed to give them the bat's ability to fly successfully at night.

Because it was magically powerful itself, the bat often served as a protective charm or amulet against the powers of evil, and as a luck bringer. Among the Hessians in Germany it was an accepted belief that the heart of a bat attached to a gambler's arm by a red thread guaranteed him success at cards. In the Austrian Tyrol the fortunate possessor of a bat's left eye could make himself completely invisible to others at will.

A Few Drops of Blood

The bat became not only the totem animal of the men of an aboriginal tribe in New South Wales but also their sex symbol. A similar association of ideas led amorous Central European girls to entice their reluctant lovers into their arms by the discreet addition of a few drops of bats' blood to the loved one's beer.

Bats have occasionally been honoured with the status of gods, the supreme deity of some of the Indians of the American Pacific coast being Chamalkan the bat. The mighty bat gods of Samoa invariably took the lead whenever the tribes marched off to war. In Europe, according to an old legend, a bat decided to join the war between the animals and birds but, being uncertain as to where its real interest lay, fought on both sides.

In the legends of a number of North American Indian tribes, the bat is given the unexpected role of hero and chivalrous champion of mankind in distress. This happier and positively virtuous aspect of the bat's character is seen in the modern American cult figure, Batman.

Voodoo Drugs

In the folklore of the countryside, bats flitting about the fields at dusk indicate fine weather. Bats were long held responsible for stealing bacon from farmhouse chimneys, and this curious bacon theme recurs in the custom, not yet quite extinct in the English countryside, in which boys, upon sighting a bat, chant:

Bat, bat, get under my hat
And I'll give you a slice of bacon.

Women, on the other hand, have always been extremely reluctant to let bats approach their heads, due to the superstition that bats are irresistibly attracted to the hair. Once entangled, they can only be released by a pair of scissors wielded by a man.

The study of electronics has shown that the mysterious ability of the bat to find its way in complete darkness without hitting any obstacles is due to a supersonic detection device not unlike radar. Nevertheless, despite every scientific effort to rationalize the bat, its image as a symbol of the Devil remains unshaken.

The traditional function of the bat in contemporary magic has been further emphasized by the edict of the New York City Council of 1962 outlawing the sale of Voodoo drugs. Bats' blood was included in the list of prohibited items, with prayer candles inscribed 'death unto my enemy', lovers' oil, and grave dust.

Bear

Human views of the bear have always been awash with misconceptions, even in areas where bears were common. Paramount among the fallacies is the idea that bear cubs are born as shapeless lumps of flesh, and that the mother bear actually moulds them into shape by licking them. This belief was held by most ancient writers and was widespread in medieval Europe. The painter Titian used as his personal signature a picture of a she-bear shaping her young. Shakespeare compares a man's lack of character to 'an unlick'd bear-whelp that carries no impression like the dam.'

The belief still exists in many rural areas of Europe and America. It is understandable because bear cubs are ridiculously tiny at birth, and mother bears (like most animal mothers) do lick their young. So an observer, standing at a safe distance from the she-bear, would see a tiny lump of flesh, half buried in maternal fur, being licked. The fallacy has given the language the useful metaphor 'licked into shape'. There are plenty of other homely superstitions about bears. In the sixteenth century bear grease was a cure for baldness, and a preventative against blight in your garden, if you rubbed it on the garden tools. Englishmen then also believed that one ride on a bear's back would immunize a child against whooping cough. And an old cure for fits involved taking fur from a live bear's belly, boiling it in aqua vitae (alcohol) and applying it to the soles of the feet.

In more recent belief, current still in parts of rural America, a bear's tooth was used as a teething implement for babies, to give their teeth the strength of the bear, and sometimes as an adult's charm against toothache. Bear grease may still be used to cure aches and pains (and in fact the massage will do some good), while sleeping on a bearskin has been said to cure backache.

Like other animals, bears figure in supernatural legends. Bear ghosts walk through some tales of the American South, and Worcester Cathedral in Britain was apparently haunted by a bear in the seventeenth century. But accounts of apparitional bears are not nearly so numerous as those of dogs,

cats, and horses. It is in the realm of mythology and ancient religion that the bear comes into his own.

It may seem odd that such a large and potentially fierce animal as the bear should be generally loved as the cuddly Teddy Bear. Desmond Morris, the British zoologist, suggests that this affection is due to the bear's round, plump, furry appearance and its ability to stand on two legs like a human being. Among the bear-worshipping Ainu of Japan, bear cubs were reared at a woman's breast until the time came to send them away to the spirit home in a ritual strangling ceremony.

Helpers and Healers

Naturally, bears are important in the myths of North American Indians. In a way the bear was the Indian's greatest competitor, for it is as omnivorous as man. Bears ate the salmon caught by Pacific Northwest tribes, the buffalo meat stored by Plains tribes, the maize grown by tribes in the southwest and, sometimes, members of the tribes. Indian myths and customs show a great respect for the creature.

Northern Indians killed bears for food but always apologized to the dead animal for the indignity, for it was thought to possess great supernatural powers, even to be a god disguised. So the bear's head and hide would be ceremonially laid out, and care would be taken with the bones (so that the bear would not be crippled in the spirit world). To some tribes, including branches of the Apache, bears were so powerful that they were not only never killed but were literally untouchable, alive or dead. In Indian myths bears often function as 'tutelary figures' or spirit helpers of the heroes. A bear acts as a healer in the myths of such widely diverse tribes as the Sioux, the Chippewa, and the Pueblos, and the shamans or medicine men of these tribes often dress as bears to take on their healing powers. The Kootenay Indians in the

Canadian Rockies believed in a group of bear gods who could be prayed to for help. The Plains Cree, Iroquois, Cherokee and others hold 'bear dances' in which they imitate bear movements and pray to the bear spirits. And Labrador Inuit believe a shaman is visited during his ecstatic initiation ceremony by the Great Spirit in the form of a polar bear.

The legend of the Bear Woman is fairly common among North American Indians, and among other primitives, too. Usually it involves a tribesman who marries a strange woman with special magical powers, and who finds that she is a bear able to take human form. Most of the tales end unhappily: the husband is perhaps unfaithful and the woman reverts to bearishness, kills him and wreaks havoc on the tribe. Or else (as in similar tales of men who marry mermaids, elves, and other immortals) she tires of humanity and returns to the forest or the spirit world, leaving her mourning husband behind.

The Bear's Son

A related class of legends tell of an alliance between a woman and a male bear. In most cases the woman produces a son, who grows up to be a semidivine hero with perhaps some vestige of bearishness (like the bear's ears in

Kwakiutl bear mask, Museum Rietberg

the Chinese version of the tale). Such tales can be found all through Europe, as in German and Croatian legend, as well as in Asian and North American Indian lore. At least two of the world's great legendary heroes are connected with bears and closely resemble the Bear-Son heroic prototype.

The first of them is the English hero Beowulf. His name seems to mean bear—'bee-wolf', translatable as 'honey-eater'. His name probably connects him with the older Bear-Son tales; and his exploits, including a descent to the underworld and his final battle with the dragon, run parallel to the basic pattern of the Bear-Son stories.

The other legendary character with possible bear connections is the Greek hero Odysseus. Recent scholarly detective work has connected the Odysseus legend with the Bear-Son stories and also with ancient bear-worshipping cults. The Odyssey refers to the family of Odysseus as the 'house of Arceisios,' which name is a variant of a Greek adjective meaning 'bearish' or 'ursine'. A very old Greek myth, credited by some authorities as belonging to the Odyssean canon, makes Arceisios the child of a union between a man and a she-bear. And Arceisios was Odysseus' grandfather.

The Great Bear

Apparently the Bear-Son legends and other myths involving the bear have their roots in the widespread ancient worship of the bear. The earliest religious expression that we know of in human history took the form of bear worship. Neanderthal men, some 100,000 years ago, carefully placed the skulls of bears on what seem to have been holy altars. The skulls were those of giant cave bears which, though vegetarian, were fierce competitors for the Alpine caves where the skulls were

found. They were fierce and imposing enough, it seems, to be elevated into gods by the men who killed them. And it is possible that the killing and the reverential disposing of the skull had in it elements of ritual sacrifice, the sacrifice not to the god but of the god, returning him to his spirit home.

The pattern recurs in later cults of the bear. The Greeks told of a bear-goddess named Callisto, who was transformed by Zeus into the constellation called the Great Bear. But behind this pretty story lay a darker fact: the cult of Zeus Lycaeus, which some authorities connect with were-wolfism and others with bear worship,

> *Again, if the Ainu kill a wild bear, its body is brought into the village to be eaten but also to be worshipped during the eating, with offerings, songs, and prayers.*

but which definitely involved human sacrifice. Lycaon himself, in legend, was the father of Callisto; and the cult grew out of his sacrifice of a boy (in most versions, his bearish grandson Arcas) to Zeus. Callisto herself came to be closely associated with the virginal goddess and huntress Artemis. There are accounts of a bear cult from Brauron in Attica that centred on the worship of Artemis in bear form. But here only traces of ritual sacrifice remain in the mock-sacrificial presentation of young girls, dressed bearlike in brown robes, as initiates. The Great Bear is a powerful god in the mythologies of a group of peoples including the Lithuanians, Lapps, Esthonians and Finns, and some nomadic tribes across the north of Russia. In these religions, as in those of some North American Indians, the shaman or priest identified himself with the bear god.

The Hairy Ainu

Many of these shamanistic religions are still alive in odd corners of the world, still with their elements of bear worship, as among the Ainu of Japan. The Ainu are themselves something of a curiosity: they are not Japanese by race but rather have fair skins and blue eyes and are exceptionally hairy. It has been suggested that their culture is at least 10,000 years old. Their religion is dominated by a fire goddess and by the ritual worship of the bear.

In Ainu tradition, when a black bear cub was caught in the mountains, he was brought to the village with all the ceremony due to a visiting god. He was nursed at a woman's breast and when he grew larger he would be caged, but still tended with care until the time came to 'send him away' to his spirit home. The sending away ceremony could be cruel, but ended quickly with a killing arrow and a ritual strangling. The dead bear's head and hide would then be arranged so that he could 'take part' in the feast held in his honour, a feast in which the main course was the bear's flesh.

Again, if the Ainu kill a wild bear, its body is brought into the village to be eaten but also to be worshipped during the eating, with offerings, songs, and prayers. The sacrifice of the young bear has largely died out among modern Ainu, though the worship of the bear god still flourishes.

The Bear's Rebirth

We do not have to look entirely to obscure primitive religions for modern remnants of ancient bear worship. There are many survivals in western countries, such as the bear festival that has long formed a part of springtime celebrations in parts of southern France. In these rites a man dressed as a bear emerges from a symbolic cave, terrorizes the town and performs a mock abduction of a woman. Other communities in western Europe and in Slav countries have parallel ceremonies which include the enactment of a bear figure emerging from its winter's sleep.

Bear worship and the tales of bear heroes tend to have this common link: that the bear's 'dormancy', or hibernation, has a powerful and timeless symbolic meaning, closely connected to one of the most fundamental patterns of all mythology. The bear's emergence from its winter's sleep is a symbolic rebirth, which parallels the death and resurrection of the hero-god in so many of the world's fertility religions. The bear's continuing presence in festivals of spring when crops are 'reborn', and in folklore and religious belief generally, testifies to the importance the animal has had through all of the ages of mythology.

FURTHER READING: Joseph Campbell. The Masks of God: Primitive Mythology. *(Viking Press, 1968); Rhys Carpenter.* Folk Tale, Fiction and Saga in the Homeric Epics. *(University of California Press, 1974).*

Beaver

In the lore of the American Northwest, the beaver is the trickster companion of the porcupine. He is also revered as a spirit who brought light to an earth condemned to darkness because Snoqalm the moon god kept the sun in a box. But when the spider wove a rope that succeeded in linking the earth with the sky, Beaver climbed up and stole the sun, which he then placed on high. In the 18th and 19th centuries the beaver was the symbol of Canada, a result of the trapping of the animals for their fur which opened up unexplored territories for human habitation.

Bee

The bee is a universal symbol of industry. According to Egyptian myth, bees originated from the tears of Ra the sun god; in the Breton tradition they are believed to have sprung from those of Christ on the Cross. In both Europe and the United States it is still customary for people to tell the bees whenever a death occurs in the family—without this communication it's believed that the bees will stop making honey and even desert the hive. The bee is the symbol of the Hindu gods Indra, Krishna, and Vishnu, who were known as the nectar-born or Madhava.

Birds

According to one Egyptian myth the god Khoum made the cosmic egg from the mud of the Nile. According to another, the sun was the egg of 'the great cackler', a goose. About 600 BC the Cretan writer Epimenides mentioned the world-egg and this concept spread to Greece.

There are other myths in which supernatural persons or beings emerged from eggs: for example, the Peruvian tradition that the orders of society came from eggs of different metals, golden for the chiefs, silver for the nobles, copper for the common people. Hawaii is said to have emerged from the sea when a deity descended and laid an egg. The number of such myths and the huge area over which they have been recorded indicates that before written history began, man was so impressed by the remarkable powers of birds that he associated them with supernatural events, including the creation of the universe.

Right up to our own time eggs have aroused amazement and awe, for the process by which what looks like a large rounded pebble produces a living creature is worthy of wonder.

The creation myths in which the nest-building of birds is involved show that this procedure intrigued mankind and inspection of nests may have influenced man's first attempts at basketwork and pottery. An amphibious creature, often a bird, is said to have brought the earth into being by fetching up mud from the water. This myth is found in India, is widespread in northern Asia and occurs in similar form in North America, to suggest that it spread across the Bering Strait. Among the Chippewa Indians the story was that various mammals tried to bring up mud but only the diver bird succeeded. Iroquois myth speaks of the tribal ancestress descending from the sky and amphibious creatures bringing up mud to make an island on which she could live. The Mandan Indians believed that two pigeons flew back and forth across the water until a blade of grass appeared and dry land followed, a tale vaguely reminiscent of the story of Noah's Ark.

The Beat of Heavenly Wings
Of all flying creatures birds are the most conspicuous and impressive. As some soar into the heavens until they disappear from sight, they were regarded as having a close relationship to the sky powers, the sun and the heavenly bodies, the weather powers and the gods dwelling on high. These powers might be thought of as appearing in bird form, or it might be believed that a man could get in touch with them by transforming himself, using magical means, into bird form.

In those regions where there are pronounced seasonal changes, there is an obvious correlation between increasing temperature, day length and the path of the sun, on the one hand, and the growth of vegetation and the breeding of animals on the other. As a result, the sun and those creatures believed to be closely associated with it were viewed with particular awe.

Brass statue of Garuda in Javanese art, National Museum of Indonesia, Jakarta

The eagle's soaring flight, mounting in a huge spiral, gave it solar affinities. Zeus, the supreme Greek god, was said to have appeared as an eagle and also as a swan, another large, powerful and high-flying bird which has retained importance in mankind's beliefs to the present day.

Other large birds, such as vultures, became linked with this complex of ideas and imagination fashioned gigantic winged creatures controlling or causing clouds, wind, thunder, and lightning. The Simurgh of the Persians had wings like an immense rain-bearing cloud, while the Indian

Garuda, with the head and wings of an eagle and the body and legs of a man, typified the wind. In the account of the Roc in the Arabian Nights which swoops into the Valley of Snakes to retrieve lumps of meat to which diamonds adhere (and are thus secured by crafty men) the magico-religious

bird has become a storybook character, but originally the great bird gripping a snake represented the victory of the beneficent fertility-bringing powers over the evil forces of drought and sterility.

As a bird so naturally became the symbol of higher power, winged creatures became associated with gods and other sacred figures in various ways, sometimes as vehicles of humanized representations. Zeus in later Greek art rides an eagle, Aphrodite is borne by a goose, and Apollo is conveyed in a swan-drawn chariot. Asian divinities are commonly portrayed mounted on large birds. Skanda, the Indo-Chinese warrior god, rides a peacock; the Hindu god of love, Kama, rides a parrot, a bird with erotic associations.

Messengers of the gods are often winged. Mercury has diminutive symbolical wings attached to his heels and in Christian art angels have birds' wings. Evil powers and emissaries may also be winged but in the West they are sometimes associated with darkness by being equipped with bats' wings. In Christian art the Holy Spirit is commonly depicted as a dove because of the reference in the story of Christ's baptism: 'And when Jesus was baptized, he went up immediately from the water, and behold the heavens were opened and he saw the Spirit of God descending like a dove' (Matthew, chapter 3).

If the heavenly powers may visit men in the likeness of birds, men can also visit the gods by pretending to be birds. This belief finds its fullest expression among those Siberian tribes in which the shaman in trance utters bird calls and flaps his arms like wings.

Leda and the Swan — the painting depicts the Greek myth in which Zeus, in the form of a swan, comes to Leda and seduces her.

It is widely believed that the soul may depart from the body, either temporarily during life or permanently after death, in the form of a bird. This notion is not a thing of the past, nor is it confined to peoples in a low state of culture. It still persists, or did until recently, around the coasts of the British Isles where it is said that seagulls are the souls of drowned seamen. There are various related beliefs. In ancient Mesopotamia the dead were described as existing in the form of birds in the underworld; among the Bantu in Africa there is a belief that the spirit of a murdered man haunts his killer as a bird, and in Germany ravens were thought to be damned souls or the steeds on which witches rode.

The Language of Birds

Apart from man, birds are the most vocal of all animals and as a group far surpass him in variety of utterance. Their calls and songs constitute a language of signals, limited but efficient. A very widespread belief, common in folktales, is that in certain circumstances men can understand the speech of birds or other animals, or that birds can understand human language. Folklore tells of occasional persons born with this gift but more often it is acquired by some device such as eating snake's flesh or magical herbs. In Iceland a hawk's tongue was carried under the tongue of the person seeking this power.

The concepts of the bird which brings news, for example in the Flood myths, and the bird which brings intelligible vocal messages are sometimes linked. Odin had two ravens which roved around the world to pry into events and gather news. They returned to perch on his shoulders and whisper what they had learned into his ear. In folktales, overhearing the conversation of birds sometimes provides the hero with valuable clues. In the Scottish ballad *The Twa Corbies* a person 'walking all alone' overhears the corbies (crows) discussing their grisly feast on the body of a dead knight. The 'Bird of Truth' motif is also widely known. The theme is that a bird reveals important information, for example, the identity of a traitor.

Connected with these ideas is the

Figure with feathered shields, National Museum of Anthropology, Teotihuacán

MAN, MYTH, AND MAGIC

belief that birds may serve as oracles or guides, as in augury. The belief lives on in the Shropshire superstition that to see a magpie going widdershins (to the left) is unlucky, and in the tradition in the Faroes that a girl can foretell where her future husband will come from by throwing stones at a crow and observing in which direction it flies. The Masai believe that if a grey woodpecker is heard on the right it is a good omen, but if heard on the left it betokens evil, while if heard behind a traveler it indicates that he will have a favourable reception.

In some places in the United States a bird entering a house is auspicious, unless it is a white bird, in which case it is a portent of death, for pure white birds are so unusual as to be considered uncanny. The calls of birds with sinister associations, such as owls, tend to be feared. On the other hand, in most of Europe the first calls of the cuckoo are welcomed as heralding spring.

Birds, being regarded as messengers of higher powers or as possessors of secret knowledge, were said to have led people to the site on which to found a new city. Similarly a bird might indicate to a saint the location for a hermitage or monastery. The diver was supposed to be a guide to the otherworld. According to legends, obliging birds have helped individuals in various ways, from feeding children to rescuing them from the sea, bringing food to prophets and saints, or carrying away poisoned food.

The Bringers of Spring

The annual appearances and disappearances of birds have long aroused mystification. Their return in spring inspired rejoicing, and linked some birds, especially larger species such as the goose and crane, with the sun. Apparently such birds were thought of not merely as heralding spring but, in a practical sense as emissaries of the

gods, as bringing it. They were sometimes greeted with ceremonies. Siberian tribes honoured the arriving geese ritually by preparing an artificial nest, and on the island of Rhodes the swallow was welcomed with a song. The disappearance of birds in the autumn aroused speculation and disquiet. It was said of some birds that they visited the land of the dead.

Red Beak and Yellow Eye

The courtship and other social displays of birds are often conspicuous and sometimes spectacular, especially when the birds concerned are adorned with brilliantly coloured plumes or perform in groups. Primitive peoples assumed, on seeing a number of birds engaged in a social performance, such as cranes, the blackcock and the cock of the rock, that they were enacting a magical ceremony. Regarding birds as wiser than themselves in some respects, they copied them, believing that such dances ushered in the fertility of spring or brought rain. The Hopi of the southwestern United States perform an eagle rain dance and the Taruhumare Indians of Mexico imitate turkeys in their rain-making ceremony. In the Alpine Schuhplattler dance the male dancers wear blackcock feathers in their hats and gambol in opposing pairs as blackcock do at the lek, or courting arena. It is probable that the dance arose in imitation of the birds. In ancient Crete there was a crane dance, as there is in modern Japan, and in Yugoslavia on Shrove Tuesday boys perform a fertility dance, imitating a cock.

The folklore of many birds has been determined or influenced by their colouring. Red being the colour of fire, lightning and blood, birds with conspicuous red markings are sometimes connected with one or more of these. The cock crossbill's red crown and its twisted bill inspired the legend that the bird acquired these characteristics

through its efforts to remove the nails from Christ's Cross. And the American robin's red breast comes, says a tale, from Christ's blood when the bird pulled thorns from his Crown.

In antiquity the colour yellow was associated with jaundice and consequently also with its cure, and it was supposed that if a patient fixed his gaze on the large, staring yellow eye of the stone curlew the disease would be transferred to the bird. Black birds, such as crows, have often been connected with the Devil or witchcraft as black has commonly been associated with evil magic and wickedness.

Comparatively few birds are pure white, although albinos occur in some species. Being exceptional, they are regarded as uncanny and can awaken fear. Pied birds were viewed with disquiet, because people could not decide whether they were good or evil. The folklore of these birds, such as the magpie and the pied wagtail, reflects this ambivalent reaction. The exception to this attitude was the oyster catcher which was regarded as benevolent. Although pied, this bird appears to be white when it is in the air, and in the Hebrides it was thought to look, in flight, like a white cross. This distinction was said to have been bestowed upon the oyster catcher because it concealed Christ from his enemies by piling seaweed over him.

The Hoopoe's Crown

Folktales provide explanations for the unaccountable physical or behavioural peculiarities of animals. Tales of the type, 'How the . . . got its . . .', are found all over the world. They are probably told to entertain rather than explain. For example, an Arabic tale explains that the swallow acquired its forked tail when the serpent of evil took a bite out of it.

The hoopoe's crest, a striking physical characteristic, was linked with the rays of the sun and in folktales the hoopoe appears as a solar bird. Birds' crests were used as symbols of royalty and the hoopoe, because of its distinguishing mark, also became linked with legends about kings. Both associations are found in an Arab legend about Solomon, which explains how the crest was given to the hoopoe. When Solomon was traveling on a magic carpet, hoopoes sheltered him from the sun. Solomon offered to reward them but they foolishly asked to be given golden crowns. When they were persecuted for the gold, the hoopoes implored Solomon to have pity on them so he changed their crowns to feathered crests. The gold-crest, peacock and crested lark are other species with ornamental crowns or crests associated with royalty.

When birds are not known to breed in an area where they are usually found, stories are told to explain the absence of nests. The fable that the barnacle goose is hatched from shellfish could not have persisted for centuries had not the breeding grounds of the birds in the Arctic long remained unknown. Similarly when a bird's shape seems inadequate to account for its behaviour odd explanations are concocted. Because the quail, which is a skulking bird when seen in its nesting habitat, seemed incapable of sustained flight over the sea, the belief arose that it rode on the back of the crane. The osprey's ability to catch fish by plunging into the water seemed extraordinary, and it was supposed that this bird of prey had the power to fascinate fish.

FURTHER READING: E. A. Armstrong. The Folklore of Birds. (Dover, 1969). E. Ingersol. Birds in Legend, Fable and Folklore. (Gale, 1968); W. Harter. Birds: In Fact and Legend. (Sterling, 1979).

Boar

The power and fury of the 'sovereign beast' have given the wild boar a wealth of symbolism, from Iceland to India, and a vast and tenacious body of folklore and legend. The ancient words of the Boar's Head Carol recall the traditional festivities of Christmas and its pagan predecessor, the winter feast of Yule.

A boar is a sovereign beast
And acceptable in every feast;
So might this Lord be to most
  and least;
Nowell, nowelle.
This boar's head we bring with song
In worship of him that thus sprang
Out of a virgin to redress all wrong;
Nowell, nowelle.

From antiquity to the Middle Ages and later, the boar was first of all a symbol of the fertility of the Earth. In Germany when the corn waved, it was once said, 'The Boar is rushing through the corn' and children were warned, 'Don't go through the corn, there's a boar in there.' The last sheaf at harvest (sometimes called 'the Sow') was saved, and from it was made a loaf in the form of a boar; this was placed on the Yule table until the end of the festive season. It was then kept until the spring sowing, when part would be eaten, and part mixed with the seed-corn to ensure a healthy crop. A comparison may be drawn with the Scandinavian Yule custom of drinking and eating to a good agricultural year and to peace.

The idea of sacrifice in the dead of winter to the fertility deities was not far off, though there is little direct evidence on this point. But the boar was the sacred animal of the fertility god Freyr in Scandinavian mythology. Snorri's Edda tells how Freyr rode to Balder's funeral behind the boar Gollinborsti (golden bristles), also known as 'the one with terrible tusks'. Another boar mentioned in the Eddic literature (the source books of Scandinavian mythology) is Saehrimnir, the boar which was killed and eaten afresh every day by the heroes in Valhalla.

Fertility and Death

The boar was thus also connected in the mythology of many peoples with the symbolism of death and the dead. In Northern Europe and Scandinavia the boar, representing the souls of the departed, was believed to run on the storm clouds as part of Odin's wild hunt. Here we can recognize the curious tension between fertility and destruction that was characteristic of many early mythologies. The Roman historian Tacitus said that the Aestii (a tribe in northeastern Germany) 'worship the Mother of the gods. They wear, as emblem of this cult, the masks of boars, which stand them instead of armour or human protection and ensure the safety of the worshipper . . .', which suggests this ambivalence. The dual, life and death, aspect of the mother goddess and related fertility deities is well known.

The wearing of armour, especially helmets, shaped in the form of a boar's head or ornamented with boar's tusks, is attested at least as far back as Mycenean Greece. The position of the boar in Greek mythology, and its connection with the gods, is illustrated by such episodes as that of the Calydonian boar hunt in the *Iliad* (book 10). Among European archeological finds of recent years was the boar's head helmet found at Sutton Hoo in Suffolk in 1939. The object of this ornamentation was probably magical. The boar symbol was also emblazoned on shields and standards even in pre-Christian Europe, and the use of the boar emblem (sanglier) in European heraldry is to be traced back to this source. The most famous wearer of this device was the English king, Richard III.

The Boar of Evil

In the ancient Near East, the boar's various aspects as a fertility symbol, symbol of death, and animal of the hunt were also well marked, though among Semitic and Egyptian peoples its character as an embodiment of evil tended to be stressed. Semitic peoples, it seems, have always regarded the pig as unclean, and have refused to have anything to do with it. This was probably because it was originally a sacred animal: the Greek writer Plutarch could not decide whether the Jews worshipped or abominated it. Among peoples who refused (and in some cases still refuse) to eat pork were the Cretans, Syrians, Phoenicians, Egyptians, and Ethiopians, as well as the Jews and Moslems.

Legends of gods slain by boars, or while boar hunting, are numerous. Adonis, consort of Aphrodite and Attis, consort of Cybele, both met their end in this way. The same may be true of the Egyptian god Osiris, though the evidence here is scanty. The Cretans held that Zeus himself was a prince ripped up by a wild boar and buried in their midst. This assertion is supposed to have earned them their traditional reputation as liars.

Thus the boar came to be the incarnation of the enemy of the gods; in Egypt, for example, the evil god Set was porcine in form. Traces of a similar conception in the West can be found in traditions of Odin's wild hunt, and in the story of King Arthur's boar hunt, in which the fabulous boar is the emissary of Satan, to be overcome not by force, but by prayer. Comparable accounts of boar hunts are found in many medieval texts, among them the French *Song of Roland*, the Anglo-Norman *Boeve de Haumtone*, the *Romance* of Sir Eglamour, and the German *Nibelungenlied*.

In India, though the volume of material is far less than in Europe, one of the incarnations of the god Vishnu was as a boar, while an Indian creation legend tells how the god Brahma, in the form of a boar, lifted up the earth on his back from the waters of the primeval flood.

The power and potency of this sacred animal was believed in many parts of the world to be a source of magical aid. Boars' tusks and hooves were used as amulets, while an infusion of boar's tusk could help cure all manner of ailments, from epilepsy and toothache to 'the twinges'.

Buffalo

The American bison, on whom Plains Indians depended for survival; a major supernatural power in their myths, such as Buffalo Old Man and Old Woman in Kiowa or Apache tales; great buffalo dances as of Mandans, with full headdresses from buffalo heads and mime of herd movement, used to lure herds for hunters; associated with rain, buffalo was prayed to by Sioux and others when rain was needed.

Bulls

Contemporary man in Western society has but one basic interest in bulls: their role in the production of beef. For most of us, even this knowledge is quite indirect since in urban society we rarely encounter bulls except piecemeal of the butcher's. It is natural then if we do not know of the lengthy, intensive and dramatic involvement of our ancestors with these creatures, or realize that millions of people in the world today still closely relate their lives to them.

The story of men and bulls begins in the Paleolithic or Old Stone Age. Man was a hunter, and some of the most widespread and frequently hunted animals were various types of wild cattle. Those best known to ancient man in Europe and the Near East were a species now called *bos primigenius*, *urus*, or *aurochs*—a huge, savage creature with shaggy hair and long, curving horns, from which Spanish fighting cattle are descended. Of all the animals hunted by our forefathers, the aurochs were probably the most valuable. Not only were they a plentiful source of meat but their bones were used for spear points, harpoons and fishhooks, and their skins were fashioned into clothing, boats and tents.

Wild cattle are herding animals, the aurochs herd consisting of a number of cows and calves dominated by a single fierce bull. Consequently, he who would successfully hunt the aurochs had first to kill this dangerous paramount bull. And ancient bulls, like their modern descendants, were powerful, swift, sharp-horned creatures. Standing six feet high or more at the shoulders, they were assuredly a most difficult animal to kill. These ancient bull hunts, these Stone Age corridas, must certainly have been savage, bloody affairs in which members of both species perished. Thus, while the aurochs were one of early man's primary benefactors, he was a dangerous and unwilling one; a benefactor who produced profound awe and fear in the hearts of those who hunted.

The Supreme Bull

During early Neolithic times, when cattle were domesticated, a new dimension was added to the relationship of man and bull. Precisely how this happened is not known, but it was a tremendous forward stride for humankind. It released man from the bondage of the hunting culture. No longer was he a virtual slave to the arbitrary movements of wild animal herds. Now he could keep a ready supply of meat and later milk on hand at all times.

Bullfight in Madrid, Spain

A rhyton, an ancient drinking vessel, in the shape of a bull's head

Perhaps the most interesting aspect of animal domestication, however, was that it appears to have been directly responsible for our ancestors' first learning that sexual activity is connected with pregnancy. While he had undoubtedly witnessed copulation among animals through the years, there is no evidence that man saw the relationship between the exuberant sexuality of the bull and the subsequent calving of the cow, or in his own sexual activity and the childbearing of his women.

Once animals began to be domesticated, however, proximity and daily observation allowed him to perceive the cause and effect relationship in procreation. Further, when Neolithic man made this discovery, bulls came to assume a new value in his eyes. Still a symbol of boundless strength and power, bulls were then esteemed for their sexuality as well, for it was obvious that a single animal could impregnate an entire herd.

During this time man also learned the rudiments of agriculture that seeds when sown would produce plants. But it was many years before the value of breaking the Earth became known and before the plough was invented. For most of this period, cattle raising and agriculture were separate spheres of activity. Cattle were for meat and milk; grain was for bread and beer. Late in the Neolithic Age, however, man saw a relationship between his cattle and his crops. He believed that the great fertility of the bull could influence the successful growth of grain. As a cattle raiser he knew the tremendous fertilizing power of the bull. From this it was but a step to believe that the fertility of the bull could be as efficacious for grain as it was for cattle.

One of the first recorded hymns shows clearly that praise is given to 'the great bull, the supreme bull which treads the holy pasturage planting corn and making fields luxuriant'. This is not homage to the Earth or to seeds, but to the bull for his aid in walking among the plants and causing them to grow by emanating fertility. The plough plays only an incidental part; it opens the Earth to receive the fertile force.

Exalted Overpowering Ox

Historians agree that all the first great civilizations of the Tigris-Euphrates region and those of the Nile and the Indus rivers were built upon the broad, firm base of stockbreeding and agriculture. In the hunting cultures, all able bodied men hunted; there was little division of labour or specialized tasks not involving the hunt. With animal domestication and planting, however, one man's effort could feed several other men, whose time and labour were then released for other pursuits. In time the inevitable enrichment of culture thus resulted in the first civilizations.

During this period, the bull continued to play a central role in man's life, as the obvious inseminator of herds and the imagined fertilizer of the fields;

both archeological relics and records of early civilizations relate repeatedly to the bull. In the analysis of these materials, however, a most surprising fact emerges: one or more of the central gods in the religions of each of these peoples was a bull god. Hymns and prayers to these deities indicate that as well as being a symbol of great strength and fertility, the bull was believed to be directly responsible for thunder, storms, rain, and floods. In fact, for water in any form. Other evidence, especially from Egypt, links the bull god with the sun and the moon.

The Bull in Heliopolis, an Egyptian hymn to the great bull god:

Hymn to Amen-Ra, the Bull in
  Heliopolis,
president of all the gods,
beneficent god, beloved one,
the giver of the warmth of life to all
  beautiful cattle,
Hail to thee, Amen-Ra,
Lord of the thrones of . . . Thebes,
Bull of his mother,
Chief of his fields . . .
Lord of the sky,
eldest son of the earth,
lord of the things which exist,
establisher of things,
establisher of all things,
One in his times among the gods,
Beautiful Bull of the company of
  the gods,
father of the gods,
maker of men,
creator of beasts and cattle,
lord of the things which exist,
creator of the staff of life,
master of the herbage whereon
  cattle live,
Form made by Ptah,
beautiful child,
beloved one.

From E. A. W. Budge, *The Gods of the Egyptians*

Throughout ancient Sumeria, a bull god called Enlil was worshipped as god of the storm and supreme god of fertility. It was through his power that there was water, the fields were green, and all things grew. Mankind itself drew life and sustenance from him. Praising Enlil as their father, the 'exalted overpowering ox', 'Lord of the world of life', 'powerful chief of the gods', the Sumerians of about 3000 BC addressed him with stirring invocations.

Similarly, in ancient India, a wealth of evidence indicates a bull-oriented religion among the earliest inhabitants of the Indus valley. The Aryans who conquered them, moreover, c. 1500 BC, left an eloquent literary testimony concerning bull worship. Hundreds of hymns by these people, originally passed on orally from generation to generation, were ultimately written down and compose a sacred Hindu literary work known as the Rig-Veda. The Aryans worshipped a number of bull gods—Dyaus, Parjanya, Rudra, Indra, and Agni—and many of the Rig Veda hymns are devoted to them.

The archeological testimony from Egypt is even more compelling. Not only do we know that the people worshipped a variety of bull gods, but that two cults, those of Apis and Mnevis, were probably the oldest, most widespread and enduring of all Egyptian religious sects. The worship of both bull gods was quite similar. Each was considered to be a god of fertility and strength, each had celestial aspects, and each had elaborate connections with other gods. Each god was believed to have an earthly manifestation, Apis being immaculately conceived by the impregnation of a special cow by a ray of moonlight, while Mnevis was the incarnation of the sun-god Amon-Re. Upon the death of each divine bull, it was embalmed like a king and interred in large tombs which were known as Serapea.

An additional association between men and bulls appeared in both early Mesopotamia and Egypt; kings related themselves to bulls and bull gods. Thus in Sumeria the great Sargon called himself the patesi or 'tenant farmer' of Enlil. King Rimush acknowledged that he was appointed by Enlil. Naram-Sin, who wore the horns of bulls into battle, presented captive kings to Enlil in recognition of the bull god's sovereignty. This close association between king and god in Sumeria had many interesting facets. Both bull god and king came to share the title 'Wild Bull'. Sargon was so called, and the seal of his servant shows a man watering a bull. Kings wore bull-horned headdresses as a symbol of their divine appointment and power. And to make the interrelation complete, there arose the custom of placing long, curled beards upon images of the bull god. This practice, probably ritualistic in origin, was rooted in the conception common in Mesopotamia that the beard was a sign of strength and masculinity. Consequently, only Sumerian kings were allowed to grow long beards.

The relationship in Egypt between kings and bull gods was even closer. Narmer-Menes, the king who forcibly united Upper and Lower Egypt into a single kingdom not long before 3000 BC, worshipped Apis and spread the gospel of the bull god throughout the land. Moreover, either his adroitness or his simplicity led him actually to conceive of himself as a bull. In either case, at a very early date bull worship in Egypt became identified with king worship.

Since bull worship was such a characteristic of all the earliest civilizations, it was inevitable that many of the other culture centres throughout the Mediterranean, facing similar problems and holding similar values, would

sooner or later focus attention on the bull. Thus in Crete, in Greece and in Rome, man's relations with bulls reflected both his Near Eastern heritage and his own particular cultural needs.

In Crete, for example, while the bull god was primarily connected with the sun and fertility, he was likewise linked with the force, the deep-throated roar, and the destructiveness of earthquakes, which were common to the island. Crete also developed the first public, ritualized bullfights. In Greece, the bull became the focus for socially ap-

One or more of the central gods in the religions of each of these peoples was a bull god.

proved rites of sexual abandon which evolved directly into Greek theatre. And in Rome, as the foremost rival of Christianity for centuries, Mithraism introduced the ritualistic washing away of sins and purification of the body with a bath in the blood dripping from a dying bull.

The Minotaur's Prey

Cretan kings, called Minos, were supreme in both the spiritual and material lives of their subjects, like the kings of Egypt. Apparently revered as the incarnation of the island bull god, Minos stands at the centre of all Cretan legends and myths. As natural leader of the bull cult, the king was the focus of activity during celebrations.

Stories of Minos and of the ceremonies and practices of Cretan bull worship spread widely about the Mediterranean. Eventually many of them became part of the mythology of neighbouring groups in the Aegean area, such as the Greeks. There is, for example, the Greek legend of Europa and the Bull in which the maiden

Europa was seduced and taken across the sea to Crete by the god Zeus in the form of a bull. Here she gave birth to Minos, who later became the bull-god-king of the island.

Another early Greek myth refers to Minos as the tyrant who ruled over Crete and who demanded tribute from Athens every nine years in the form of seven young men and seven maidens. On arrival in Crete, these youths were taken into a giant maze and released. Here they became the prey of a ferocious man-bull or Minotaur who roamed the confines of the maze in search of such human tribute. This Minotaur was the result of the union between Pasiphae, wife of Minos, and a bull with which she had become enamoured. By concealing herself within a wooden cow, constructed for her by the master craftsman Daedalus, she had seduced the bull. The man-bull creature that she bore was imprisoned by Minos in a labyrinth at Cnossus, and it was here that the young Athenians met their end. Long did Athens live in fear of Crete and its Minotaur until one of her heroes, Theseus, entered the labyrinth, and slew the beast.

Scholars have interpreted the myth with the aid of other myths and have concluded that it is an account, albeit garbled and distorted, of early bull cult practices. These included three major groups of ritualistic observances: fertility dances, bullfights or bull fertility rites, and sacrifices.

Bull Dancers of Crete

Each spring, just at the time when all nature revived, Minos held the spectacular island corrida, or running of the bulls. Every phase of these great rituals, from the chase and capture of the wild bulls to their final death in the arena, appears in hundreds of

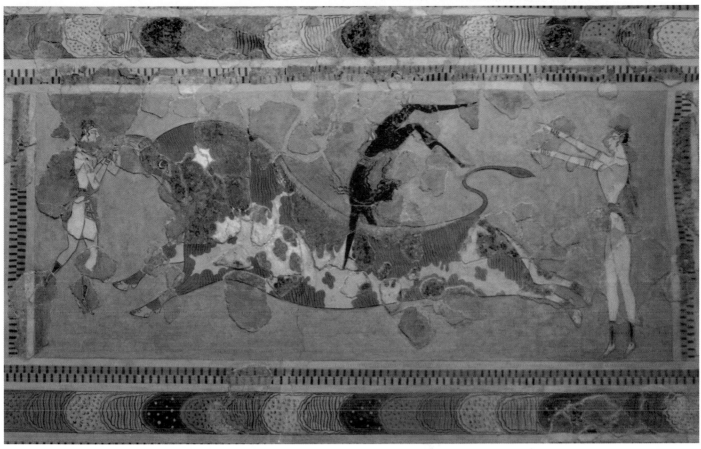

Bull leaping, fresco from the Great Palace at Cnossos, Crete

Cretan art forms. From this evidence we know that these were great fertility rites which were performed in an effort to impregnate the land with new life. This impregnation was accomplished at the arena in two ways: by horn grappling and by bull sacrifice.

The Cretans, like the ancient Sumerians, considered the horns of a bull to be the focus, the concentrated essence of the bull's strength and fertility. At the corrida it was the magic, fertile horns of the wild bull which became the centre of religious interest. The initial part of the Cretan bullfight was consequently composed of a series of ritual actions designed to procure a portion of this tremendous power for the benefit of mankind. To do this, specially trained male and female athletes went into the arena unarmed. Standing before the onslaught of a bull, the sacred performers had neither cape nor sword, and in fact did nothing until the beast was almost upon

them. Then by grasping the horns of the charging bull a split second before the lowered head snapped upward in a mighty toss, the athlete was catapulted into the air. Performing a forward somersault in mid-air, he landed with his feet on the back of the bull or on the ground.

That the feat was extremely dangerous is obvious. There are, in fact, numerous Cretan depictions of athletes trapped under the hoofs and caught between the horns of raging bulls. The aim of this and other horn-grasping methods was nonlethal contact with the horns of the sacred bull. With every grasping, every swing, every toss, the bull cult devotees believed that their champions were absorbing strength and fertility for the ultimate benefit of all men.

The Cretan obsession with male virility is further evidenced by the numerous images of bulls showing erect phalli found at Cnossus. An even more

striking indication of Cretan pride in male sexuality is the fact that all female performers in the bullring wore a breech cloth bunched together toward the front to give the appearance of the male organ. In the spring then, as the warming sun quickened the land, Cnossus held its sacred bullring ceremonies designed to fructify the earth and its creatures with the exuberant sexuality of the bull.

The spread of the bull cult from Crete was inevitable. Assimilating elements from bull religions all over the Near East and Africa, Cretans used them in creating many spectacular bull rituals of their own, and in turn spread these throughout the Mediterranean world. These practices were usually modified by those who adopted them, but many of them took root around the shores of the Mediterranean and became the hybrid systems of bull ritual that were to develop into the modern Spanish bullfight.

FURTHER READING: J. R. Conrad. The Horn and the Sword. (Dutton, 1957). See also F. Altheim. A History of Roman Religion. (Dutton, 1938); L. Cottrell. The Bull of Minos. (London: Evans, 1953); Sir A. Evans. The Palace of Minos. (Biblo and Tannen, 1921); E. E. Evans-Pritchard. The Nuer. (Oxford University Press, 1969); H. Frankfort. Before Philosophy. (London: Penguin, 1949); W. K. C. Guthrie. The Greeks and Their Gods. (Beacon Press, 1968); L. Spence. Myths and Legends of Ancient Egypt. (London: Harrap, 1949); R. Whitlock. Bulls through the Ages. (Lutterworth Press, 1977).

Butterfly

Symbol of the soul and of attraction to the light: in Europe, North America and the Pacific it was widely believed that the soul has the form of a butterfly, which gave the creature uncanny and sometimes ominous connotations; in northern Europe to see one flying at night was a warning of death, and some said that the soul butterfly's ability to leave the body in sleep accounts for dreams; medieval angels were sometimes depicted with butterfly's wings and fairies are often shown with them.

Buzzard

Scavenger bird, associated in much mythology with cleanliness and curative powers; Pueblo Indians used its feathers in curing rituals, and to 'sweep away' evil; American superstition says a buzzard feather worn behind the ear will prevent rheumatism, buzzard grease will cure smallpox; also associated with death in the Old South, where beliefs say that witches sometimes take buzzard form, and that a buzzard shadow will do harm if it passes over you.

Camel

Synonymous with stubbornness, slyness, and even stupidity, in animal fables the camel appears as a creature tricked and eaten by wilier beasts such as the panther, jackal, and crow. To Beduins a camel is a sacrifice of massive value. Most prized are creatures with ten offspring, which are neither mounted nor milked. In India, camel bones are buried at the entrance to a home, making it impossible for ghosts to cross the threshold. Today the mosque at Koba (Aqaba) marks the spot where Mohammed's favourite camel Al Kaswa knelt, in a God-sent sign on the prophet's flight from Mecca, prompting him to rest in safety for four days.

Cat

During the thousands of years in which the cat has lived among human beings it has been venerated at one period as a deity, and at other times cursed as a demon. In parts of ancient Egypt where the cat was regarded as sacred to the cat-headed goddess Bast, spiritual ruler of the city of Bubastis (now Tell Basta) to the east of the Nile Delta, to kill one might be punishable by death. Diodorus Siculus, the Greek historian, described how a Roman who committed this crime was murdered by a mob despite the pleadings of high Egyptian officials. If a cat died, from any cause whatever, its owner went into mourning, shaving his eyebrows and performing elaborate funeral rites. Cat cemeteries were established on the banks of the Nile, where the sacred animals were mummified and then laid to rest, together with vast quantities of cat mascots and bronze cat effigies.

The cat was invested with this aura of holiness elsewhere in the ancient world. The Roman goddess Diana sometimes assumed the shape of a cat, and the chariot of Freyja, the Scandinavian fertility goddess, was drawn by cats. This reverence was due not so much to the animal's importance as the guardian of the granaries against mice (as in ancient Egypt) or to its role as the traditional enemy of the serpent, but to the beauty of its eyes which were strangely reminiscent of the moon.

In her *Cult of the Cat*, Patricia Dale-Green says, 'Like the moon it (the cat) comes to life at night, escaping from humanity and wandering over the housetops with its eyes beaming out through the darkness.' Many people believed the cat was the child of the moon and it was said that 'the moon brought forth the cat'. This curious link has been regarded as due to 'the changeableness of the pupils of the eye, which in the daytime is a mere narrow line, dilatable at night to a luminous globe.' From the magic of their eyes arose the belief that cats were seers with strong mediumistic powers. In the East the cat is said to bear away the souls of the dead, and in some parts of West Africa natives accept that the human soul passes into the body of a cat at death.

An Italian legend tells of a cat that gave birth to her kittens beneath the very manger in which Christ was born. But the cat was not destined to be venerated in Christian Europe, for the Church with its violent repudiation of paganism succeeded in reducing the status of this once sacred animal to that of a devil.

The gods of one religion almost invariably become the devils of the next, but there has rarely been so dramatic a fall from grace as that of the once holy cat. During the persecution of the heretical sect of the Cathars the belief was fostered that these heretics had worshipped the Devil in feline form, and the stage was set for the cat's participation in the witchcraft tragedy.

In the Middle Ages the English scholar Gervase of Tilbury stated a popular belief when he wrote, '. . . women have been seen and wounded in the shape of cats by persons who were secretly on the watch and . . . the next day the women have shown wounds and loss of limbs.' In 1718, toward the end of the witchcraft mania in the British Isles, William Montgomery of Caithness, driven berserk by a vast crowd of cats which gossiped outside his house in human language, attacked them, hatchet in hand, killing two and wounding others. On the following day, two old women were found dead in bed while another had an unexplained gash in her leg, proof that both had changed shape during the night.

At the height of the witchcraft delusion it was generally assumed that a witch could take the shape of a cat only nine times, presumably because of the belief that a cat had nine lives.

More often, cats were given the comparatively minor role of witches' familiars. The villain of one of the first important trials of English witches, in 1566, was a white spotted cat called Sathan, which fed on its mistress's blood. The cruelties inflicted upon a cat caught in the mesh of witchcraft could be dreadful, for the wretched animal was likely to be burned alive, both in England and on the European Continent.

Some people have an intense fear of cats, and in the seventeenth century Increase Mather, the celebrated New England Puritan divine, observed, 'There are some who, if a cat accidentally comes into a room, though they neither see of it nor are told of it, will presently be in a sweat and ready to die away.' It was generally assumed that if a cat was allowed near a corpse it would steal the soul, and the dead person would then become a vampire. Vampire cats were common in Japan, but were easily recognizable, as they had two tails.

One superstition, hardly extinct today, held that cats crept into the cradle to suck the breath of young babies. Nursemaids stood permanent guard against them.

In parts of Europe where many of the old pagan ceremonies were preserved relatively unchanged, a cat often personified the spirit of the corn. At Briancon in France a cat ceremonially garbed in ribbons, flowers, and corn ears presided at the harvest, while near Amiens one of these animals was ritually killed when the last sheaves of corn were cut. It was customary to roast cats alive to drive away evil spirits at the European Easter and Shrove Tuesday fire ceremonies. In the English Guy Fawkes celebrations sacks of living cats were placed on the bonfires.

Until the close of the eighteenth century black cats were burned alive in the Highlands of Scotland, in a ceremony called Taigheirin, to secure from the gods the gift of second sight; and the Irish Hellfire Club is said to have celebrated one of its orgies by igniting a huge tomcat.

Almost as unfortunate was any kitten born in the month of May. Rarely a good hunter, it would bring home glow worms and snakes instead of mice and, because of this, was usually drowned. Needless to say its 'melancholy disposition' made it easily recognizable.

Lore of the Black Cat

Legendary lore has had a particularly dramatic influence on feline fortunes. In Britain the 'blackberry' cat's reputation for devilment and mischief is due solely to the fact that it is born at the end of the blackberry season, this being the time of year when, according to an old tradition, Satan was thrown out of heaven into a blackberry bush (which he then defiled with his urine and spittle).

The sins of the blackberry cat pale into insignificance when compared with those of the black cat which, in the United States and most of Europe, is regarded as the embodiment of the Devil himself. In Britain, it is the white cat who plays this role. The brindled cat was notorious in England as the familiar of the witch, hence the witches' cry in Macbeth, 'Thrice the brinded cat hath mewed', while the black cat, generally speaking, symbolizes magic minus malice.

Even today cat lore, particularly the correct approach to the black variety, is extremely complicated. The black cat should be gently stroked along the spine and never chased away, or it will take the luck of the home with it. To come across such an animal out of doors is highly favourable in most parts of Britain, but in Yorkshire, as in the United States, it is unlucky; at the same time it is lucky to own a black cat.

One supernatural skill attributed to these animals is their ability to forecast the weather. When cats scamper wildly it means wind; when they wash their ears, rain; and when they sit with their backs to the fire, frost or storms. The Indonesians believe that it is possible to produce rain by pouring water over a cat.

Observers in the past have tried to rationalize the weather forecasting element in the feline make-up. An early attempt suggested that 'the moisture which is in the air before the rain, insinuating itself into the fur of this animal, moves her to smoothe the same and cover the body with it so that she may feel less the inconvenience of Winter as on the contrary she opens her fur in Summer that she may better receive the refreshing of the moist season.'

The cat has always been credited with that most important function of divinity, the art of healing. The instrument for this is its tail, which will cure a 'queff or stye if drawn downward over the eye, while the following charm is recited:

I poke thee. I don't poke thee.
I poke the queff that's under the eye.
O qualyway, O qualyway.

'Tail cure' is equally effective in the treatment of warts, whitloes and the itch. Catskin properly dried and applied to the face is believed to relieve toothache, and in the seventeenth century a whole cat boiled in olive oil was thought to make a first class dressing for wounds. If a disease resisted ordinary methods of treatment it was at one time customary to transfer it to the family cat, by dousing the animal with the patient's washing water and driving it from the house. When any member of the family was ill, the cat's every movement might be scrutinized for signs and portents. Its leaving home was an omen of death.

It was noticed that cats were extremely sensitive to the presence of an unburied body in the house, and that they left home immediately after someone died, returning only after the funeral. A cat that stood its ground but was caught leaping over the coffin was always killed at once, as such behaviour was thought to bode ill for the prospects of the departed in the hereafter.

It was a rule in many households that a sick or dying cat be put out of the house, to prevent death from spreading through the family. When moving house in the northeast of England it was traditional to abandon the family cat in order to preserve the luck.

Seamen were invariably kind to a cat, believing that it brought luck to any ship it boarded. In addition cats were infallible weather guides and were thought to be invaluable when

a ship was becalmed, as a wind could be raised by placing a cat under a pot on the deck. To throw a cat overboard, particularly if it were black and without a single white hair, was unthinkable, since this could cause a storm.

Actors also welcome cats, regarding their presence as a good omen, and they believe that kicking a cat causes the worst possible luck. But if a cat runs across the stage during a performance, it is thought to be an extremely ominous sign.

Many cat superstitions and fears have survived in the United States. The lore of the Old South tends to see the cat as a devil, a witch, a witch's imp but at the same time its whiskers were often used in 'conjure' magic and charms. Southern belief also says that if you kick a cat you will get rheumatism, and if you drown a cat the Devil will get you. Yet a broth made from boiling a black cat was believed to cure consumption. New Englanders long believed that they could tell time from a cat's eyes, for the pupils supposedly contracted at low tide, dilated at high tide. Pennsylvanians boiled black cats to keep the Devil at bay; Ozarkians, afraid to kill a cat, might chop off its paw and throw it out of the house.

In modern times, although the cat has not yet recovered its lost status as a goddess, there have been other compensations. Television stardom has come its way and it would sometimes appear that the entire economic life of the nation is geared to the production of its food. Yet, quite unspoiled, the cat remains serene, civilized, godlike, and utterly mysterious.

FURTHER READING: Patricia Dale-Green. Cult of the Cat. (Houghton, Mifflin, 1963).

Cock

The proud strutting, aggressiveness, and sexual ardour of the cock, together with its striking appearance and loud crowing, are the reasons for this bird's particularly widespread involvement in folk customs and traditions. It has retained its association with ancient lore, and has also tended to accumulate new beliefs and practices wherever it has been introduced.

The cock appeared in southern Europe in post-Homeric times, probably about the 5th or 6th century BC. Early in the fifth century a cock was depicted on a Sicilian coin. The Persian wars were fought during this period and there can be little doubt that the bird's introduction was due to this Asian incursion. The cock was sacred in Persia: to kill one of these birds was regarded as a sin, and its Persian name indicates that it was considered oracular. Aristophanes, in The Birds, called it 'the Persian bird' and compared its crest to the headdress of the Persian king.

The Persians, in their turn, called the Carians, who came from a region in Asia Minor, 'cocks' because they wore crested helmets. A Greek writer compared the cock's adornments to the magnificent robes of Croesus, the proverbially wealthy king of Lydia. Pliny, too, commented on the remarkable comb. Because of the bird's pugnacity and courage, a cock was placed on the head of the statue of Athene on the Acropolis, as a symbol of battle.

The crowing of the cock attracted special attention among the Greeks because it occurred about dawn, al-

though the bird does, of course, crow at other times. There was a Greek story that when Mars chose to spend a night with Venus in the absence of her husband, Vulcan, he commissioned Alektryon (the Greek for 'cock') to watch at the door. He fell asleep and Mars, surprised by the returning husband, punished Alektryon by transforming him into a cock. He has been vigilant at dawn ever since.

Because evil spirits, 'the powers of darkness', have always been believed to be particularly active at night, the dawn crowing of the cock was usually a welcome sign, and the belief arose that the bird itself was effective in exorcizing evil. In the Persian sacred books it was stated that the cock's crow awakens the dawn, arouses mankind to praise the perfect Holiness and drives away specters and demons. This tradition persisted in Europe.

The belief arose that a bird that could frighten devils must be able to scare wild animals, and travelers in Libya carried a cock with them to frighten lions and basilisks. The basilisk was a fabulous monster, hatched by a serpent from a cock's egg, and alleged to be able to kill with a glance. The Greek writer Aelian, who died in about AD 222, remarked that the basilisk dies in convulsions on hearing the crowing of a cock. It is widely believed that a crowing hen is a sinister omen.

The Healing Bird
Another Greek author, Heliodorus, writing in the 3rd to 4th centuries AD, stated that the cock crows because of its affinity for the sun. The bird's solar connection dates from ancient times in Europe as well as in Asia, and we may assume that this association was introduced at the same time as the bird itself. The Greeks believed that the cock was sacred to Apollo, god of the sun, and it became associated with Asclepius, the god of healing, Apollo's

Two cocks face each other on either side of a jar with a cone-shaped base filled with gold coins.

son by the nymph Coronis. This was the outcome of its connection with the sun and the life giving powers, and its opposition to the powers of darkness. In the *Phaedo* Plato records Socrates's request before drinking the hemlock that a cock should be offered to Asclepius on his behalf, although this request was not connected with any desire to escape the effects of the poison.

The practice of sacrificing cocks has been widespread. Cocks were sacrificed to the sun in Mexico, and elsewhere served as ritual sacrifices after the erection of a building or bridge (probably instead of human victims). In the East a cock may be killed over an invalid's bed and the blood sprinkled on the sufferer. It was the custom in Ceylon for a red cock to be dedicated to a sick person and sacrificed if he recovered. In Scotland, the blood of a red cock was administered in a flour cake to the invalid.

There were places in Germany where it was believed that illness and bad luck could be warded off by hiding the head, heart and right foot of a cock in the house. In both Germany and Ireland a cock was sacrificed on 11 November, St. Martin's Day (or Eve, in Ireland). In Athlone in Ireland the blood was sprinkled on the threshold and the four corners of the house. D'Arcy Thompson in *A Glossary of Greek Birds* (1936), states that he himself remembers a cock being sacrificed to St. Nicholas to cure a sick cow.

Many ideas concerning good and bad luck involve the cock. American lore says if a cock crows on a porch visitors will come; if in the rain, the rain will stop. A cock crowing facing a house, at the front door, on a banister, or inside the house, is an omen of death. In Germany it was an ill omen if a wedding procession met cocks fighting while on its way to church.

Bronze statuette of *Der Hahn* (the cock)

Cock fighting is an ancient amusement, popular in some eastern countries and all over Central and South America, and still carried on illegally in certain regions of Europe and the United States. As early as the 3rd century AD the Christian writer Lactantius had declared cock fighting an unsuitable spectacle for Christian people, but the compassion for animals shown by many saints had little effect in encouraging humane treatment.

Cockroach

Large beetlelike insect infesting many houses, dark-coloured and nocturnal, so acquiring supernatural attributions. In the Old American South, it was believed that a witch could be caught by leaving a jar in the hearth ashes overnight, and a cockroach found in the jar was the trapped witch. Folk medicine used cockroaches to treat urinary ailments, epilepsy, and worms in children. United States lore suggests ridding your house of roaches forever by sweeping them out on Good Friday.

Cow

The cow for centuries has been looked upon as a tangible symbol of life and fertility by nomadic and pastoral peoples, who depend on this uncomplaining beast for nourishment and prosperity. In mythology the cow has come to be associated in particular with the divine givers of life, the mother goddesses, either of the sky or of the earth.

In ancient Egypt the goddess Hathor, mother of the sun god, was frequently represented either as a cow, or as having a human face, with cow's horns and ears. It was believed that every night she engulfed the sun god, only to give birth to him again every morning. Similarly Nut, another Egyptian sky goddess, was depicted as a cow, supported by the other gods, and with the stars on her underbelly.

In many ancient religions, however, the cow as a source of fecundity took second place as an object of worship to the bull as a source of generative power. The male symbol thus took precedence over the female. This is true of ancient Near Eastern religion generally. In Greece and Crete, too, the bull cult

of Minoan-Mycenean religion was far more important than any corresponding veneration of the cow, though in some traditions the sky god Zeus was said to have been nursed by a cow. His consort, Hera, is described by Homer as boopis, 'cow-eyed'.

This idea of divine nourishment is also found in ancient Scandinavian mythology. Snorri's Edda tells of the primeval giant, Ymir, who was nourished by four rivers of milk from a cow. The beast, Audumulla, was herself created out of condensing frost. Being thirsty, she licked the blocks of salty ice around her and as the ice melted under her warm tongue, the head and then the body of a man appeared. This was Buri, grandfather of Odin, greatest of the gods.

Accept the Cow

It is in India and in Hinduism that the cow plays the most striking role, both in mythology and in the day-to-day practice of religion. In practice, Indian cow worship is restricted to one species of the animal, the East Indian humped zebu. The roots of this worship are certainly Indo-European, and have much in common with features already mentioned. The cow is thought of as a symbol of the divine bounty of the Earth, and as the 'mother' of gods and men. The high god Varuna is called 'son of Aditi' in the oldest of the four chief Hindu collections of prayers and hymns, the Rig Veda, while the goddess Aditi is called 'the Cow, the sinless'.

The myth of the Earth taking the form of a cow receives its first detailed expression in the Vishnu Purana, an ancient Sanskrit collection of legendary lore. In this, Prithu, the monarch of all, approached the Earth in order to make her yield plants. The Earth assumed the form of a cow and ran away, but was finally caught and persuaded to nourish the Earth with her milk. Then Prithu milked the Earth into his own hand, and there grew up

all manner of corn and vegetables for man's food.

Although there was no express prohibition of cow killing or the eating of beef in early Indian history, by the time of the great epic, the *Mahabharata*, of the 3rd century BC, it was stated categorically that the killing of a cow was the greatest of all crimes: 'All that kill, eat, and permit the slaughter of cows, rot in hell for as many years as there are hairs on the body of a cow so slain.' The Laws of Manu, the greatest of the Hindu codes of law, are less extreme. They lay down that slaying cows is a 'minor offence'. Provided the killer lives in a cow house, bathes in urine, and follows the cows all day, standing when they stand and sitting when they lie down, he may expiate his crime in three months. It may also be noted that Zoroastrianism knew of

Facsimile of a vignette from the Book of the Dead of Ani. Hathor, as the Mistress of the West (a goddess of the afterlife) emerges from a hill representing the Theban necropolis. She is depicted as a cow, wearing her typical horns and sun-disk, along with a menat-necklace. Her eye is shaped like the sacred Eye of Horus. At bottom right is a stylized tomb.

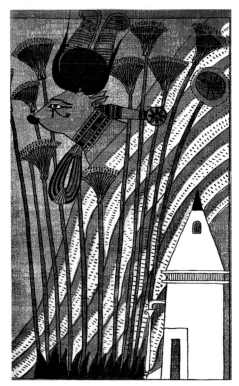

White cows decorated for Diwali celebrations

similar prohibitions: Ahura Mazdah is the lord of all cattle, and therefore 'all robbery and violence against the (sacred) Kine' is forbidden.

The cow, by reason of her sacredness, is also a practical means toward the expiation of other sins. Again according to Manu: 'He who unhesitatingly abandons life for the Brahmanas (the priestly caste) or cows, is freed from the guilt of the murder of a Brahmana, and so is he who saves the life of a cow, or of a Brahmana.' Similarly, he who has committed a mortal sin can be purified by attending cows for over a year. On a somewhat different level, a birth at an inauspicious time can be remedied by passing the infant beneath the body of a cow—thus bringing about a symbolic rebirth from the source of holiness.

Death Clutching a Cow's Tail

Not only the cow itself, but also its products, are powerful sacred instruments in Hinduism. They are especially effective in purifying a person from the stain of sin. There are five of these

products: milk, curds, clarified butter, dung and urine; none must be wasted. All were important in the sacrificial rituals of early Hinduism, and have increased in significance down the ages.

Of the many reasons for the tenacity of the cow cult within Hinduism, special mention must be made of the association of Krishna, the most popular of Hindu gods, with the cow. A legend told of Krishna's youth depicts him as a cowherd, devoted to their care, and yet dallying with the maidens who shared his responsibilities. Their devotion to him is a pattern of human devotion to God; but the setting, amid the cows, is also significant. Cow worship was further strengthened in opposition to the Moslem invaders who had no compunction about the slaughtering of cattle. Again, it received fresh impetus with the development of the doctrine of *ahimsa* (harmlessness), with its implicit reverence for all forms of life, animal as well as human. A more modern development has been the symbolical identification of the cow with India as a nation—a local-

ization of the original identification of the cow with the Earth.

At present, the cow plays a variety of roles in the religious life of Hindu India. In some Hindu temples, a cow is brought in every morning, placed with her back to the image of the deity and solemnly milked. In Hindu rituals generally, every part of the cow—as well as the five products mentioned earlier—has significance.

At an annual festival, the Gopastami (cow holiday), women attend an adorned cow, placed in the temple courtyard. They move around it four times, each time pouring water on the tail from a jug, and then lifting the tail to their eyes and head. Finally each woman kisses the cow, whispering, 'Truth belongs to you, and it is our duty to keep our promises.'

It is widely believed among Hindus that the cow is able to act as a pathfinder in the world beyond the grave, and that it is highly auspicious to be able to die clutching a cow's tail. For the lower castes, often forbidden direct access to temples, a cowshed has come to fill the function of a temple in their daily lives.

The protection of cows in India because of their sacredness has led, ironically, to the neglect of their welfare, partly because controlled breeding and the exercise of ownership and restraint is virtually impossible. The traditional Hindu attitude, however, is summed up in Gandhi's well-known words: '"Cow Protection" to me is one of the most wonderful phenomena in all human evolution; for it takes the human being beyond his species . . . Man through the cow is enjoined to realize his identity with all that lives . . . "Cow Protection" is the gift of Hinduism to the world; and Hinduism will live as long as there are Hindus to protect the cow.'

Coyote

Major trickster figure in myths of Plains Indians and other tribes throughout North America; sometimes described as taking human form in a mythic past when animals lived like men. A creator and a central culture hero, he appears in many origin myths, teaching basic skills, bringing fire and so on, but his dual nature also places him in tales of entertainment where he appears mischievous, violent, erotic, or merely foolish.

Crab

Sometimes a symbol of the union of opposites, because it is at home both on land and in the water. In the Tarot card called the Moon a crab crawls up onto land from a pool, a symbol of the depths of the mind revealing themselves. In some of the Pacific islands crabs are gods, or the shadows or messengers of gods. The fourth sign of the zodiac is Cancer, the Crab.

Crane

Cranes flying in large, clamourous flocks attracted much attention in ancient times. The Greeks noted that the cranes travel in a wedge formation, which reminded them of the triangular shape of their letter D (Δ); and so a connection arose between cranes and the alphabet.

There was also a mythological or symbolic association between cranes and trees. On a Celtic altar of the first century AD, found in Paris, the god Tarvos Trigaranus is shown felling a willow tree in company with three cranes and a bull. In Eastern symbolism the crane and the pine tree, signifying long life, are often depicted together. In Irish legends there are indications that the crane was once regarded as having supernatural qualities. St. Columba, who was called 'crane cleric' was said to have turned some women into cranes. In the West the lofty 'alphabetical' flight of the birds connected them with Apollo, the god of sun and poetry, and with Hermes, the patron of communications. But the association between long-necked birds and the sun is very ancient. Such birds appear frequently as a design on early pottery in the Middle East and it seems that not only cranes but other long-necked birds such as geese, egrets, and even flamingoes were associated with the sun.

The migrations of cranes and geese have been connected with the coming

Ceramic coyote head at the Anahuacalli Museum in Mexico City

of spring, and with increasing warmth and fertility, since time out of mind. Even today, when the numbers of cranes breeding in Europe are much reduced, the migrating flocks arouse excitement as they pass noisily overhead.

As happened not infrequently in the bird lore of antiquity, accurate observation merged into myth. Aristotle noted that cranes when sleeping stand first on one leg, then on the other. Aelian, the Roman writer of the 3rd century AD, improved on this; he stated that they posted sentinels and that these birds held a stone in the raised foot to help themselves to stay awake. Horapollo, a Greek grammarian living in the 4th century AD, referred to the crane as a symbol of vigilance. Thus the stone-grasping belief is probably an addition to much earlier tradition, based on the fact that the crane is indeed a wary bird.

Dancers Entombed Alive

During the mating season, cranes perform an elaborate and impressive type of dance, and this was interpreted by some ancient peoples as a form of magical ceremony. The crane's curious movements during its 'dance' were imitated in human dances in Crete, China and elsewhere. Describing the courtship display of the American whooping crane, now a rare species, Margaret Rawlings wrote (in *The Yearling*): 'The cranes were dancing a cotillion . . . two stood apart, erect and white, making a strange music that was part cry and part singing. The rhythm was irregular like the dance. The other birds were in a circle. In the heart of the circle, several moved counter-clockwise . . . The outer circle shuffled around and around. The group in the centre attained a slow frenzy . . .' A crane dance was performed by human dancers in ancient

Cranes on a hanging scroll, colour on silk

Crete in connection with the labyrinth, the home of the Minotaur. The layout was circular and apparently the performance was enacted on an arena of swastika pattern. The circle and the swastika are both symbols of the sun so we may assume that the dance was a solar ritual, which is in agreement with evidence that the crane was a bird of the sun.

In ancient times crane dances were also performed in China. According to historical records Ho-lu, king of the ancient kingdom of Wu in the Yangtze Valley, offered his daughter a fish of which he had already eaten a portion, thereby breaking a taboo. She committed suicide, whereupon the king in order to propitiate her spirit and avert evil, sacrificed dancers by burying them alive. He constructed a magnificent tomb, furnished with objects of priceless value, for her remains. An underground passage led to the sepulchral chamber. The dance of the white cranes was enacted in the marketplace of the capital. The crowd was ordered to follow the funeral cortege and boys and girls were instructed to enter the passage following the crane dancers. Then a machine was set in motion to close the passage and bury the dancers alive.

In the Far East crane dancers were associated with a group of ideas—thunder, rain, fertility, and reincarnation. In Chinese records it is stated that black cranes and demons danced during times of drought. A picture of a crane is placed on the catafalque when coffins are carried to the grave in parts of China; a crane fashioned from paper is sometimes harnessed to the sedan chair containing an image of the deceased. Such a paper crane may be suspended from the window of the dead man's house during Taoist funeral ceremonies. The patriarch of Taoism, Lao-Tze, is shown wearing a red robe embroidered with white cranes and riding a one-horned monster, not un-like a water buffalo. Thus in China, as in Crete and Gaul, there is an association between a supernatural being, a horned beast and the crane.

The crane figures in a number of fables. The story of a war between cranes and pygmies goes back to Homer's reference in the *Iliad* and is mentioned, among others, by Aristotle and, in English literature, by Milton. It was constantly repeated by Greek and Latin writers. It even traveled to India, where a tradition became current that dwarfs fought the monstrous mythical eagle of Hindu mythology, Garuda.

FURTHER READING: W. Harter. Birds: In Fact and Legend. *(Sterling, 1979).*

Crocodile

The crocodile is the embodiment of hypocrisy—the creature who 'smiles' then gobbles you up. According to ancient lore, the crocodile, described by one sixteenth-century explorer as 'cowardly on land, cruel in the water', first lures its prey with moaning sounds then, having devoured its meal, sheds tears of false remorse. Crocodiles do make mournful noises, though the 'tears' they produce are probably their mechanism for getting rid of excess body salt.

The Egyptian god Souchos (Sebek) took a crocodile form, and was revered because of the membrane that covers its eyes; like a deity this allows the animal to see but not be seen. Within his temple at Faiyum, sacred crocodiles were even decorated with jewels by their attendant priests. During the seven days of the year sacred to Apis, the bull of Memphis, it was said that the crocodile would harm no one.

For many African peoples the crocodile is an ancestor spirit with a role in the genesis of the cosmos. It takes the supreme cunning of a fox to foil a

Relief of crocodile at the temple of Kom Ombo

crocodile, as in the South African folktale which relates how a king's cattle and sheep—and herders and travelers—were saved from being devoured by crocodiles when the fox ate them while they were still eggs.

Crow

The crow family forms a group of conspicuous, large birds with a wide distribution throughout the world from the arctic to the tropics. In particular, ravens and crows of Europe and Asia have attracted man's attention, and much folklore is connected with them. These associations arose primarily from their carrion-feeding behaviour; hunters in ancient times, aware that the presence of the birds provided clues to the whereabouts of game, and often of carcasses, would regard them as endowed with knowledge and insight surpassing their own. As death has long been a mystery to mankind the observed close association between carrion-feeding birds and corpses meant that they aroused disquieting responses.

The raven's habit of picking out the eyes from a corpse before eating the flesh was commented on by Aristophanes in *The Birds*. In the Bible, in Proverbs (chapter 30) it is said: 'The eye that mocks a father and scorns to obey a mother, will be picked out by ravens of the valley.' In Bohemia it used to be said that crows picked out the eyes of St. Lawrence. One of the crows in the Scottish ballad 'The Twa Corbies' says of the fallen knight, 'I'll pike out his bonny blue e'en.' By the odd kind of inversion which sometimes occurs in folklore it was said in Wales that blind people who showed kindness to ravens would regain their sight. In Czechoslovakia there was a tradition that a man who ate three ravens' hearts reduced to ashes would become a crack shot. The notion that by partaking of the heart or flesh of a creature one could acquire some of its qualities was extremely widespread and in this instance it was evidently supposed that the raven's farsightedness could be acquired. According to the Greek writer Porphyry (3rd century AD), by eating the hearts of crows one might acquire the birds' prophetic powers.

Why the Raven Croaks

Black, the colour of the crow, has long been associated with death and disaster; and because large birds of this colouring are relatively uncommon, a need was felt to explain their dark hue. A number of legends purport to explain how they acquired it. Thus, according to the Greek geographer Pausanias (2nd century AD) and other writers, when Apollo became the lover of Coronis, the mother of Asclepius, he commissioned a snow-white crow to mount guard while he went to Delphi. Despite this Coronis, although already pregnant by him, became unfaithful with Ischys. Before the crow set out with the news Apollo divined what had happened and, infuriated

that the crow had not picked out Ischys's eyes, turned the bird black.

Another story relates that the gods were sacrificing, and the raven was sent to bring water from a fountain for a libation but he dallied, waiting until some figs were ripe. So the bird was condemned to suffer from thirst in summer—and that is why the raven croaks so hoarsely.

The frequent allusions in folklore to the association between the raven or crow and water might seem unaccountable, for these birds are not especially partial to damp habitats and, indeed, sometimes frequent rocky outcrops and ruins in desert country. The association has apparently arisen through ravens being frequently seen circling among black storm clouds. Thus the species was credited with some of the qualities of a storm bird such as were attributed to large high-flying, and sometimes mythical, birds in Asia and elsewhere. Among the Greeks and Romans the crow was likewise considered to be a weather prophet. Many Greek writers refer to the raven as presaging tempests, though some characteristics of its behaviour

were interpreted as prognosticating good weather. The raven's association with clouds and rain meant that it was often regarded as a thunderbird.

Perhaps the most familiar episode in which the raven is associated with water is the account in Genesis of the sending forth of a raven by Noah from the Ark to search for land. This is derived from an older myth of the Deluge originating in the ancient city of Acre in Israel, in which the dove, swallow, and raven are sent forth in turn to discover whether the waters had subsided. It is recorded that at Krannon in Thessaly there were two ravens and never more—a detail perhaps based on observations that the birds pair for life—but at Krannon the ravens were connected with a magical rain-making ceremony. Coins of the 4th century BC depict two ravens on a small wagon containing a jar of water with pieces of metal suspended from it. By jolting this contrivance the jangling sounds and splashing water simulated a miniature thunderstorm. It was believed that in this manner rain could be induced.

The carrion crow, *Corvus corone*

Messenger and Guide

In common with the eagle and some other conspicuous, large birds the raven was regarded as being in contact with higher powers; and in this capacity it was regarded as entrusted with carrying information, water or fire, or performing other missions. In what seems to be a variation of the Deluge story the culture hero of a Siberian tribe, the Koryak, comes to the rescue during a period of incessant rain by flying up to heaven and stopping the leak. The mythical association with water was apparently carried to the New World where we find an American Indian culture hero Yetl transforming himself into the form of a raven in order to obtain and escape with fresh water. He was surprised in the act and was turned from white to black. However, he succeeded in flying to Earth and disgorging the water to become streams, rivers, and lakes.

The mythological figure Raven is of course the major culture hero and trickster of all tribes of the North Pacific coast. (Crow is a lesser figure in Indian myth, being a minor trickster of the Canadian Chipewyan and some Plains tribes.) For the Kwakiutl, Haida, and other North Pacific tribes, he is the transformer who brought mankind into being (out of a clamshell), gave them fire, water, game, and the wealth of Nature. As a trickster, he is a great stealer of food, usually thwarted laughably. Raven appears too in Jicarilla Apache myths, where he is responsible for making man mortal; while in Iroquois and other woodland Indian ceremonials Raven is often evoked for curing rituals.

Death is a Hooded Crow

As a wise bird flying hither and thither and at times reputedly in touch with the gods the raven was said to act as messenger, informant, and guide. Ravens led the Boeotians to where they founded a new city and they guided Alexander to the shrine of Jupiter Ammon in the oasis of Siwah in Egypt and later foretold his death. It was said that when the people from the island of Thera in the Aegean emigrated to Libya ravens flew alongside their ships to guide them. The Emperor Jimmu of Japan marched to war in the seventh century with a golden raven as guide. Pausanius recorded that a crow indicated the grave of the Greek writer Hesiod; according to Aelian a crow carried messages for King Marres of Egypt. Odin's two ravens, Huginn and Muninn, went forth each day prying into what was happening in the world and returning to perch on his shoulder and whisper their news into his ear.

In Celtic areas the importance of the raven and crow was once great though it is uncertain to what extent we are justified in speaking of a raven divinity or crow god. Various supernatural female figures appeared in the form of ravens or crows. Odin was called Hrafna-gud, god of the raven. The goddess of slaughter who came to the Celtic hero Cu Chulainn when he was mortally wounded appeared with her sisters as hooded crows and perched on his shoulders as he was dying.

Scottish folklore still holds reminiscences of these ferocious beings in the person of the dread Cailleach, a female who can appear as a raven, hooded crow or other birds. In Anglo-Saxon poetry the raven is constantly associated with battles. The similarities between Germanic and Celtic raven and crow traditions are such that we may assume with some confidence that their origin dates from the period when the peoples concerned lived in close proximity to one another. According to the Prose Edda, while his body lay sleeping, Odin could take the shape of various creatures, including that of a wild beast or bird. Odin's ravens were not fierce flesh-eating birds; Huginn and Muninn represented Thought and Memory—the mind's ability to go roving as in a shaman's trance. On a seventh century helmet from Sweden he is shown on horseback with two birds presumably ravens flying round his head.

In Christian Europe the raven had sinister significance, derived from Roman ideas concerning augury, dim recollections of the raven's connection with pagan gods, and from its dark plumage and deep croaking. Shakespeare refers several times to the ominous raven, and its association with death and fortune. In 1650 Dr. Nathaniel Hone wrote: 'By the flying and crying of Ravens over their houses, especially in the dusk of evening and where one is sick, they conclude death.'

Apparently, there has been a transference of oracular beliefs from the crow to the magpie, another member of the family, and the sayings and rhymes, and even minor ritual, such as taking off one's hat to it in Wales, seem to be derived from Roman crow augury.

The raven and grey (hooded) crow still retain in parts of the British Isles something of their reputation as oracles. There is an Irish phrase 'raven's knowledge' meaning to see and know all. It is also said in Ireland that the raven and grey crow 'tell the truth'.

The references in the Bible to Elijah being fed by ravens and to ravens being fed by God predisposed Christians to regard the bird as benevolent but, on the principle that the gods of a defeated faith may become the evil spirits of its successor the raven was sometimes viewed with suspicion—not surprisingly in view of its many heathen associations. St. Ambrose wrote at length on the bird's impiety in not returning to the Ark. Jewish, Moslem, and Christian legends regarded it as blameworthy for remaining to eat carrion and it was said that henceforth it was condemned to eat carrion. In

—an extension of the story of Elijah's ravens.

The ravens at the Tower of London remind those who are interested in ancient traditions of the significance which these birds have possessed in the British Isles and elsewhere for many centuries. It is said that disaster to these ravens would presage Britain's downfall. At one point in the Second World War, people were disquieted by the rumour that the Tower ravens had not croaked for five whole days.

Sun-Crow of China

The most interesting of the many fables concerning ravens and crows is 'The War of the Owls and Crows' which appears in Indian as well as classical sources. It seems to embody reminiscences of very ancient beliefs with regard to the heavenly bodies, the owl representing the moon and the crow the sun. In China the three-legged sun-crow is an important symbol. The tradition that a crow never enters the Acropolis at Athens appears to be based on the tradition of the enmity between Athene, whose symbol was an owl, and the crow.

The raven and crow have been the subjects of a number of heterogeneous beliefs. Parts of the raven were used in medicine, according to Pliny, and raven's eggs were used by the Greeks in homoeopathic magic. Ovid, in Metamorphoses, refers to the witch Medea infusing into the veins of the elderly Jason a decoction of an aged deer and the head of a crow that had outlived nine generations of men. Folklore attributes a very long life to birds of the crow family. Aelian states that raven's eggs dye the hair black but unless you filled your mouth with oil while you applied this remedy for grey hair you would find that your teeth also had become indelibly black.

the Koran the raven is sent by God to show Cain where to bury Abel but this is a version of an older Jewish legend. We hear of desert saints being assailed by devils in the form of 'black stinking ravens'. In Germany, witches were said to ride on them. When St. Vincent was thrown to the beasts at Saragossa his body was defended by ravens and when at length it was buried at Cape St. Vincent ravens kept guard. Shakespeare makes use of both traditions malevolent and benevolent. In a single scene of *Titus Andronicus* (Act II Sc. 3) he mentions the 'fatal raven' and quotes 'ravens foster forlorn children'

MAN, MYTH, AND MAGIC

FURTHER READING: E. A. Armstrong. The Folklore of Birds. *(Dover, 1969).*

Cuckoo

The loud call of the cuckoo, heralding the arrival of spring, is of greater importance in folklore than its other well-known habit of laying its eggs in the nests of other birds. None of the familiar birds visiting Europe announces the advent of spring with so loud, reiterative, and distinctive a call—a call whose pitch and other characteristics make it easily imitated by the human voice. Other birds with call notes having some resemblance to the human voice, such as the great northern diver and some owls, are commonly regarded as mysterious and have also achieved prominence in folklore.

The thirteenth century song 'Sumer is icumen in, Lhude sing cuccu' reminds us that to our forefathers, as to us, the cuckoo was a welcome harbinger of increasing sunshine, warmth, and growth. Its arrival was a notable date in the calendar, as is indicated by traditions in the English counties that the cuckoo arrives for the local fair—for example, in Hertfordshire, where it is said to come to Sawbridgeworth fair. In Siberia some of the tribes timed their spring ceremonies by its call.

It was a small step from noting correlations between birds' calls, weather, and farming operations to assuming that correspondences between the cuckoo's calling and human affairs were such that personal fortunes could be predicted by noting the bird's behaviour. Thus, in England, Scotland, and on the European Continent it was said that a person could tell how long they had to live by noting how often the cuckoo called. All was well if, as often in spring, the cuckoo called incessantly—but probably such sayings were never taken very seriously. It was also said that a girl could ascertain how long she would remain unmarried by counting the calls; but in Germany, if the cuckoo called more than ten times in such circumstances, it was generally regarded as bewitched and unreliable. In the United States it is said that a cuckoo's call, especially if from low-lying lands, is a forewarning of rain. And another American superstition states that, whatever you are doing when you hear the first cuckoo of spring, that activity will predominate in your life for the rest of the year.

A belief dating from the time of Aristotle or earlier, and still lingering in the countryside today, is that the cuckoo turns into a hawk in winter; this arose, no doubt, to explain the bird's disappearance. Plausibility was given to the notion by the similarity between the cuckoo and the merlin, a kind of falcon, together with the disappearance of the merlin from much of its winter range to its breeding haunts about the time the cuckoo arrives.

There was a widespread belief in Europe and North America that on hearing the first cuckoo of the year one should wish, and there are still people who make a ritual event of the occasion by turning the coins in a pocket, for luck. It is said that if you have money in your pocket when hearing the bird, you will not want for it throughout the year. In parts of Germany it was the custom for rustics to roll on the grass when the bird was first heard, claiming that by so doing they could avoid suffering from lumbago. In Norfolk and Sussex it was unlucky to hear the first cuckoo while in bed, as this was a warning that someone in the family would become ill. In the Scottish islands and in France it was undesirable to hear the cuckoo before having broken one's fast. The Scots expected bad luck to follow, but the French said that the person who heard the cuckoo while fasting would suffer from numbed limbs or become a good-for-nothing idler.

The yellow-billed cuckoo (*Coccyzus Americanus*). Some cultures believe you should make a wish upon hearing the first cuckoo of the year.

There appeared in print as far back as 1685 a procedure for obtaining a clue to one's future spouse. It was said that if a man looked under his left shoe on first hearing the cuckoo he would find a hair of a similar colour to that of his future wife; a woman could discover her future husband in the same way. There were various other somewhat similar procedures.

Prophetic Bird

Augury and ornithomancy are based on notions that bird behaviour has ulterior and sometimes supernatural significance. Thus in Cornwall, England, to hear the cuckoo on the right presaged good fortune, while to hear it on the left boded ill. In Norway more elaborate prognostications were made according to the point of the compass from which the bird was heard calling. As bird augury was practiced on a considerable scale by the Romans, some of the associated notions may have been carried north and have influenced regard for the cuckoo. They must also have been carried to the New World, for an old rural American belief reads similar meanings into the location of the bird—especially the first of the year. If it calls from the south, a good harvest is presaged; if from the north, death or other tragedy; from the east, luck in love; from the west, general good luck.

The similarity of the cuckoo's two syllable call to words in various languages has formed a basis for some traditions. A Bohemian legend relates that the cuckoo is a metamorphosed girl calling for her lost brother or, alternatively, if the words are interpreted differently, announcing that he has been found. The theme of a Serbian song is that the spirit of a dead man could not find release because his sister

Cuckoo Flying Under a Full Moon, Utagawa Hiroshige (1797–1858)

wept so incessantly at his grave. So she transformed herself into a cuckoo and cries continually, 'Ku ku, Ku ku,' meaning 'Where are you?' There may be some connection between these two stories and a belief that the cuckoo goes to a mysterious realm, the land of the dead, in winter. This is supported by an odd Estonian legend according to which Christ came to a cottage after a wicked stepmother had murdered two children and told the father that they would appear in spring as two living creatures. They emerged as a cuckoo and a swallow.

The cuckoo has often been associated in the past with cuckoldry: Shakespeare speaks of the cuckoo who 'mocks married men'. In the *Asinaria* of the Latin dramatist Plautus (c. 250–189 BC), a man's wife, finding him in adultery, shouts at him: 'What? is the cuckoo lying there? Get up, gallant, and go home.' The connection between the cuckoo and cuckoldry appears to have arisen from its nesting behaviour and its consequent reputation as a usurper.

Dog

From the bones of dogs discovered in caves, burial grounds, and lake dwellings in Europe it is known that a breed existed here in the New Stone Age, and in the Bronze and Iron Ages. The domestic dog is probably descended from the grey common wolf, *Canis lupus*.

From the earliest recorded times the dog has been intimately associated with man, his home, and his family. The first mention of the dog in the Bible may be found in the account of the Israelites in Egypt (Exodus, chapter 11) and an early reference to his being man's companion occurs in the Book of Tobit (in the Apocrypha), when Tobias sets out on his journey, accompanied by an angel, 'and the

Hercules and Cerberus, by Antonin Pavel Wagner, Michaelertor, Hofburg Palace, Vienna, Austria

young man's dog with them'. Both cats and dogs were held in high esteem in ancient Egypt; the city of Cynopolis took its name from cynos, a dog. Its citizens were forced by law to provide for all their stray dogs, and they even went to war with a neighbouring city when someone ate one of their dogs. It became customary to name dogs as monuments to the dead: Pharaoh Rameses II (13th century BC) gave his pet dog the name of Anaitis-in-Power, and other dogs which were commemorated by name in this way included Ken, Abu, Akna, Tarn, and Temas. Several paintings of King Tutankhamen's dogs have been discovered, elegantly depicted on the furniture of his tomb. One shows the boy king riding in his golden chariot, chasing deer, with two great mastiffs accompanying him, wearing gold collars.

It is believed that the Egyptians worshipped the dog because of their regard for the dog star, Sirius, the brightest star in the skies. Sirius was venerated by all the people of the Nile, who depended on the rise and fall of the great river for their livelihood. The rising of the river marked for them the most important feast day of the year, and when the time for the flood drew near they watched with anxiety for the rise of Sirius, the dog star, over the horizon. This told them that the floods were soon to be expected, and that their new year was beginning. Falling down on their knees in the light of the star, they worshipped Sirius, faithful as the dog, which never failed them.

Another reason for this dog-worship may have been because the dog-headed god Anubis, or Apu, was said to guide the souls of the dead to the underworld, the abode of Osiris. Thus the god—and the creature whose head he wore—had to be placated and worshipped.

The Smell of an Infidel

The dog was also revered by the early Babylonians, Assyrians, and Chaldeans, who were the people living between the two great rivers, the Euphrates and the Tigris. History relates that the Governor of Babylon owned so many dogs that four towns were made exempt from taxes provided the inhabitants fed their dogs properly. Terracotta statuettes of these ancient creatures may be seen in the British Museum, and their names have a familiar ring even today. The last of the great kings of Assyria in the 7th century BC gave such names to his hunting mastiffs as 'He-Ran-and-Barked', 'The Producer-of-Mischief and 'The Seizer of His Enemies'.

Because the Egyptians worshipped dogs, the Hebrews hated them, and scorned the belief that animals could detect the presence of spirits and ghosts, or were familiar with the world beyond the grave. But the Hebrews, although disliking the dog, were aware of their value. 'Dwell not in a town where no barking dog is heard', they said. According to legend, when the Jews made their silent, secret exodus from Egypt to find the Promised Land, not a single Egyptian dog stirred: 'they did not move their tongues against man or beast'.

Islam abhors the dog for one of the same reasons as the strict Jew. The animal is held to be an unclean eater, a devourer of refuse, and must therefore be classed with the pig. Yet Mohammed allowed dogs to be used for the chase, and the animals captured were eaten, provided the name of Allah was uttered when the hunting dogs were slipped from their leads. The Muslim creed admits two dogs into heaven, Tobit's dog, already mentioned, and

The Hound of Heaven

Behind the image of the watchdog that guards man's possessions, lies that of the personal dog-ghost that protects him on lonely roads; and, deeper still, lies the image of the divine dog that protects man's soul on its way to paradise. Behind the image of the guide dog that leads the blind is that of the personal dog-ghost that guides its master to treasure, and ultimately the divine dog that guides souls through the darkness of the Underworld. (Harnesses moulded on the clay images of dogs found buried with their masters in Chinese tombs are similar to those used by the blind.) Behind the image of the dog that hauls medicine and food to outposts is that of the personal dog-ghost that brings these commodities to the bereaved, and—on the deepest level—that of the divine dog-physician and the suckling bitch-goddess. Dogs on all three levels guard treasure, hound criminals and provide faithful companionship: all three take the initiative in approaching man.

Dog-deities provided the light of the sun, moon and stars, and the waters that fertilized the earth. They were responsible for the potency of man and fertility of women, and they gave protection against all evil influences.

The dog received the souls of dying men. It also judged souls after death, and maintained equilibrium between the light and dark elements. As an incarnation of the Buddha, the dog brought man enlightenment.

Finally, we come to the Hound of Heaven —Chris—the Guide, the Protector, the Healer, the Light of the world, the Judge—who everlastingly pursues man's soul, and operates in the individual psyche as the will toward 'Life more abundant'; as the drive toward greater consciousness.

Patricia Dale, *Green Dog*

the great watchdog Katmir, said to be the Dog of the Seven Sleepers, who appears in the Koran and whose descendants are prized by the Bedouin tribes to this day.

The Country of the Dogs

A number of strange beliefs concerning dogs are held in the East. In various parts of the Orient it is—or was, until very recently—believed that

there are tribes of men whose heads are fashioned in the shape of a dog. Bilad el Kelb, the Country of the Dogs, said by the Sudanese to exist near Uganda, is a land where all the men become dogs at sundown and run around barking fiercely and hunting in the woods. Arabic superstition maintains that there is a tribe called Beni-Kelb (the Sons of the Dog), in which housewives and daughters look like fair women, but the males have no speech, because they are all white hounds. Some say these hounds 'dwell not in the land of Arabia, but inhabit a country beyond the flood, where they devour their old folk as soon as their beards are hoary'. When these fabled animals catch sight of a guest approaching, the story goes, 'the hospitable men-dogs spring forth to meet him, and holding him by his mantle with their teeth, they draw him gently to their nomad tents, where they give him drink and refreshments.'

The Emperors of ancient China hunted tigers, deer, and boar with greyhounds, mastiffs, and chows. The chow, still the commonest dog of China, is traditionally the village guardian, sleeping in the sun by day, on watch at night. In Tibet, the lamas placed images of 'dog-lions' in their sacred temples.

It is clear that the ancient Persians venerated dogs because of the many references in their sacred writings. Three kinds of dog are mentioned in the Zend-Avesta: the house dog, the shepherd's dog, and the vagrant. The stray, prowling around the camps in search of carcasses and unwanted food, was a scavenger well-provided for, being compared to the begging holy man, and was protected by religious laws. In the Zend-Avesta the stray dog is described as being 'self-clothed and self-shod, watchful, wakeful, and sharp-toothed, born to watch over man's goods.'

There are only five sins, according to this work, which carry with them

The Hindus believe that the dog is equal in status to man. 'The wise will look upon a Brahmana possessed of learning and humility, and on a dog'. The dog is therefore a responsible creature, and must pay for his mistakes. Thus, a mad dog that bites without first barking or warning, and wounds a man or sheep, must pay for his crime as if it were willful murder.

In the sacred books of the Hindus there are two four-eyed dogs of Yama, the God of Death of early Vedic mythology. These dogs guard the gates of hell, a myth which has a parallel in Egyptian mythology, in which Anubis, the dog-headed (or jackal-headed) god, was given the same task, and also in Greek myth in which Cerberus is the monstrous watchdog of the underworld.

Superstition in connection with the dog dies hard. In many parts of central Europe today, and in most Slavonic countries, the dog-spirit is said to live in the fields of ripening corn, so that when the wind rustles the corn like

the penalty of being cast into outer darkness. Two of these concern the dog—giving him food too hot to eat, or refusing him food while humans are eating. The faithful, said the holy law, must 'set aside three mouthfuls of bread and give them to the dog'.

When a man dies, as soon as the soul has left the body, the corpse-demon falls upon the body from hell, and this demon can be expelled only by the glance of a four-eyed dog. As the Parsees could never find such a creature, they interpreted the doctrine as meaning a dog with two spots over the eyes.

A yellow-eared and four-eyed dog was believed by many Persians to watch at the head of the Kinvad bridge, the gateway to the next world, and with his fierce barking he was said to drive out the Devil from the souls of the holy ones who walked over the bridge into eternity. This yellow-eared dog, according to the Parsees, was the first creature allowed to guard man's body before God had animated it.

'Arise, O thou yellow-eared dog, arise!' cried God, and the dog immediately barked and shook his ears, so that the Devil, seeing the fierce creature, fled down into hell.

The Watchdogs of Hell

It was considered a serious crime, according to the Zend-Avesta, to kill a sacred water dog, the holiest of dogs. This impious act was believed to bring on a terrible drought which would dry up all the pastures, the drought lasting until the dog's killer was discovered and put to death. Then the holy soul of the dog was offered as a sacrifice for three days and three nights, in front of a blazing fire. The slayer had to endure 20,000 lashings on his back, and then to carry 20,000 loads of wood. He must also kill 10,000 snakes, 10,000 tortoises, 20,000 frogs, 10,000 cats, 10,000 earthworms and flies, and after further punishment he was finally considered to have atoned for his crime.

The Dog Husband

One of the five daughters of an old woman owned a dog. That girl became pregnant, for the dog changed itself into a young man to become her lover. Her family, ashamed, cast her out. But the girl made fire and survived. Eventually she gave birth to four male pups and one female. They grew quickly. One night months later the girl heard sounds like children playing. She spied on the pups, and saw that they had removed their dog coats and were playing in human form, an ability they had kept secret from her. She quickly took the coats and flung them into the fire. From then on the children walked upright as humans. When the girl's family learned that the children were real people, they were all reconciled.

Abridged from *Folk-Tales of the Coast Salish*, ed. Thelma Adamson waves the older folk say, 'Look—the mad dog is in the corn.' This dog is supposed to stay in the cornfield until the last sheaf is left standing. He runs in front of the reapers, seeks sanctuary in the last sheaf, but is finally caught. If a reaper falls ill during the harvest, he is said to have stumbled upon the corn spirit, who has punished him with sickness.

Many legends and superstitions surround the close bond between man and the dog. The Spaniards relate how three dogs, Cubilon, Melampo, and Lubina, went with their masters to worship the infant Christ at Bethlehem, so that even today in Spain it is considered lucky to call dogs by these names.

In the United States, a yellow dog following you awhile, or a strange dog going home with you, means good luck. A dog rolling over continually means visitors coming; a dog eating grass foretells rain. And as elsewhere, a dog howling at night is a death omen —because of the old belief in the dog's supernatural perceptions, enabling it to see the approach of Death himself.

FURTHER READING: Patricia Dale-Green. Dog. (Houghton Mifflin, 1967) with a complete bibliography.

Dolphin

As at the present day, the belief that dolphins were especially friendly to mankind was popularly widespread in the ancient world, and there are many stories of boys riding dolphins and of dolphins saving men from drowning. Perhaps the most famous of all these is the story of Arion, the legendary poet and musician of the 7th century BC, who was threatened with death by sailors who coveted his wealth. He persuaded them to let him sing one last song, then leapt into the sea and was carried safely ashore by a dolphin that

Pot-bellied dog figure, Mexico, State of Colima (200 BC–500 AD). Ceramic, pre-Columbian collection, Worcester Art Museum

had been attracted by his singing.

Many similar tales are told of heroes and demigods, and it has been argued that they represent local versions of the myth of the god who dies and is re-born. Sometimes the dolphin conveys the god safely to the underworld, or brings him back in the spring; sometimes the body of the god is carried to the place that will eventually become his cult centre.

According to one myth about Dionysus, the god hired some sailors for a voyage and the crew, unaware of their master's identity, plotted to abduct him and sell him as a slave. Discovering this, he manifested himself by filling the ship with wild music and flowing wine, turning the oars into serpents and causing a vine to grow up the mast. Terrified, the sailors leapt into the sea, whereupon Poseidon turned them all into dolphins.

The dolphin was associated not only with life and death but with divine

wisdom and love. Apollo sometimes appears as a dolphin god, and the foundation of his celebrated oracle at Delphi was attributed to Cretan sailors who had been led there by a dolphin that Apollo had sent to guide them. Aphrodite and Eros are frequently portrayed riding dolphins, and Poseidon found an amorous task for the dolphin when he sent it in pursuit of the nereid Amphitrite, who had spurned his advances. As a reward for bringing her back to him, according to one account, Poseidon placed the dolphin in the sky as a constellation.

The idea of the dolphin as a guide or guardian on a journey, particularly by water or to the underworld, was widespread among the Greeks and probably throughout the Mediterranean area. At the Greek settlement of Olbia, on the northwest coast of the Black Sea, tokens in the shape of dolphins have been found in the hands of the dead. Dolphins and deities with dolphin attendants, often in forms that resemble the Greek myths, have also been found at many Roman sites as far apart as Libya and Britain.

Classical dolphin beliefs survived into the Christian era and were assimilated to at least one Christian legend. The body of Lucian of Antioch, who was martyred in 312 AD, was thrown into the sea but brought ashore by a dolphin, and Symeon Metaphrastes, the biographer of the saints of the Orthodox Church, tells how the saint's corpse was carried upon the dolphin's back laid out as if resting upon a bed, and it was a marvel to see how the corpse remained immovable upon such a slippery and round body.

Dolphins are found not only in the Mediterranean but in temperate waters elsewhere, and they appear in the folklore of various maritime peoples. In Annam, for example, it was believed that dolphins would save shipwrecked sailors from drowning, and to find a dead dolphin at sea was a sign of bad luck.

That ancient beliefs may not be entirely mythical is suggested by twentieth century reports of drowning people pushed ashore by dolphins, and of dolphins making friends with swimmers and even allowing children to ride them. In recent years, scientists have begun to investigate the reputed intelligence of these creatures and have reported that dolphins seem to have imitated human speech and responded intelligently to certain experiments. However, the possibility that the dolphin is an intelligent species with which man will one day communicate remains a dream. It is a dream in which the dolphin is as benign, and as mysterious, as in the ancient myths.

FURTHER READING: R. Stenvit. The Dolphin. (Dent, 1969); N. Glueck. Deities and Dolphins. (Cassell, 1966).

Dove

A number of different strands have contributed to the folklore and symbolism of the dove, and so various themes are involved. This is understandable when we consider that the folklore concerns more than one species and that different aspects of the bird's behaviour have caught the attention of people in various communities. In most ancient writings the bird referred to is commonly the domestic *Columba livia*, but species are not always clearly differentiated; when the allusion is to migratory species the turtle dove *Turtur communis* is concerned, or in Asia Minor *Turtur risorius*.

The domestication of the dove (or pigeon) dates from remote times, as early Egyptian tomb paintings testify. There was a 'pigeon post' in Babylon and according to Pausanias, the Greek

Dolphins adorn a fresco in the Minoan Palace in Knossos, Crete, Greece.

traveler and geographer of the 2nd century AD, a winner at the Olympic Games sent news of his success to his father by homing pigeon.

The Saracens also used pigeons during the Crusades to maintain communications. But in the Middle East as well as in Europe dove cotes were built and the breeding birds were often exploited for food. Such dove cotes dating from the Middle Ages may still be seen in the English countryside.

Although the flesh of doves has been found appetizing by many peoples and pigeon pie was a popular dish in England, there were inhibitions among the Semites against eating it; this was probably because of the birds' associations with divine beings. At Hierapolis in Syria, one of the chief centres of the worship of Atargatis, a deity similar to Astarte and Ishtar, the statue of the goddess was surmounted by a golden dove. The birds were regarded as so holy that a man who was impious enough to touch one was regarded as defiled for a whole day.

The Greeks explained in a myth how the dove became associated with Aphrodite, the goddess of love. The goddess and her son Eros were playfully competing in picking flowers and as Aphrodite was winning because she had the help of a nymph named Peristera (Dove), so Eros turned the nymph into a dove and henceforth she remained under the protection of Aphrodite.

A Greek writer mentions that as Adonis had been honoured by Aphrodite, the Cyprians cast doves into a pyre to him. The mythology of the goddess, whose names Aphrodite Anadyomene signify Sea Foam Rising from the Sea, and especially the story that she was born from an egg brooded by a dove and pushed ashore by a fish, suggest that her cult came from across the sea to Greece.

Like a number of other birds with religious associations, the dove came

to be regarded as oracular. According to Virgil two doves guided Aeneas to the gloomy valley where the Golden Bough grew on holm oak. There was a tradition at Dodona in Greece that the oracle was founded by a dove, and the oracle in the oasis of Siwa (Amnion) which Alexander the Great sought out was similarly reputed to have owed its origin to a dove. The Romans sacrificed doves to Venus, goddess of love, whom Ovid and other writers represented as riding in a dove-drawn chariot.

The Roman worship of Venus was to a large extent derived from a Phoenician sanctuary (Eryx), where the dove was revered as the companion of Astarte. Thus European beliefs concerning doves were mainly derived from Asia. It may be that the association in the Middle East between doves and goddesses of fertility arose from the conspicuous courtship and prolific breeding of the birds.

The use of the dove as a symbol of peace, in which role it commonly appears today in cartoons, is derived from the reference in Genesis (chapter 8), describing the return of the dove to the Ark. On being sent out the second time, the bird reappeared with an olive leaf in its beak 'so Noah knew that the waters had subsided from off the Earth'. Thus the dove became associated with future prosperity and tranquility, and hence with peace.

Symbol of the Holy Spirit

The importance of the dove in Christian symbolism is derived from the account of the appearance of the bird at Christ's baptism (Matthew, chapter 3; Mark, chapter 1). From the time of the early Church to the present day it has been the symbol of the Holy Spirit, and from the fifth the dove was shown in pictures of the Annunciation. It also appears in representations of the Creation as the spirit of God 'moving over the face of the waters'.

The white dove has long been an emblem of purity and doves were offered in the Jewish rite of purification (Luke, chapter 2). In Malory's *Morte d'Arthur,* as the Holy Spirit appears to Lancelot, a dove carrying a tiny golden censer in its beak enters by the window, impressing the Knights of the Round Table with the purity of the castle of Pellas in which they are assembled. The incident is represented in Wagner's opera *Parsifal.*

Doves feature in the biographies of Saints and Christian personalities down the centuries. In the third century the election of Fabian as Pope was regarded as divinely indicated by a dove landing on his head, and when Clovis was consecrated on Christmas Day, 496, a pure white dove was said to have brought a vial filled with chrism (anointing oil). Probably because of its association with the Virgin Mary, the dove became an emblem of innocence.

The Mourning Dove

For some North American Indians, though, it was an emblem of improvidence or incompetence. California and Great Basin tribes tell many proverbial fables about a dove's inability to build a sound nest, or to profit by the teaching of the thrush.

The voices of doves have contributed to their folklore—which, in the United States, seems often to have been transferred from the English cuckoo. In Georgia, a girl hearing the calls of the returning doves in spring performs a ritual derived from an English cuckoo ritual. After taking some steps she looks in her right shoe for a hair which will match the colour of the hair of the man she will marry. Rural lore also says that the dove's call (like the cuckoo's) predicts rain. Unlike the cuckoo, a constant call of a dove is an omen of death.

Doves have been widely associated with death and mourning, probably due to the soul-bird belief—which is shared by many North American Indian tribes. An English folk belief suggests keeping a live pigeon or dove in the bedroom of a dying man, to prolong his life till the family gathers, apparently because 'the soul, with an affinity for the bird, might thus be made to linger. But in the United States the bird is also a health bringer: turtle doves nesting near, a house keep off rheumatism, and a dead dove placed on the chest cures pneumonia.

FURTHER READING: E. Ingersoll. Birds in Legend, Fable and Folklore. (Singing Tree Press, 1968); D'Arcy Thompso. A Glossary of Greek Birds. (Oxford University Press, London, 1936).

Eagle

Many place names such as 'Eagle Rock' and 'Eagle Mountain' remind us that these magnificent birds were once a familiar sight in the mountainous areas of Europe and North America. Even today when the numbers of birds of prey have been greatly reduced in Europe there are localities, as for example in the eastern Mediterranean, where at times of migration considerable numbers may be seen.

It is significant, not only for the natural historian but also for the folklorist, that species and individuals decrease northward, and it is not surprising to find that eagle lore is most deeply rooted in the mountainous regions of Asia. In religion, magic, and literature the eagle achieved prominence in that continent and the European folklore of this great bird is in large part derivative.

Bird with Two Heads

In antiquity the eagle had a more significant role in Mesopotamia than in Egypt, where Horus, the falcon god, was of considerable importance. This is understandable when we take into consideration the differences in climate and topography between the two regions: such geographical factors had much influence on religion. Ancient Egypt was a land of sunshine dependent on the annual rise of the Nile, whereas the Mesopotamian city states came into being in a region fringed by mountains and menaced by storms and floods. As far back as the 3rd millennium BC a double-headed eagle was associated with Ningursu of Lagash, the Babylonian god of fertility, storm and war. These associations are explicable when we remember the eagle's habit of soaring powerfully among the clouds, which were regarded with the greatest concern in such an area, as they brought fertility to the fields but might also be responsible for disastrous flooding. The double-headed eagle was adopted by the Hittites and later cultures down the centuries. Evidence of the prolonged continuity of tradition is apparent in its having been the emblem of Austria-Hungary.

The sculpture *Ganymede* (Bertel Thorvaldsen, 1817) features Ganymede feeding an eagle, perhaps Zeus in bird form.

Zeus with eagle. Tondo from a black-figured Laconian cup (c. 560 BC)

In the Old Testament the eagle typifies swift and high flight and is noted as frequenting battlefields, but in most contexts the vulture is not clearly distinguished from the eagle. Through inadequate observation and the misunderstanding or deliberate embroidery of texts, eagle lore became increasingly divorced from natural history.

Myth of Rejuvenation

Eagles which survive to maturity are long-lived, as Aristotle, Plato, and Pliny noted. The references in the Old Testament, such as 'youth renewed like the eagle's' (Psalm 103.5), together with observations of sea eagles plunging into the water to secure prey, contributed to the myth of the bird renewing its youth; this became elaborated and embellished as it was transmitted from scholar to scholar down the centuries.

Albertus Magnus (1200–1280 AD), quoting earlier authorities, wrote: 'They say that an old eagle, at the period the young ones are fledged, as soon as she has discovered a clear and copious spring, flies directly upward even to the third region of the air, which we term the region of meteors, and when she feels warm, so as to be almost burning, suddenly dashing down and keeping her wings drawn back, she plunges into the cold water, which by the astringing of the external cold increases the internal heat. She then rises from the water, flies to her nest, and nestling under the wings of her warm young ones melts into perspiration, and thence with her old feathers she puts off her old age, and is clothed afresh; but while she undergoes the renovation she makes prey of her young for food.' Like so many medieval scholars Albertus feels constrained by the weight of authority to quote this account but remarks that as he has known two captive eagles moult in the normal way he must regard this as a miraculous occurrence.

Another example is provided by the eagle-and-serpent motif. It appeared among the Hittites in the myth of the strife between the weather god and the serpent Illuyankas and has continued throughout many centuries and cultures. It appears today in the lectern of Peterborough cathedral, in England, and also in the arms of Mexico. In nature, it is not uncommon to see an eagle carrying a snake in its talons in regions where the snake-eating, short-toed species of this bird are found. In antiquity the conflict between the bird which soars high and the reptile which creeps into holes in the Earth impressed people who looked on it as expressing the tension between the forces at war in the universe. Interpretations varied but the motif remained a dramatic portrayal of life's warring opposites.

In Indo-Iranian mythology, the eagle had an important role. It was associated with two themes, both of which had wide ramifications; in the Hindu text the Rig Veda, it figures as the bringer of the sacred soma, an intoxicating spirit distilled from a plant of this name. In the Avesta, the holy book of the Parsees, it is said to dwell on the 'All-healing Tree Light' which in religion and art is related to the Tree of Life. From the cults in which these large symbolic birds were involved emerged beliefs in monstrous mythical winged creatures, such as the Arabian Anka, the Persian Simurgh, and the Roc which carried off Sinbad the Sailor, as well as composite part-bird beings like the Indian Garuda. There are reminiscences of these strange creatures in the Book of Daniel where we read of a lion with eagle's wings and in Revelation in which other composite creatures are mentioned, underlying such concepts is the attempt to symbolize supernatural power.

Asian influence may be detected in the exalted status of the eagle in Greek mythology, as the attribute or associate of Zeus. His eagle-surmounted scepter at Olympia was in the tradition of Babylonian processional scepters and such signs of authority continued into the Middle Ages.

Probably the beliefs that the eagle's feathers are incorruptible and that if placed with other feathers they consume them are extensions of the tradition of longevity. There may be another such extension in the legend current in Inishbofin at the mouth of Killary Bay, Co. Galway, and also in the Shiant Isles in the Hebrides, that Adam and Eve continue to live on in these islands as eagles.

European eagle lore originated in the mountainous regions of Asia, and the bird features prominently in Indo-Iranian mythology: in one particular illustration from a sixteenth century Persian manuscript the legendary Kai Ka'ns is borne aloft in his flying machine by eagles attracted by the raw meat impaled on the four spears.

The myth of the eagle stone, a nodule said to be brought to the nest by eagles to assist in ovulation, appears to be a variant of a motif in which birds such as the cock, swallow, hoopoe, raven, crow, jay, crane, adjutant stork, and the mythical Roc are associated with stones to which magical properties are frequently attributed.

Companion of the Sun

The eagle, because of its upward soaring flight, is a bird of the sun and therefore associated with solar, sky, and weather powers, but it also has obscure connections with the stars. The constellation Aquila (Eagle) is opposed to Cancer (Crab) and this was represented on ancient coins by showing a crab on the obverse to the eagle. It was also associated in some circumstances with lightning and the thunderbolt. The Romans believed that the eagle was never struck by lightning—hence the practice of burying an eagle's right wing in the fields or vineyards to ward off the hailstones accompanying thunderstorms.

These ancient associations continued in a somewhat disguised form in the legends attached to various Christian saints. St. Medard, bishop of Noyon in the sixth century, was protected during a tempest by the outspread wings of an obliging eagle—and when St. Servatius of Tongeren in Belgium was in discomfort from the hot sun, as he slept by the wayside, an eagle shaded him under its wings. In the Christian church the eagle has long been the symbol of St. John because, as St. Jerome wrote, 'he ascends to the very throne of God'. For this reason most lecterns in cathedrals and churches are in the form of an eagle with outspread wings.

Relief with the two-headed eagle of the Holy Roman Empire near the south entrance of the cathedral of St. Vigilius, Trento, Italy

In the British Isles eagles occur in the folklore of Wales where it is said that King Athur lives on in a cavern guarded by these birds. In stormy weather Welsh people used to say: 'The eagles are breeding whirlwinds on Snowdon. In the neighbourhood of that mountain the cries of eagles were regarded as foretelling disaster. The Greeks and Romans also drew auguries from the behaviour of eagles. Plutarch mentions an eagle's nest with seven eggs as a portent. At the battle of Arbela in Anatolia (331 BC) a sooth-sayer rode close to Alexander the Great assuring him that he had divined by an eagle that he would be victorious over Darius. An eagle is said to have lifted the headgear from Tarquinius Priscus and then replaced it, thereby indicat-ing that he would be king of Rome, as indeed he became in about 616 BC.

Roman legions regarded a site as suitable for winter quarters if there was an eagle's eyrie in the vicinity. Shakespeare, who was well acquainted with the lore of the eagle, referred to a number of classical ideas throughout his plays. The eagle is no exception to the rule that auspicious birds may occasionally predict evil. The appear-ance of one of them was a favourable portent at Alexander's birth, but eagles could also foretell death.

Since the eagle was a powerful aerial creature associated with the gods, por-tions of its body were considered to have medicinal or magical properties. Its feathers, cooked together with a special herb, were said to cure demo-niacs, its liver pounded with honey and balsam cured cataract, presum-ably on the assumption that as the bird's sight is keen a concoction from some organ should be a remedy for poor vision. Its heart served as a love charm but its marrow could be used as a contraceptive—a somewhat ineffec-tive prescription as birds' bones do not contain marrow. The eagle is promi-nent in fables and folktales. A number

of these stories, such as The Eagle and the Tortoise and The Eagle Shot with its Own Feathers, go back to classi-cal sources, and the story of the wren which outwitted the eagle and won the competition as to which bird could fly highest is found in Aesop's Fables.

Egg

The sight of a young bird suddenly breaking out from what seemed a lifeless object encouraged ancient peoples to speculate about the nature of creation. The egg became a symbol of life. Early man was unable to grasp an abstract idea like the creation of the world but he could watch a parallel process in the hatching of an egg. The idea of a 'world egg' which produced the first creator followed from this, and it appears in many early creation myths. Ancient Egyptian writings describe how the sun god Re was born from an egg. In Hindu mythology

To Sea in an Egg-Shell
Many people in the United States invert the shell of a boiled egg after they have eaten it, and smash the other end. This is a relic of the idea that witches used unbroken shells as a means of transport — to fly through the air or sail over the sea. Reginald Scot in The Discoverie of Witchcraft *(1584) says: 'They (witches) can go in and out at auger-holes, and sail in an egg-shell . . . through and under the tempestuous seas.'*

the golden world egg is called hiran-yagarbha; it hatches Brahma, the sun, and he forms the universe from its component parts. The Chinese have a legend that the first being, P'an Ku, appeared from the cosmic egg, and in Oceania various legends ascribe the origin of man to birds' eggs.

The emblem of life became a popu-lar fertility symbol. In some countries peasants carry eggs into the fields as a magic charm to increase the crop and double the yield of grain. The Scots

used to put a nail and an egg in the bottom of the basket and pile seed corn on top. The egg represented the corn 'as full of substance as an egg is full of meat'. Slavs and Germans smeared the plough with egg on Green (Maundy) Thursday, a festival of re-newal, hoping to ensure a good crop.

Eggs are seen as such powerful fertility charms that they are used to correct various types of impotence and sterility. In Pec, a town in Serbia, pain in the testicles is relieved by an application of fried eggs sprinkled with sal ammoniac. The same treatment is said to restore lost virility. In Mo-rocco, a man wishing to increase his sexual capacity eats an egg yolk every morning for forty days. A childless Hungarian woman mixes a little of her husband's blood with the white of an egg and the white speck from the yolk. This mixture is stuffed inside a dead man's bone and buried in a spot where the husband will urinate; then the woman will conceive. According to a traditional Hungarian saying, a man with a big family has 'mixed his blood with eggs'.

Because they contain new life, the seeds of the future, eggs are often used in divination. A popular method of discovering one's future husband was to pierce the shell at Hallowe'en, New Year, or some other significant occa-sion, and catch the white in a glass of water. The shapes which formed were studied carefully and interpreted; in France the egg was broken on some-one's head. Girls in Scotland and Ireland removed the yolk from a hard-boiled egg and filled the cavity with salt. If the charm was to work effec-tively it all had to be eaten, including the shell. This was done at midnight and no water might be drunk before the morning. If the girl dreamed that her lover was bringing some, it meant she was going to be jilted.

Ceremonial burial of an egg is quite common in the Middle East. Moroccans who wish to drive someone insane empty an egg and write the name of a jinn, or spirit, around the shell with a mixture of saffron, fig juice and egg white. The contents of the egg are then mixed with gunpowder and put back. If the egg is buried where the victim habitually walks, the charm will drive him out of his mind. Should the parents of a newborn Moroccan baby omit the customary gift of money to the local schoolmaster so that his pupils can have a holiday, the boys take their revenge. They secretly dig a hole outside the parents' door and steal an egg from their chickens. The egg is interred and a chapter of the Koran recited over it, as is the custom at a funeral. When the mother walks over this her child is doomed to die and she herself will be permanently afflicted with an issue of blood.

In parts of the United States, folk medicine gives a way to erase a birthmark: rub it with a fresh egg each morning for seven days, burying the eggs under the doorstep.

Eggs are also used in protective magic as a guard against the Evil Eye. In north Albania, when a child is born the neighbouring women call and bring eggs to the mother as a gift. If the new arrival is a boy they take an even number: two, four, six, or eight. If it is a girl the number will be odd: one, three, five or seven. One of the eggs is smashed and thrown across the infant's face to guard it from the Evil Eye. In southern Macedonia (Greece), forty days after a birth the mother takes her baby to be 'churched'. On her way back she calls at the homes of the sponsor and closest relations. If the child is a boy the woman of the house takes an egg and, passing it over the infant's face, blesses it, saying, 'Mayest thou live, my little one. Mayest thou grow old, with hoary hair and eyebrows, with a hoary beard and moustache.' The ancient Mayans used eggs to cure, or counteract, the Evil Eye in

Hanácké kraslice, a traditional way of decorating Easter eggs with straw in the region of Haná, in Czechoslovakia. The photograph was taken on an exhibition of egg decorating in Delkovice-Last'any in Czechoslovakia.

a simple ritual where the priest would break the egg and the victim would gaze at it as if it were an eye, burying the egg afterward.

The Easter Egg

A great number of traditions have grown up around the custom of giving Easter eggs, but we do not know precisely when or where this custom originated. A grave excavated at Worms, Germany, and dated about 320 AD, contained two goose eggs painted with stripes and dots, but local archaeologists were unable to say whether the burial was Christian. As early as the time of Pope Gregory the Great (590–604 AD) eggs were forbidden during Lent: hence they became a special treat when the long fasting period was over. Decoration of eggs for Easter existed in Poland before the eleventh century and, in England, the household accounts of King Edward I contain an entry for 18 pence spent on the purchase of 450 eggs, to be coloured or covered with gold leaf and given to the royal household.

In England before the Reformation eggs were used in church ceremonies. The appearance of the new bird from its shell compared to Christ arising from his tomb at the Resurrection. In Old Russia we find similar ideas. The tradition of giving Easter eggs was immensely important and one legend traces the custom to St. Mary who, it is said, was arrested by a centurion in Alexandria. She left a basket of plain eggs at the foot of the cross on the original Good Friday. They were a gift for the soldiers there, so that they might be a little kinder to her son. But the basket was ignored and after a time the blood of Christ flowed down and stained the eggs red. Even today Balkan peasants say that the red colour represents the blood of Christ.

Apart from these plain eggs, peasants of Central and Eastern Europe produce very elaborate patterns with the wax-resist technique. The artist uses a crude wooden pen filled with melted wax to trace patterns on the shell. Areas covered by the wax remain undyed when the egg is dipped in colouring. Designs utilizing as many as seven colours can be created by this method. Other types of decoration involve applique work.

The Poles glue paper shapes to the surface of the shell, and in Serbia they use little circles of coiled metal or tufts of brightly coloured wool. These elaborate eggs were sometimes presented as tokens of love by a young girl to her sweetheart. As many as a hundred might be given and, if a girl felt that the work was beyond her, she employed a local woman to do it. Factory-made chocolate eggs are a comparatively recent innovation.

A traditional English technique for colouring eggs was to tint them with dyes made from plants or to press flowers against the shell. The Wordsworth Museum in Grasmere contains a few eggs decorated for the poet's grandchildren in the 1860s by the family gardener. It is unusual to see such historic specimens, since they generally became casualties of the Easter games. Egg rolling is the best-known game, still practiced in United States and in England and Scotland.

Many superstitions concerning eggs prevail in the United States. Farmers advise against setting a hen in May, or placing an even number of eggs under a hen. Eggs set by a woman will be pullets, but those taken to the nest in a man's hat will be cocks. An egg marked with a black cross will keep weasels away. Eggs laid on Friday are said to cure stomachache. It is unlucky to take hen's eggs in or out of a house after sunset, or to bring birds' eggs inside at any time. Dreaming of eggs foretells good luck, or a wedding; a dream of broken eggs portends a lovers' quarrel; a dream of a lapful of eggs is an omen of riches to come. An old belief from the South says that placing eggs under your parents' bed will make them quarrel.

FURTHER READING: Mircea Eliade. Patterns in Comparative Religion. *(London: Sheed & Ward, 1958); S. G. F. Brandon.* Creation Legends of the Ancient Near East. *(Verry, Lawrence, 1963); Alan W. Watts.* Easter, Its Story and Meaning. *(Schuman, 1950); Christina Hole.* Easter and its Customs. *(Barrows & Co., 1961).*

Elephant

Revered in the East for its strength and stability, the elephant was held to be a symbol of wisdom, moderation, and pity associated with kings and royal authority. In Indian tradition the Earth is held in the universe by eight pairs of elephants which, as they grow tired and shake their burden, cause earthquakes. In Hindu legend Indra, the king of the heavens, rides an elephant called Airavata, while the elephant-headed, single-tusked Ganesha, god of worldly wisdom and prosperity, is regularly petitioned for success before any enterprise or journey; his image is often included on the opening page of students' notebooks. In Siam (now Thailand), sacred white elephants were once reared by human nurses.

In African fables the elephant is a wise chief who impartially settles disputes among the forest creatures. In one story, a hunter finds an elephant skin and hides it. Soon after, he spots a beautiful girl crying because she has lost her clothes. The pair marry, but one day the wife discovers her elephant skin in a barn, puts it on and returns to the bush. Thereafter her sons become ancestors of the clan which has the elephant as its totem and have nothing to fear from these creatures who are their kin.

Elephant hairs are plaited together to make talismans worn to protect against the deadly powers of the Evil Eye.

Opposite page:
Statue of Ganesha, Ahmedabad, India

Falcon

In ancient Egypt the falcon or hawk was sacred to the falcon-headed god Horus and a symbol of the sun, probably because it was able to fly so high in the sky and to look unflinchingly at the sun's orb. Dead falcons were so revered that they were ritually buried in costly coffins. To the Greeks, the falcon was sacred to Apollo, while in Japan the peregrine falcon is a symbol of victory featured in the story of Jimmu Tenno—the bird is believed to have landed on his ship when this mythical ancestor first reached the country's shores.

Feather

The proverbial lightness of the feather—so sensitive that held to the lips of a dying man it betrays whether he is still breathing or not—is the aspect which the ancient Egyptians associated with the hairbreadth balance between truth and lying. In the old Egyptian picture language, the hieroglyph for Maat, goddess of truth and therefore also of justice, was the ostrich feather, and in their ritual beliefs about death and the consequent journey to the underworld, the symbolic feather plays a vital role in the Judgment of the Dead. The deceased entered the Hall of Judgment, which was presided over by Osiris seated on his throne, clad in a tight-fitting robe of feathers, emblem of righteousness. Around the hall sat the forty-two judges, each with the feather of truth on his head. The heart of the dead man was placed in one pan of the scales and in the other was placed Maat, or her symbolic representative the feather, to test the truthfulness of his testimony. Only if the two pans were perfectly balanced,

Many Native Americans use bright plumage in ceremonial dress.

Piegan man, half-length portrait, dressed in war bonnet and holding a feathered coup-stick, facing front

did Osiris give favourable judgment: 'Let the deceased depart victorious.'

Symbol of Peace

Of course many American Indian tribes also used feathers in this way, adding an extra feather to their headgear for every slain enemy. From this practice grew the superb traditional war bonnets of the Plains Indians—cascades of feathers (usually from the golden eagle) down warriors' backs.

The bonnets seem to have originated with the Siouan tribes; other Indians had their own sort, such as the Blackfoot war bonnet, a crown of feathers standing upright around a headband. But the usual inter-tribal borrowings led to the widespread adoption of the Sioux bonnets.

Feathers also functioned most centrally in American Indian religious practice—there reflecting a basic mythological idea, that birds are links and mediators between men and gods.

Feathers had a mostly ornamental use for many northwest Pacific tribes, though such ornaments would indicate rank and status in highly status-conscious communities. Similar considerations operated with the magnificent feather cloaks worn by Mexican and southeast American Indians; and the Creeks and others had turkey-feather fans to be carried during ceremonies as a sign of leadership. But the northwest tribes also brought feathers into religion, in the form of down—which, as a symbol of peace, according to P. E. Goddard, was strewn over men's hair on all religious occasions.

More importantly, feathers were a major part of the ceremonial decorations on many of the objects used in Indian religious worship. Feathers decorated the calumet pipe that was smoked in so many rites of the Plains—and that was borrowed (from the Pawnee and others) by eastern tribes, Iroquois, and Cherokee. The

eastern Indians also borrowed an important rite called the Eagle Dance, in which feathers naturally functioned—mainly in the form of fans made from four eagle, turkey, or wild goose feathers which were carried by the dancers.

Feathers have, predictably, many magical and ritual roles in the complex religious activity of Southwestern Indians. But their greatest prominence is as the primary symbolic decoration on the 'prayer sticks' that are so important to such tribes as the Pueblo or Navaho. The feathers seem to be the specific 'carriers' of the prayer that is being offered up by means of the sticks. Sometimes, indeed, a cluster of feathers on a stick can have the property of carrying a prayer.

And it seems that different feathers can have different associations. So (to oversimplify the symbolism) eagle feathers that are tinted red are linked with curing societies, but in natural colours they are associated with the dead, as are turkey feathers; hawk feathers are connected with war, and so on.

In Hungary during the fifteenth century struggles against the Ottoman Turks, only a man who had slain a Turk was permitted to sport a feather. The so-called Prince of Wales' feathers, the crest consisting of three ostrich feathers, has a similar provenance. It was taken by the Black Prince from John of Luxembourg, whom he left dying on the field at the Battle of Crecy in 1346 and it has remained the badge of the Heir Apparent to the English throne.

Fish

Many meanings are embodied in fish, reflecting the various facets of its nature. Because of its affinity to the sea, from which all created life originated, it was widely held to be sacred. Like the Leviathan, the fabulous fish that bore the whole weight of the world upon its back, the cosmic fish is the symbol of the physical universe. The fish is also a symbol of sexual activity, because of its fecundity.

In the lore of the ancient Chaldeans, the swallow-headed fish was the expression of psychic regeneration, as was Pisces, the sign of the fish and the last sign of the zodiac. Pisces is closely bound up with the symbolism of water, while those born under the sign are said to have some of the characteristics of the fish.

In Asia certain cults practiced fish worship and to their priesthoods the flesh of fish was taboo. Even at the most primitive level fish worship has persisted until modern times. The Indians of Peru not only revered those fish which came to their nets in the greatest profusion but held the doctrine that the first fish created in the world above bore the name 'Heaven'

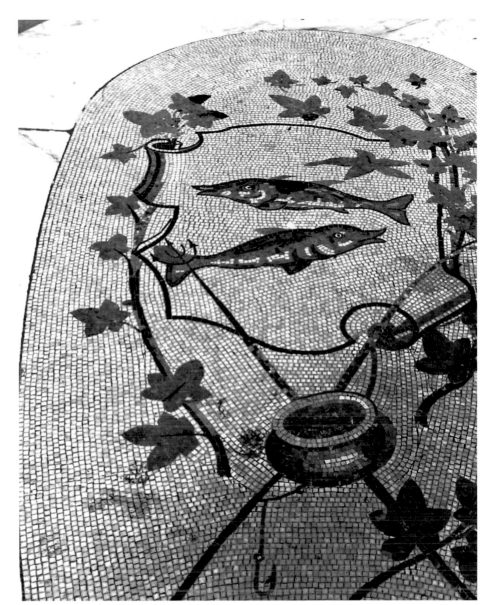

Fish mosaic, Naples Gallery

and was the mother of all the others. The zoologists of the ancient world tended to the belief that fish were the spontaneous creations of the water itself, and in a Sumerian legend the first fish to rise from the primordial waters became the teacher of the arts of civilization to men.

Innumerable are the legends of creatures half-human and half-fish haunting the rivers and coasts of the world. It is significant in this respect that the Sumerian god Ea, god of the waters, had a body like a fish, the tail of a fish, and feet below like a man's.

The existence of a fish cult in the Near East is by no means conclusive,

although it is strongly suggested by the fact that the Syrian form of the goddess Derceto was a fish and also that her son Tammuz was probably associated with a fish. Under the name of Atargatis this deity has been identified as a local form of the Semitic Ishtar-Astarte, goddess of fertility and water. There were sacred fish ponds at Edessa and Ascalon and at Hierapolis where the fish grew to an immense size and would answer to their names. Atargatis is said to have descended into the sacred pond at Hierapolis and to have returned to heaven bearing a fish—the ancestor of the Pisces sign of the zodiac.

Although permanently in the vernacular as a whale, stricter translations from the Old Testament scripture refer to Jonah's culprit as 'a very large fish'. *Jonah and the Whale*, Pieter Lastman

Dagon, god of the Philistines, has been considered a fish god. This idea probably arose from a confusion between *dag*, meaning fish, and *dagan*, meaning corn, for there is every reason to believe that he was a corn deity. In Assyrian monuments, however, a god named Dakan or Dagan is represented as a man with the tail of a fish. Nina the divinity of Lagash, who was the patroness of fishermen and goddess of maternity, was in fact a corn spirit who received offerings of fish. Egypt, where the harvest was the gift of the River Nile, provided a fusion of aquatic and agricultural symbolism in the Egyptian fish deity Rem, who wept fertilizing tears over the land. In India the creative gods Brahma and Vishnu could take the forms of fishes. The first man, Manu, is told by a fish in the Indian version of the flood story to build a ship to save himself from the coming deluge.

Fish have been consumed as holy food, and at the heart of Jewish fish symbolism is the belief that at the end of the world Messias will catch the great fish Leviathan and divide its flesh among the faithful. It would appear that the Jewish custom of eating fish was subsequently adapted by the Christians, who partook of a sacramental fish meal. The fish in Christian symbolism represents Jesus Christ, and in the old Roman catacombs the fish symbol appears frequently. The Greek word for fish is ichthus and the early Christians saw in the letters of this word a monogram summarizing their faith: Iesous CHristos, THeou Uios Soter (Jesus Christ, Son of God, Saviour).

Certain fish of a sacred character, possessing the power of fore-knowledge and of healing, had considerable influence on the divinatory rites of

Celtic peoples. At Ffynnon Beris in Wales the appearance of a trout was always considered a favourable omen, and as recently as the eighteenth century the movements of sacred fish or eel indicated the matrimonial prospects of young girls at Ffynnon Ddwynwen in Anglesey, where an old woman was always present to interpret the oracle.

The Mighty Kraken
Some fish had the power to heal the sick from contact with their divinely 'charged' bodies. To this day, tench applied to the soles of the feet are used for the treatment of yellow jaundice in peasant Ireland; the tench also has the reputation for healing other fish, being known as the 'physician of fishes'.

Even more remarkable were nautical freaks, the monstrous squids, sea serpents, and the mighty kraken of the northern waters, described by Erik Pontoppidan in his *Natural History of Norway* (1752–1753) as 'the largest and most surprising of all the animal creation'. The kraken was said to be about a mile and a half in circumference and so vast as to be frequently mistaken for an island, yet fishermen were often kindly disposed toward it, for its presence at the bottom of the sea was thought to drive shoals of fish into their nets. According to one legend, which would appear to link the kraken with the great cosmic fish of antiquity, only two of these fish existed and these were created at the beginning of the world and would die at the world's end.

The sea monk of Norway, described by Guillaume Rondelet in his *Books of Sea Fishes* in 1544, was a grotesque creature which derived its name from its monklike cowl and tonsured head. The Chinese sea monk raised storms and attacked and capsized junks and was the terror of the Eastern seas.

The inclusion of the fish in the totemic systems of many peoples from Alaska to Africa has led to corresponding taboos. A Polynesian would not eat eel or shark if it happened to be his own individual totem. Anthropologist Margaret Mead reported how certain brightly coloured fish were taboo until they had water poured over them; then they could be safely presented to the tribal chiefs. In Serbia fish is taboo for a pregnant woman; the Tasmanians rejected fish with scales, and the Bantu reject fish absolutely. On the banks of the Seine the John Dory is taboo and in Co. Sligo in Ireland it is the skate. The monk fish, if caught, was always nailed to the masthead, for its presence aboard, like that of priests and clergymen, was believed to bring disaster.

Fish have provided the theme of many legends. Innumerable are the tales of fishes that return lost rings, perhaps the best known being that of the ring recovered from the body of a salmon, as recorded in the life of St. Kentigern, patron saint of Glasgow. This miraculous fish found further immortality by being incorporated in the arms of the city. In the Chinese versions of the Cinderella story a girl receives help from a fish, and in the legend of the cathedral of St. Pol de Léon in Finistère a fish brought a bell to the Ile de Batz from England in the sixth century. There are other curious legends of human souls imprisoned within the bodies of fish and of fabulous reward being offered to fishermen for their liberation.

Some of the most surprising beliefs still form part of the contemporary lore of fishermen. Even the most prosaic of anglers can be victim of the superstition that a fish returned to the water will convey a warning of danger to its fellows. American anglers share this and other fishermen's superstitions: that an offering should be made, perhaps a coin put into the water; that fishing is best in a south or a west wind; that changing poles is unlucky, as is talking about how many fish they caught.

Creature with Principles

Generally speaking, the fish has been thought of as on the side of the angels, although there is a solitary incident in the annals of English witchcraft in which a fish played the part of a familiar spirit, in Leicester in 1616. There seems to be a universal belief that fish are endowed with a kind of pre-knowledge, and also that they have an instinctive moral sense. Thus, blood shed by human beings in anger has been known to result in fish deserting a particular fishing ground.

Most fish superstitions contain vestiges of ancient modes of thought. One of the most interesting of these relates to the system of correspondences, in the belief that every land creature has its marine counterpart. Well-known examples are the sea horse and the sea cow, while the swordfish,

---

The Almighty Fin

Fish (fly-replete, in depth of June,
Dawdling away their wat'ry noon)
Ponder deep wisdom, dark or clear,
Each secret fishy hope or fear.
Fish say, they have their Stream
  and Pond;
But is there anything Beyond?
This life cannot be All, they swear,
For how unpleasant, if it were!
One may not doubt that, somehow,
Good Shall come of Water and of Mud;
And, sure, the reverent eye must see
A Purpose in Liquidity.

We darkly know, by Faith we cry,
The future is not Wholly Dry.
Mud unto mud!—Death eddies near—
Not here the appointed End, not here!
But somewhere, beyond Space
  and Time,
In wetter water, slimier slime!
And there (they trust) there swimmeth
One Who swam ere rivers were begun,
Immense, of fishy form and mind,
Squamous, omnipotent, and kind;
And under that Almighty Fin,
The littlest fish may enter in.

Oh! never fly conceals a hook,
Fish say, in the Eternal Brook,
But more than mundane weeds
  are there,
And mud, celestially fair;
Fat caterpillars drift around,
And Paradisal grubs are found;
Unfading moths, immortal flies,
And the worm that never dies.
And in that Heaven of all their wish,
There shall be no more land, say fish.
    Rupert Brooke, *Heaven*

---

which really exists, was the opposite number of the mythical unicorn. A suggestion of spontaneous generation appears in the superstition that the eel springs to life from river mud or from a horse's hair in water, and of sun worship in the belief that it cannot die until sundown.

A considerable body of mythological lore survives in the British Isles in connection with that once staple article of diet, the herring. According to an article in the journal Folklore, it was a Yorkshire fisherman's belief that the herring evolved from the sea anemone. More common was the belief in the Royal Herring, the monster leader of the shoal on sea journeyings, a creature so sacred that fishermen refused either to catch or harm it. Herrings eaten raw were reported to bring visions of a future bride to Tyneside bachelors. Optimistic sea fishermen had the custom of wrapping inedible portions of herring in a piece of paper before discarding them, in the hope that the bones would knit together again and that the reconstituted herring would then summon its fellows from out of the sea.

Misinformation marches hand in hand with mythology in the lore of individual fishes: the shark is aware of forthcoming death at sea and follows the ship in anticipation of a meal; the skate loves music and can be caught by playing the fiddle. Crustacea and other forms of marine life possess their own individual mythologies. In Tahiti the sea-hermit crab is a god and if eaten without the proper rites can cause death; the shadows of the gods also take the form of crabs.

Harvest of the Sea

As with agriculture on land, the opening of the fishing season is accompanied by special rites, including blessing the boats and sometimes laying salt in the nets to placate the water spirits. In the Caroline archipelago in the Pacific there is ceremonial chanting followed by an obligatory silence; if this silence is not observed, the season will be a failure. Indeed success in fishing must never be mentioned as this constitutes a form of arrogance that is highly objectionable to spirits. Greediness among fishermen is always unlucky. One must never fish every day, as this might be construed as an expression of dissatisfaction with the bounty of the gods.

Inevitably the fish harvest is an occasion for thanksgiving ceremonies, a curious example being the mimetic dance of the Yuchi Indians of North America suggestive of the movements of a fish. More sophisticated are the various modern festivals like the 'harvest of the sea' services at Brixham in Devon, when the churches are decorated with fishing gear and offerings of the catch.

Aids to Love

Preaching to the fish takes place in certain American Indian tribes, based upon the assumption that fish are more likely to submit to a friendly rather than unfriendly group. The preacher, it is said, must utter his words 'in full voice' to be effective. In Scotland at one time fishermen would make pretence to hurl a fellow fisherman into the loch and then haul him out as if he were a fish, so as to provide a clear hint to the fish of precisely what was expected of them.

Certain fish are luck bringers, a well-known example being the fiddle fish, which is never eaten but instead towed behind the fishing boat until it falls to pieces. Even the eating of fish has its appropriate ritual. Mackerel, herring, and pilchard must always be eaten from tail to head, never the reverse way or the main school of fish in the sea will turn tail and desert the fishing waters for the open sea. American belief says that goldfish are lucky, and that whooping cough can be cured by swallowing a live fish.

Fish as prolific breeders could hardly escape becoming sex symbols and as such they were incorporated in the monuments of the ancients. Symbolically the fish represents the male principle in an active state, while the head alone symbolizes the female. (Freud also conceived the fish to be the symbol of the male organ.) Fish have therefore been thought to influence the sexual activities of both men and women. To eat certain fish in Greenland led to pregnancy in either sex, and in Java the husband of a childless woman who ate fish from 'the Children's Sea' was likely to have offspring. It is quite common to prescribe fish for women during pregnancy, and virgins in Brazil, India, and Samoa are said to have been fertilized by presents of fish.

Such aphrodisiacs as oysters and the sepia octopus were favourites in classical times. The book of Tobit, written in the 2nd century BC, describes how the burning of a fish drove away a demon that impeded love. It is not surprising therefore to learn that in medieval love rites fish were often burned rather than eaten, since the acrid smell of burning fish could be calculated to drive away the demonic enemies of love.

The presence of phosphorus in fish is said to have been responsible for the choice of this form of food as an aphrodisiac. More surprising is the widely held belief that fish as a food is good for the brains, a superstition which possibly arose from the fact that the monks, the educated class of an earlier age, ate large quantities of fish. Or perhaps it arose from the half-understood fact that phosphorus is a prominent constituent of human nerve and brain cells.

Frog

In mythology, the frog appears comparatively rarely but, when he does, he seems to evoke either extreme repulsion or respect. The ancient Jews, for instance, regarded him with abhorrence. In the book of Revelation, seven angels 'pour out on the earth the seven bowls of the wrath of God'; when the sixth does so, 'three foul spirits like frogs' appear; 'demonic spirits, performing signs'.

The Jewish attitude to frogs doubtless goes back to the early days of their culture, when these creatures were called up by Moses and Aaron as

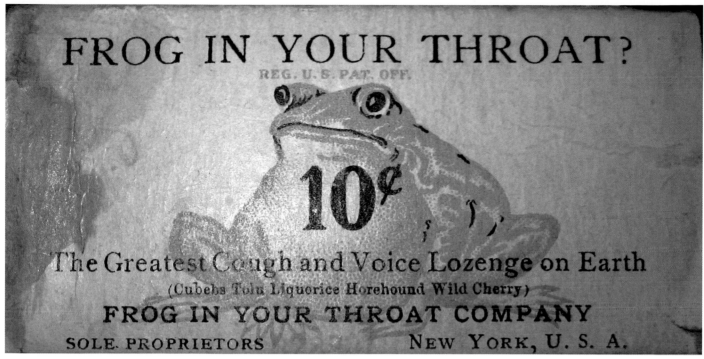

FROG IN YOUR THROAT?

REG. U. S. PAT. OFF.

10¢

The Greatest Cough and Voice Lozenge on Earth

(Cubebs Tolu Liquorice Horehound Wild Cherry)

FROG IN YOUR THROAT COMPANY

SOLE PROPRIETORS   NEW YORK, U. S. A.

Although associated with the ailment, the frog here advertises a cure.

the second plague of Egypt (Exodus, chapter 8). The Egyptians themselves, on the other hand, clearly regarded the frog in quite a different light: Heket, their gentle goddess of childbirth, had the head (and sometimes the entire form) of a frog and, in a variant of the Egyptian myth of the creation of the world, she and her ram-headed hus-

Pygmy riding a frog representing the goddess Ḥāqit. Hellenistic, Lower Egypt

band Khnum were the first to 'build men and make gods'.

The frog also plays an important part in a central Asian creation myth, in which Otshirvani the creator and his assistant Chagan-Shukuty came down from heaven and saw a frog playing in the primeval waters. Chagan-Shukuty picked it up and put it on its back on the surface. Otshirvani sat on the frog's stomach and told his assistant to dive and see what he could find beneath the waters. After repeated attempts, Chagan-Shukuty brought up some earth. At Otshirvani's behest he sprinkled it on the frog which sank, leaving the little earth, just big enough for the divine pair to rest on, afloat on the deep. As they slept, Shulmus the devil came and saw his opportunity to destroy the gods and the still tiny Earth by flinging them into the waters. But when he picked up 'the Earth' it grew so that he could not see around him; he ran, but the more he ran the bigger grew the Earth. Finally, he gave up and dropped the now-enormous Earth just as Otshirvani awoke. Shulmus escaped to continue his evil work in new ways. In other Asian myths the frog supports the

world (as he does in Ceylon, beneath a turtle, a snake, and a giant).

The frog is also connected with the deluge myths found in many parts of the world. In Queensland, Australia, the aborigines say that a great frog once swallowed all the water in the world, causing great drought and suffering. It occurred to the people that if only they could make the frog laugh, he would bring up the water and all would be well again. Several animals did comic turns and dances for him; but he remained unamused until the eel, by squirming and wriggling about, made him roar with laughter. As he laughed the waters burst out, flooding the world and drowning mankind.

The Huron Indians of North America have a similar story saying that all water was in the belly of a huge frog until Ioskeha, the great hero of creation, stabbed him and returned the waters to the lakes and rivers. In other North American legends animals brought order to the world, which was then destroyed by monsters bearing fire and flood; according to the Alaskan tribes, one of these demons was a monstrous frog-woman.

Naturally enough, for many peoples the frog is associated with rain. This is especially so, it seems, in India and South America. Orinoco tribes in Venezuela have kept frogs captive and beat them in time of drought. A hymn in the Hindu Rig Veda seems to show that frogs were worshipped for bringing rain or that, awakened themselves by showers, they brought long life and prosperity; the gods granted rain when the frogs croaked but the moon killed them with the dew. It was also thought that the much-needed moisture could be summoned from the skies by pouring water over a frog or by hanging it up. In Malaya the same result could be achieved by swinging it on the end of a cord. Some Chinese tales say the dew brings frog spawn down from the moon; the frog is called the 'celestial chicken'. By contrast, the Shan and the Karen tribes of Burma regard the frog as the enemy of the moon, the demon that swallows it at eclipses.

In Europe, the frog figured chiefly as an ingredient of magic and was highly regarded in the 'medical' half-world between magic and science. Although toads were preferred to frogs in the practices of witchcraft, the latter were certainly credited with magical qualities; in some countries frogs were always killed on sight because they were thought to be witches. In America and other countries, though, it was deadly bad luck to kill a frog; at the very least it would make your cow's milk bloody. Here the frog is a creature of positive magic; it is lucky if one enters your house, or if you dream of frogs. You make a wish on the first frog heard in spring; and gamblers will be winners if they meet a frog in the road on their way to gamble. American superstition still retains the belief that a hook-shaped bone of the frog will act as a love charm, if placed among the clothing of the person whose love is being sought.

Few animals are more closely associated with the Devil, demons, and witchcraft than goats

Beliefs in the frog's medicinal powers go back a long time. Pliny the Elder, who died in 113 AD, discusses the 'magic' (which he himself professed to regard as silly or wicked) introduced from the East into the Greco-Roman world. In this magic the frog had a variety of uses. It would be carried around a cornfield and buried in the centre before sowing, and dug up before harvest. It would be hung up in orchards and vineyards to protect them from fog and storms, or in a granary to preserve the grain. A person found to be suffering from acute inflammation of the left or right eye could be cured by hanging the corresponding eye of a frog round his neck. The physician Galen considered that to hold a frog, boiled in water and vinegar, in the mouth for some time is quite good for toothache. A later Latin physician, Marcellus, who lived in about 400 AD believed toothache could be cured by spitting in a frog's mouth and asking it to take the pain away. An Arabic text of the ninth century recalls an ancient belief that a woman who performed the same action would not conceive for a year. On the other hand, the primitive Wends, Slav tribes, maintained that it was the frog and not the stork that brought newborn children.

The frog was used in medicine until the seventeenth century. Sufferers from epilepsy were said to have been cured by a powder made of frog's liver; and the eye of a frog, plucked before sunrise and swallowed, or worn as an amulet, was a remedy for fever. It still functions in folk medicine today. In American belief a soup made from nine frogs will cure whooping cough. In other cures the disease has to be 'transferred' to the body of a frog by some magical and usually inhumane process. For instance, to cure headache, you must bind a live frog to your head and keep it there until it dies.

Goat

The goat is a symbol sometimes of agility and sometimes of an obstinate insistence on having one's own way (and so its Latin name is enshrined in the word 'caprice'). In popular traditional astrology those born under Capricorn are assigned the goatish characteristics of leaping over difficulties and butting away obstacles. But the goat is far better known for its proverbial lechery, its stench, and its link with the Devil, all of which are connected in the reports of the witch trials in Europe.

One of the earliest representations of what is claimed to be a witch is to be found in the western doorway of Lyon cathedral in France. In an early fourteenth-century sculptured panel, a hag is shown riding on the back of a goat, and whirling what appears to be a cat in her left hand.

An attack on the witches of Arras in 1460 says that the Devil appeared to them as a goat, a dog, or a monkey, but never in human form. They made offerings to him and worshipped him. 'Then with candles in their hands they kiss the hind parts of the goat that is the Devil . . .'

The statement that the Devil never appeared in human form was contradicted all over Europe, but that he was frequently an animal, especially a goat, was confirmed in many confessions extorted from suspects (though not in England and Scotland, where there is no trace of the Devil as a goat). A character in Martin le Franc's Champion des Dames, of the mid-fifteenth century, says that at 'the obscene synagogue' the witches gazed upon the Devil in the form of a cat or a he-goat.

Some of the descriptions suggest a man dressed up as an animal. At Poitiers in 1574 the Devil was 'a great black goat who talked like a man'. At Avignon he was a man until the time came for him to mount a rock to be worshipped, when he turned into a goat, described in the sentence pronounced in 1582 as filthy, stinking, and black.

Witches were sometimes accused of riding to their sabbaths on demonic goats. The Italian witch judge Paulus Grillandus said that in 1525 a suspect told him that she went to witch meetings riding on a he-goat which would be waiting for her at her door when she wanted to set off. In the Compendium Maleficarum of Francesco-Maria Guazzo, an early seventeenth-century friar who prepared this encyclopedic work on witchcraft at the request of the bishop of Milan, a woodcut portrays a witch riding off in this manner.

Pan and Satyrs

To judge from some of the confessions and the pictures which artists based on them, the Devil often looked not unlike the Greek god Pan, who had a human body with the horns, ears, loins, legs, and hooves of a goat. He was an amorous god and his function was to make flocks fertile. At an annual festival in February in Rome, the Lupercalia, goats and a dog were sacrificed to Faunus, who was identified by classical writers as Pan. Two young men, naked except for girdles made of the skins of the sacrificed animals, ran round the boundary of the old city of Rome on the Palatine hill. They struck at anyone they met with strips of goatskin. They themselves were popularly called 'he-goats' and a woman struck by them was supposed to be delivered from barrenness.

The name of the festival suggests warding off wolves or propitiating a wolf god. It is thought that the ceremony was a rustic ritual mingling purification and fertility magic with the beating of the bounds.

Some writers have assumed a connection between the Devil of the witches and Pan or the satyrs, the lustful goatish creatures who revelled in the train of Dionysus. Dionysus himself, also a god of fertility in some of his aspects, was sometimes connected with the goat (though more often with the bull). At the village of Eleutherai outside Athens he was called Melanaigis, 'he of the black goatskin', and the 'goat-song' in his honour eventually developed into the Greek tragedy.

It is unlikely that the witch religion was a survival of the worship of Pan, Dionysus or any particular pagan deity, but the figure of the lustful man-goat may have influenced the linking of the goat with the lord of witches, who were renowned for their transports of animal lechery.

Another possible source of the goat's link with the Devil can be found in both classical and Jewish traditions, and is again connected with one of the features of witchcraft which most obsessed the persecutors—the orgy in which the worshippers copulated with their master and sometimes with his subordinate demons. There were plenty of classical myths in which human beings had intercourse with gods—who to Christians were devils—and the belief that the powers of darkness desired the love of women also occurred in Jewish lore, especially in the legend of the Watchers, the fallen angels who sinned through their lust for the daughters of men.

A Goat for Azazel

The leader of the Watchers (according to Enoch, a Jewish apocryphal book) was Azazel, who was associated with Mars, the planet of war, and who, after his descent to Earth, taught men evil by showing them how to make weapons of bloodshed. This same Azazel was connected with the Jewish scape-

The Sabbath of Witches, Francisco de Goya (1746–1828)

goat ritual. Down to 70 AD, a goat was selected each year 'for Azazel'. It was formally loaded with the sins of the people and sent away into the wilderness 'to Azazel' (Leviticus, chapter 16). The ritual was not forgotten and in the thirteenth century Rabbi Moses ben Nahmen explained that:

God has commanded us, however, to send a goat on Yom Kippur to the ruler whose realm is in the places of desolation. From the emanation of his power come destruction and ruin; he ascends to the stars of the sword, of blood, of wars, quarrels, wounds, blows, disintegration and destruction. He is associated with the planet Mars. His portion among the peoples is Esau, a people who live by the sword; and his portion among the animals is the goat. The demons are part of his realm and are called in the Bible seirim (he-goats); he and his people are named Seir.

The scapegoat ritual tended to connect the goat with evil and, through the link with Azazel, with the fallen angels and the Devil. This association was hammered home by St. Matthew's gospel (chapter 25) in which Jesus likens the righteous to sheep and the wicked to goats, and says that the goats will be condemned to 'the eternal fire prepared for the devil and his angels'.

The seirim or goat-demons assigned to Azazel by Rabbi Moses ben Nahmen are mentioned several times in the Old Testament. Azazel and the Watchers lusted for mortal women and it seems that the seirim may have done so too, for Leviticus 17.7 says, 'So they shall no more slay their sacrifices for satyrs (seirim), after whom they play the harlot' (and, 'neither shall any woman give herself to a beast to lie with it' (18.23). The translation 'satyrs' itself indicates the mingling in Western Europe of classical and Jewish tradi-

Brahma on Hamsa, Tibet, seventeenth to eighteenth centuries

tions about goatish beings which desire women.

The link between the scapegoat, Azazel, the Watchers or fallen angels, and the lecherous goat-demons may have influenced the medieval belief that witches adored the Devil by copulating with him in the form of a goat. The belief was probably strengthened by the passage in Exodus (chapter 22) which was so frequently cited as a justification for witch-hunting: 'Thou shalt not suffer a witch to live', followed immediately by, 'Whosoever lieth with a beast shall surely be put to

death. He that sacrificeth unto any god save the Lord only, he shall be utterly destroyed' (King James version).

The copulation of women with a divine goat is reported in antiquity from Egypt. In the 5th century BC, Herodotus (book 2) says that the people of Mendes in the Nile Delta venerate all goats, especially male ones. 'One of them is held in particular reverence, and when he dies the whole province goes into mourning . . . In this province not long ago a goat tupped a woman, in full view of everybody—a most surprising incident.'

Herodotus identified the divine he-goat as Pan. Writing much later, Plutarch (died c. 120 AD) says that the most beautiful women were selected to lie with the divine goat of Mendes. Much later still, the goat turns up as Eliphas Levi's Goat of Mendes or Baphomet of Mendes, which he identified with the heathen idol honoured by the Templars and suggested was the Devil of the witches' sabbath.

Goose

In many parts of Europe and Asia the goose has played an important role in local folklore, custom and mythology, and in the British Isles it is one of the few birds still involved in ritual observances. The preservation of such folk rites in a sophisticated society usually indicates the very great antiquity of the beliefs originally associated with them.

The principal goose ritual in England is a goose dinner which is eaten at Michaelmas (29 September), a custom which persists in the Yorkshire Dales and used to be much more widespread. A similar feast is held in Denmark on or near Martinmas (11 November). It might at first seem absurd to regard having goose for dinner as anything more than enjoying a good meal but customs which are observed at specific times of the year often have an interesting history and there is plenty of documented evidence to attest to the great age of the Michaelmas goose feast.

A record dating from the time of Edward IV states that: 'John de la Hay was bound to render to William Barneby, Lord of Lastres, in the county of Hereford, for a parcel of the demesne lands, one goose fit for the Lord's dinner on the fast of St. Michael the Archangel.' George Gascoigne wrote in 1575:

And when the tenants come to pay

their quarter's rent
They bring some fowl at Midsummer,
*   a dish of fish in Lent*
At Christmas a capon, at Michael
*   mas a goose;*
And somewhat else at New Year's
*   tide for fear their lease flies loose.*

By the sixteenth century, therefore, the Michaelmas goose was believed to be a propitiatory gift to keep landlords in good humour. It was believed that eating goose at Michaelmas brought good luck: 'If you eat goose on Michaelmas Day you will never want for money all the year round.' A cookery book of 1709 informs the housewife:

So stubble geese at Michaelmas
are seen upon the spit; next May
produces green.

'Green geese', mentioned by Shakespeare in *Love's Labour's Lost* were birds fed on green pastures and the rhyme obviously implies fertility, increase, and good fortune.

Bird of the Sun

Beliefs and ceremonies associated with the goose used to be characteristic of most northern countries. In pagan Sweden the goose figured as a grave offering; in Germany geese were sacrificed to Odin at the autumnal equinox and there was apparently a goose goddess at Cologne. During the thirteenth century the inhabitants of Friesland were accused of a form of witchcraft in which a goose was involved.

Goose beliefs and cults were not confined to Europe. Among Siberian tribes the bird figured in various ceremonies. One tribe sacrificed it to the river or sky god while another made a 'nest' for the goose god of skin, fur and cloth. Further south, in India, the wild goose is considered of great significance and the god Brahma is frequently depicted riding on a gander. Aphrodite, the Greek goddess of love,

was also shown being borne through the air by a goose. In China a goose was carried at the head of processions and a pair of geese or duck might be presented to a newly married couple; the mandarin duck is a symbol of marital fidelity.

All these beliefs and rituals appear to have originated in an association between the goose and the sun, and consequently with fertility. In early times people were greatly impressed by the spectacle of flocks passing overhead in spring and they connected the birds with the lengthening of the days, greater warmth, growth, and the mating of birds and beasts. Wild geese thus came to represent the power which wrought these changes—the sun or sun god.

Goose feasts may be a dying tradition in the British Isles but another ritual, derived from goose beliefs, is still widely observed though without realization of its origin—the custom of 'breaking the wishbone' when a chicken is served for dinner. A Bavarian physician, writing in 1455, describes the procedure by which the weather might be forecast by examining the breastbone of the Martinmas goose. He adds that the Teutonic knights in Prussia 'waged all their wars by the goose-bone'; that is, they judged by this kind of oracle whether the weather would be propitious for their campaigns. In Yorkshire it was believed that the breastbone of a goose appeared dark in colour before a severe winter and much lighter if the winter were to be mild. It is a natural corollary to belief in the supernatural powers of the goose to attribute oracular significance to its remains.

The Barnacle Goose

The remarkable Irish belief that geese hatch from shellfish relates in particular to the barnacle goose which still winters around the coast of Britain in great numbers. It is now known that barnacle geese only breed north of the Arctic Circle, and in the past the breeding of this noisy, conspicuous species of goose was a mystery, because no nest had ever been found or reported even by those who sailed up to Iceland. After a severe storm, the bodies of birds might be found drifting among flotsam on the beach, covered with barnacles, and so it could be believed that it was the shells themselves which generated the geese.

A tenth century Arab diplomat writing of a country called 'Shasin', probably Ireland, reported: 'There is something marvellous there, such as is nowhere else in the world. On the seashore grow trees, and from time to time the bank gives way and a tree falls into the sea. The waves toss it up and down so much that a white jelly is formed on it. This goes on until the jelly increases in size and assumes the shape of an egg. Then the egg is moulded in the form of a bird with nothing but both feet and the bill attached to the wood. When Allah wills, the wind that blows on it produces feathers and it detaches the feet and bill from the wood. So it becomes a bird which scuttles into the sea about the surface of the water. It is never found alive, but when the sea rises it is thrown by the water on the shore, where it is found dead. It is a black bird similar to the bird that is called the Diver.'

In 1186 the Welsh writer Giraldus Cambrensis, returning from his travels in Ireland, lectured on his experiences to members of Oxford University: 'There are in this place many birds which are called Bernacae,' he said. 'Nature produces them against Nature in the most extraordinary way. They are like marsh geese but somewhat smaller. They are produced from fir timber tossed along the sea and are at first like gum. Afterward they hang down by their beaks as if they were seaweed attached to timber, and are

surrounded by shells in order to grow more freely . . . They do not breed and lay eggs like other birds, nor do they hatch any eggs, nor do they seem to build nests in any corner of the earth. Hence Bishops and religious men do not scruple to dine off these birds at the time of fasting, because they are not flesh nor born of flesh.'

The tradition was given wide currency by John Gerard in his Herball of 1597. He was unscrupulous in his borrowing and often careless in regard to facts. As he and others copied and improved on the illustrations of barnacle geese hatching, these became increasingly realistic, showing birds issuing from barnaclelike fruit growing on a tree by the waterside.

A contributory factor to the survival of this type of myth, lay in the supporting evidence of travelers' tales of fabulous creatures, which gained wide currency and were popular. A Friar Odoric, who made a journey to the Far East in 1313, noted in his journal that he had heard of a tree reputed to bear melons containing 'a little beast like a young lamb'. He added 'I myself have heard reported that there stand certain trees upon the shore of the Irish Sea, bearing fruit like a melon which, at certain times of the year do fall into the water and become birds.'

The barnacle goose legend, as Giraldus had realized, several hundreds of years earlier, provided an excellent excuse for eating goose on fast days. The Irish sense of humour has often come to their rescue, when living was hard and food scarce, so they clung to the belief in the generation of the barnacle goose from shellfish and thus were able to conform to the requirements of church discipline without offending their consciences.

FURTHER READING: Edward A. Armstrong. The Folklore of Birds. *(Dover, 1970); W. Harter.* Birds: In Fact and Legend. *(Sterling, 1979).*

Grasshopper/ Locust/Cricket

Benign crickets and grasshoppers are welcomed for their stridulent 'voices'. In Europe it is an evil omen if crickets desert a house; if heard in a home where they have not previously resided they presage death. In the Bible, locusts were the eighth of the plagues conjured by Moses to test the Egyptians. The Romans viewed such plagues as monsters and held magical ceremonies involving bronze and copper images to quell their destructive powers; in Japan straw images of their larvae were paraded by villagers bearing torches, ringing bells and beating drums. In West Africa locusts are driven out in a scapegoat ceremony in which they are forced to follow a person being driven from an affected area.

Hare

'Now we will begin with the hare. And why Sir will you begin with the hare rather than with any other beast? I will tell you. Because she is the most marvellous beast that is on this earth.' So wrote William Twice in his fouteenth century treatise on hunting.

Marvellous indeed is the hare. As a symbolic figure from the unconscious the hare constantly recurs in dreams, and in world mythology it is closely associated with the moon. It has performed the role of deity and devil, of witch and witch's imp, and for reasons hard to comprehend this most timid of creatures has been regarded by mankind with a mixture of horror and awe.

Opposite page:
The Hares and Frogs,
Wenceslaus Hollar (1607–1677)

Carrying a hare or rabbits foot brings luck and protection.

It was generally accepted that a witch could assume the shape of a hare at will and resume her true form by an incantation. Witches in the shape of hares were notorious for ravaging the farmer's fields and for stealing the milk of cows. They could only be destroyed by a silver bullet—symbol of the moon—fired from a gun. If they were merely injured a search was at once begun for a woman with a similar injury; if such a woman was found, she was often condemned to death.

The Algonquin Indians worshiped the Great Hare, who was credited with forming the Earth. In Greece and China the hare was associated with the moon; in the former country it was connected with the lunar goddess Hecate and in the latter with the powers of augury. Buddha in one of his reincarnations took the form of a hare, which leaped into a fire and implanted its image upon the moon.

In pre-Christian Europe the hare was regarded as a symbol of fertility and therefore of the spring. The Romans divined the future from its movements and its sacred flesh was denied to ordinary mortals.

Many people feel an aversion to eating the meat of the hare and there is a suggestion of totemism underlying this objection. But it is possible that it was also based on the rules of magic: it would be extremely dangerous to consume the flesh of so timid an animal for fear that this same timidity would be transmitted to the eater.

The hare was reverenced in Europe as the spirit of the corn, particularly in Germany, Holland, France, and Ireland, where the reaping of the last of the corn was known as 'cutting the hare'. Reapers were urged on at their labours at harvest end with the cry, 'We'll put the hare out of it today.'

Many relics of the old traditions of divining the future from the movements of the hare survive in modern Europe. In the British Isles a hare running down a village street is an omen of fire. For a hare to cross the path of a traveler is highly ominous, especially if the traveler is a pregnant woman. In this case it is necessary for a piece of cloth to be torn from her clothing to prevent her from giving birth to a hare-lipped child. Fishermen were known to abandon a day's fishing after a hare had crossed their paths, and under no circumstances could the word 'hare' be uttered at sea. A fatal accident in a mine was thought to be foreshadowed by the presence of a white hare or a white rabbit; this is in itself an interesting example of a superstition originally associated with the hare becoming attached to the rabbit, a later arrival in Great Britain.

The white hare also occurs in ghost lore. A typical example was described by Robert Hunt in his *Popular Romances of the West of England*, in the legend of a betrayed girl who died from grief and returned in the shape of a white hare to haunt her lover.

Melancholy as a Hare

Hares have acquired a reputation for melancholia. Many people shunned the flesh solely from fear that by eating it they would become contaminated by melancholy. The belief that the hare's melancholy increased to the point of madness in the month of March (when this creature is especially shy and wild, this being the mating season) survives in the expression 'mad as a March hare'.

The hare strikes a happier note as one of the symbols of the Easter festival, for it was the Easter hare that laid the Easter egg. The ceremony of scrambling for hare pie, which still takes place on Easter Monday at Hallaton in Leicestershire, however, has undertones of ritual sacrifice.

Possibly the best known surviving reminder of the hare's ancient powers is the custom of carrying a hare's foot as a charm against colic, rheumatism, and misfortune generally. It is mentioned in the diaries of Samuel Pepys, who remarked after touching a hare's foot to cure the 'colic', or severe indigestion: 'Strange how fancy works, for I had no sooner handled his foot but I became well and so continue.'

Hawk

Like the eagle and falcon, hawks are frequently connected with the sun in symbolism, because of their flight, dominating ferocity, and yellow eyes. The sparrowhawk belonged to Horus in Egypt and was a solar bird in Greece and Rome. The kite was sacred to Apollo as lord of the Delphic oracle, because circling in the sky it sees everything. In Japan, there was a divine golden kite, Nihongi.

Horse

The modern domesticated horse is of Indo-European origin, arriving in Europe and the Near East as part of the vast migration westward of entire peoples. It has been truly said that in the Old World, civilization marched at the pace of the horse for the social development of primitive societies proceeded in direct ratio to the utilization of 'horse power' in its literal sense. South American civilization, in the absence of the horse, relied instead upon the ox and llama as beasts of burden. The triumphant progress of Cortez in Mexico was due as much to the alarm created among the Indians at the sight of the war horses as to the fighting capacity of the invaders.

Myths of the Norsemen from the Eddas and Sagas: Loki and Svadilfari, Dorothy Hardy (1891–1925)

Lapith fighting a centaur. South Metope 30, Parthenon (c. 447–433 BC)

As a symbol of terrestrial power, the horse was projected into the heavens in the form of the divine horses of the ancient religions, and in this manner became integrated with sky gods. In classical mythology, Poseidon or Neptune is said to have created the horse which became sacred to him, and to have invented horse racing. Among other myths concerning the origins of the horse is that which declared the horse to have been created out of an egg, the symbol of creation.

In Christian art the horse is represented as the symbol of the three saints Anastasius, Hippolytus, and Quirinus, who are shown being torn asunder by wild horses. However, to horse users everywhere, the horse has always symbolized power, speed, and pride.

In its role as a divinity the horse has played many parts, of which the divine horses of King Diomedes and the Celtic goddess Epona are prominent examples. Epona, a divinity of the Gauls, was both a goddess and protectress of horses, a tribute to the valour of the Celtic warriors.

Many gods, goddesses, and demi-gods were closely associated with the horse in antiquity and Demeter, the Greek fertility goddess, was sometimes represented with the head of a horse. In almost all of the ancient civilizations the sun was believed to have been drawn across the sky in his chariot by celestial horses. It was in this august fashion that Dag, the Norse god of day, was conveyed through the heavens by the white steed 'Shining Mane' which spread its light across the whole living world. According to Norse mythology Mani, the moon goddess, traveled across the sky in a car drawn by Alsvidur, 'the All Swift'. Diana, goddess of the moon, traveled likewise in a horse-drawn chariot. The gods Thor and Helios drove their cosmic chariots through the heavens, while the mighty Odin was borne through the clouds on the back of his eight-footed steed.

Driven over Precipices

In sacrifice we submit our most precious possessions to the gods, and the horse, the symbol of social power in ancient societies, was accorded this dreadful honour. In Imperial Rome, the October Horse was sacrificed as an offering to Mars. In some of these barbaric rites, horses were driven over precipices as offerings to the sea deities. Part of the funeral rites of the warlord of old was the obligatory killing of the war horse in order that it might continue to serve its dead master in the afterlife, a custom which continued until as late as the fourteenth century. The traditional military funeral with its riderless horse, carrying its dead master's boots reversed on either side, is a last surviving relic of this form of sacrifice. The nomadic tribes of the Altai Mountains of Central Asia continued the sacrifice of horses until well into the twentieth century, despite attempts to suppress the custom by the Soviet government. In a government poster of the 1920s the skins of flayed horses are displayed on poles above the legend: 'There are no gods. No sacrifices of horses will deliver you from your need.'

In Western Europe horses were burned alive in rural districts as late as the eighteenth century as a magical device, intended to remove disease from the remainder of the herd, or were burned alive in order to prevent the death or theft of other animals.

To ancient man the drama of the heavens was performed by demigods, animals, and men, the gigantic reflections of their pale selves on Earth. The hooves of the divine horses pulling the celestial chariots accounted for the thunder; the whiplash was the lightning that flashed terrifyingly across the sky; and there were the famous Wind Horses among whom were Pegasus and Hofvarpnir, steed of Gna, messenger of the divine Frigg. Sometimes the heavens would be agitated into a fury of terrifying commotion, as if an army was marching through the clouds. Out of this was born the legend of the Wild Huntsman with his diabolical horse and baying hounds, searching for human souls.

Satanic Steed

Allusions to mystical, allegorical, and cosmic horses find a place in many religions including Christianity. In both the Old and New Testaments occur supernatural horses. Elijah and Elisha saw visions of fiery horses and in Revelation, St. John describes the terrible horses that harry mankind, having 'tails like serpents'.

Fairy horses and horsemen were an integral part of the mystical lore of the past, whether it was the enchanted horse of the Arabian Nights or the minute mounts of the elves and leprechauns of the West. Fairies were supposed to travel from place to place at fantastic speeds once they had uttered the magical cry, 'Horse and Hattock'. In the demonic beliefs of the past the horse played a central role. There was the colt-pixie, an evil spirit in the guise of a human being which lured horses to their doom. In the annals of witchcraft diabolic colts sometimes become the familiars of witches. Satan himself had been known to manifest himself in the guise of a horse and it was perhaps for this reason that a famous performing horse of the sixteenth century was burned as a witch in Rouen when taken abroad by its English master.

It was believed that a human being could be transformed by witchcraft into a horse. If the witch approached a sleeping victim and threw a magic halter over his head, he would be immediately transformed into a mount and could be ridden to the witches' sabbath. However, the bewitched human could turn the tables on the hag if he could slip off the bridle and throw it over her head, for she would be transformed into a mare and could be ridden over the countryside until she sank to the ground with exhaustion. Devils and witches were thought to delight in tangling the manes of horses and stealing into the stables and riding them undetected into the night. As a magical defence against such intrusion an amulet in the form of a stone with a hole in it was hung inside the stable door. An example of one of these, recently discovered in Epping Forest, near London, is in the shape of a crudely formed pentacle. Verbal charms both sacred and profane were commonplace in magically-minded Europe. In the Durham Ritual the aid of Abraham is sought to protect the horse from the powers of darkness, a significant example of the manner in which Christian ideology became permeated by pagan concepts. The ever-popular horse brasses in the shapes of suns, crescent moons, hearts and swastikas, among other symbols, were originally worn as a form of defence against the Evil Eye, to which the horse was thought to be peculiarly susceptible.

The horse played a part in European fertility rites. The character of the Hodening Horse, a man disguised in a white sheet and horse's head who trots around Kent villages at Christmas and All Souls' Day, and the Welsh custom of the Mari Lwyd involving a horse skull (possibly a relic of Roman horse sacrifice), probably survive from fertility rituals. In many May Day festivals the hobby horse plays a prominent role, the best known of which is the Padstow Horse which dominates the local Spring rites. In primitive communities such as those of the North American Indians, the horse dance was sometimes performed as a rite to emphasize the importance of the horse to the tribe.

Phantom Horses

Over the centuries the sharper outlines of the old divine myths have sometimes become blurred, overlapping into traditional ghost lore. There are innumerable tales of phantom horses which often pull ghostly coaches along lonely country roads. In Devon the ghost of Sir Francis Drake still drives his horrific black hearse pulled by headless horses. At Wyecollar Hall near Colne and at Loughton, Essex, the phantom horsemen gallop down their respective beats; the last being

Dick Turpin, the infamous highwayman with the ghost of the woman he murdered clinging to his back. There are also many fascinating legends of phantom horses and riders who sleep through the centuries within caverns buried deep in the hillsides, ready to gallop forth at the clarion call of invasion in defence of their native lands. An interesting example of the fusion of ghost and elemental was the phantom white horse which was once observed at Oxwich, Glamorgan, walking upon its hind legs and then disappearing into the churchyard well. Until about fifty years ago a phantom woman riding through the skies on a white horse could be seen at Mayland in Essex, if one looked through the branches of a certain oak tree.

Horses reputedly possess certain clairvoyant powers of their own which enable them to perceive otherwise invisible intruders from the spirit world. They are notorious for obstinately halting at haunted crossroads, quite unresponsive to the proddings of spur or whip, and there are cases where horses have refused to pass a spot where it afterward transpired that a funeral was to pass that day. According to the ancient system of divination from horses known as hippomancy, the Celts made their sacred horses walk in procession behind a chariot and ascertained the future from its movements. Germanic priests drew inferences from the carefully observed manner in which their divine horses emerged from the temples; if they advanced right foot first the omen was favourable, while the left was unfavourable. Well into modern times the horse continued to play a modified role in rustic divination. In some places it is still considered lucky to meet a white horse, while in others it is unlucky. A once common ritual was the custom of spitting and

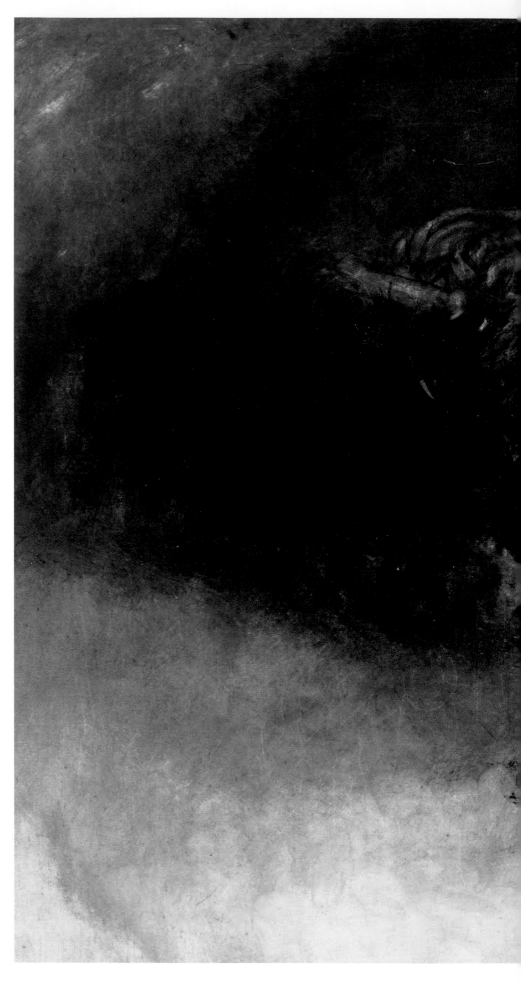

Death on a Pale Horse. J. M. W. Turner (1775–1851)

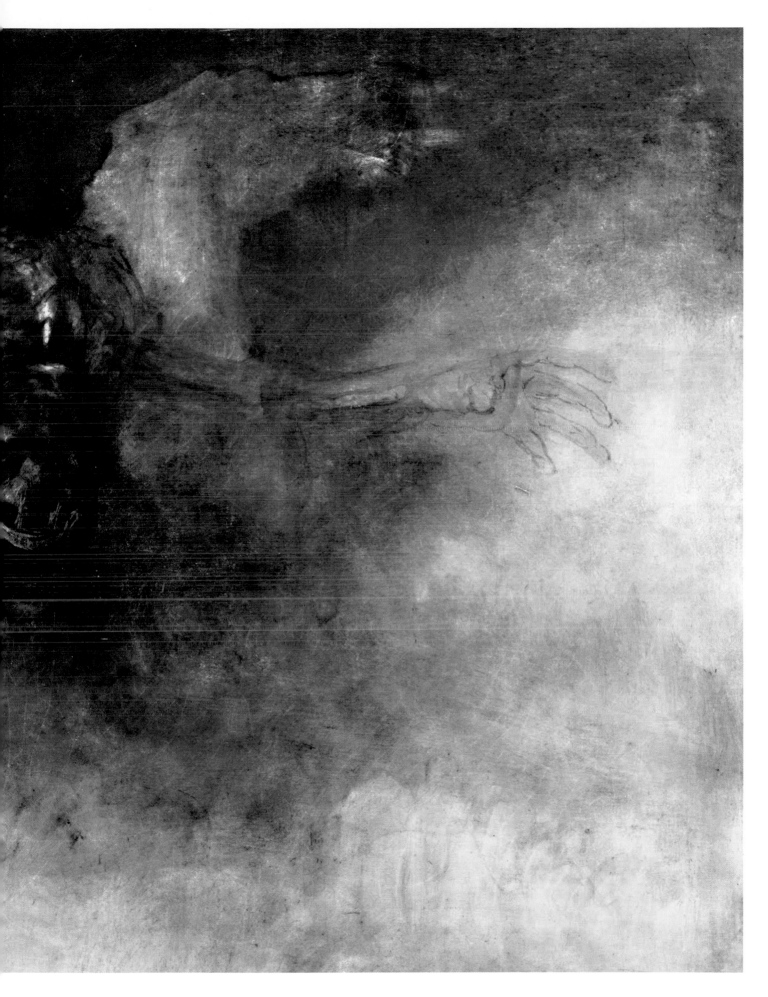

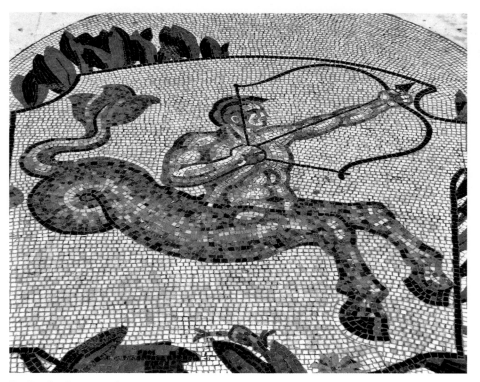

Sagittarius in a mosaic

appears in a dream is a good sign and understandably so, since it is the traditional friend and servant of mankind.

ERIC MAPLE

FURTHER READING: Arthur Vernon. History and Romance of the Horse. (Gale, 1975); M. Oldfield Howey. The Horse in Magic and Myth. (Folcroft, 1979).

Hyena & Jackal

The nocturnal wanderings of the hyena, its association with death, and the uncanny call of the striped species, which is said to resemble demonic laughter, have been responsible for the animal's importance in witchcraft. Although it is found mainly in the warmer regions of Asia and Africa, it is also credited with magical properties in European folklore.

Among the Matabele of Rhodesia it was said that wizards dug up corpses which they then turned into hyenas to use as messengers or steeds, while in Africa generally there was a widespread belief that wizards could transform themselves into hyenas. In Abyssinia tales were told of men transforming themselves into the animals while in full view of other people, and in the Sudan it was thought that magicians became hyenas at night in order to roam the countryside howling and gorging themselves. It is said that a soldier who shot a hyena followed the trail of blood to a hut where he found a wizard dying of a fresh wound; the soldier himself died shortly afterward. In England tales of this kind were told of wounded hares later discovered to be witches. The Wanika of East Africa regarded the hyena as one of their ancestors and it was an offence to imitate its call. Like some South African Bantu they exposed their dead to be eaten by these animals.

In Europe a great variety of magical properties were attributed to the

---

making a wish on seeing a white horse and crossing the fingers until a dog was seen. A similar superstition was applied to piebald horses.

Until the early years of the present century, and still surviving in some country places, there was an elite class of horse handlers known as 'Whisperers', whose members were supposed to exercise an uncanny power over horses. This mysterious art, which was known also in America, enabled the handler not only to tame the most intractable of animals but to paralyze its movements if he so desired—in other words, apparently to bewitch it. According to a recent investigation of this practice by George Ewart Evans, the Whisperers' power was due not to witchcraft, to which it was commonly imputed, but to a shrewd understanding of horse psychology and physiology, certain secret aromatic oils being used to halt or attract the animals.

The magic of the horse has had its influence upon both interior and exterior domestic architecture. Attached to the gable ends of German houses the horse's head served as a defensive charm against evil spirits, while horse skulls were often employed as household amulets.

Many eccentric theories in folklore survive in either direct or indirect examples of the supposed magical power of the horse, such as the belief that horse hairs placed round the neck cure goitre, or inserted in a sandwich will banish worms in children, or again, if left in water the hairs will become transformed into eels. John W. Tesley, who was interested in folk remedies, recommended as a cure for cancer an infusion of dried and powdered horse spurs (the callosities on the inside of the horse's leg) in warm milk and ale. Pennsylvania Germans attempted to free their children from witchcraft by passing them through a horse collar.

Many horse superstitions are still religiously observed by horsemen. To change the name of a horse, it is thought, changes its luck. It is still a common practice when entering a horse for a show to mutter 'break a leg' as a prophylactic charm against the hostile intervention of the jealous gods. To dream of a white horse is an omen of death in some places in Britain, but generally the horse that hyena. Greek writers recounted the Arab belief that if one of these animals stepped on a man's shadow it deprived him of the powers of speech and movement. They also reported that if a dog, standing on a roof in the moonlight, cast its shadow where a hyena could step on it the dog would fall to the ground. The statement by the sixteenth century writer, Bartholomew, that the hyena by circling an animal three times, could charm it into immobility may be a later elaboration of these notions.

Cure for Crocodile Bites

The supposed similarity between the hyena's howls and human cries or laughter, which contributed to African beliefs in humans changing into hyenas, also led to strange European notions. Aristotle stated that the hyena lured dogs by imitating the sound of a man vomiting, and Bartholomew elaborated on this idea in an account of how hyenas approached houses at night, mimicking the human voice and even calling men by name in order to devour them. Sir Kenelm Digby, the seventeenth century scientist, varied the theme; he wrote that the hyena could imitate the calls of all sorts of animals so that they flocked to him and were captured.

Among Pliny's prescriptions concerning the magical virtues of the hyena's body were the following: if haunted by nocturnal spirits wear a tooth from the beast suspended on a thread round your neck; to foil the charms of wizards smear the blood of a hyena around the doorposts of the house; to cause a woman to fall in love with you touch her lips with a whisker from the muzzle of one of these beasts.

Encouraged by such statements English writers of the fifteenth to the seventeenth centuries pleased people who liked to be told of the strange qualities of unfamiliar animals by providing them with far fetched ideas that owed more to imagination than to tradition. It was said that witches ate the heart and liver of the hyena in order to perform witchcraft. Top sell, whose *History of Four-footed Beasts* was published in 1607, stated that a hyena's skin hung on the gate of an orchard would ward off hail or lightning. He also remarked: 'The dung or filth of an hyena, being mingled with certain other medicines is very excellent to cure the bites and stingings of crocodiles and other venomous beasts.' According to this fanciful writer a man wearing a hyena's skin could pass unscathed through the midst of his enemies and the marrow of the animal's right foot 'is profitable for a woman that loveth not her husband, if it be put into her nostrils'.

Guardian of Cemeteries

Christian hermits living in the Egyptian desert in the fourth century were on familiar terms with hyenas and did not attribute magical properties to them. Stories are told of a hyena who led a hermit far into the desert to the cave where another was living; of another which on finding a hermit lost in the wilderness guided him to safety; and of St. Macarius of Alexandria who, when a hyena brought her blind whelp to him, cured it by applying saliva to its eyes.

In a number of biblical contexts the word translated as fox refers to the jackal, an animal that appears in folk-

Spotted hyena mask. Many African cultures tied the spotted hyena to witchcraft.

lore and folktales as crafty and shrewd rather than malicious. As a scavenger and eater of carrion it acquired in some areas an association with death: in ancient Egypt Anubis, the jackal-headed guardian of cemeteries guided the dead to the judgement of Osiris. According to the ancient Indian laws of Manu a faithless wife would be a jackal in her next incarnation. The animal's apparent timidity is the reason why the Bushmen of southern Africa protect their children against becoming timorous by forbidding them to eat the animal's heart.

In Indian folktales the jackal has a role rather similar to that of the cunning fox in Europe. In one story a crocodile seizes a jackal's leg but the jackal talks the reptile into believing he is holding a tree root. In another a Brahmin who compassionately releases a tiger from a trap is about to be eaten when a jackal persuades the tiger to re-enter the trap. In yet another, an elephant swallows a jackal but dies when it is eaten by the animal inside it. The jackal finds himself trapped in the elephant's dried-up skin but calls for rain and escapes when rain falls and softens the hide.

Insects

The insect world comprises an enormous group of organisms, many with very different characteristics. There are, for example, over 250,000 species of beetle, some of which are microscopic, while others are bigger than the smallest birds; their colouration varies from dull and inconspicuous to brilliantly iridescent. The characteristics of insects have become associated with mythology and folklore and have given rise to remarkable beliefs and superstitions.

Humanity has been interested in insects not just out of curiosity, but because some have forced their attentions unpleasantly upon it as parasites, pests,

and destroyers of crops. The locust, the tsetse fly, the plague-disseminating flea and the mosquito have profoundly affected human history and economy. Only the bee and the silkworm have been 'domesticated'. The mythology of insects has been mainly concerned with their origins, transmigrations, oracular significance, explaining their characteristics, devices for expelling noxious species and the use of insects in magic and medicine.

From ancient times ants have been mentioned in proverbs and fables as paragons of industry. In Thessaly their digging activities caused them to be associated with agriculture through the myth of the nymph Myrmex, who falsely claimed to have invented the plough. Athene, who had actually done so, transformed her into an ant. There was also an ancient belief that the ants of Ethiopia and India dug for gold. An ancient German belief was that they could be driven away by ringing bells. In England it was said to be a sign of rain when ants were seen carrying their pupae, but in Germany this was interpreted as indicating fine weather. In ancient and medieval times, treatment in various ways with ants was believed to have medical value, especially for people suffering from fever.

Thunder Chrysalis

It was a common belief, mentioned by Aristotle and persisting well into the seventeenth century, that insects were spontaneously generated. Beetles were said to arise from putrefying flesh and from dung, where they were often seen to gather. The ancient Egyptian belief in the scarab as a symbol of life beyond the grave appears to have arisen from observations of beetles emerging from the ball of dung in which some beetles place their eggs. The ladybird is called by names which associate the insect with Our Lady, such as Marienkäfer (Mary beetle) in Germany. It is still the

custom in Britain for children to place a ladybird on a finger and say to it:

Ladybird, ladybird, fly away home,
Your house is on fire and your children are gone.

In some areas it was thought that the direction in which a ladybird flew indicated where a girl's 'true love' could be expected; in Sussex, when a ladybird landed on someone, its spots were counted to ascertain how many happy months to expect. In the Hebrides its five spots are said to represent the wounds of Christ, although the number of spots varies with different species.

Beliefs concerning the cockchafer have some similarities to ladybird beliefs and seem transferrable from one to the other. The cockchafer is regarded with favour in France and Germany; in Bavaria it was considered a good omen if a beetle settled on a person's hand; in France it was often carried in processions. Like the ladybird, it appears to have been anciently associated with spring and fertility.

The stag beetle was connected with thunder and in Germany was called Donner-puppe (thunder chrysalis), perhaps through its association with the oak tree, the tree most often struck in a thunderstorm. In Scotland blindfolded boys struck at it, probably on the assumption that a black-horned creature must be devilish. According to a Hebridean legend, the burying beetle betrayed Christ during the Flight of the Holy Family into Egypt by telling his pursuers that he passed by the previous evening, but the dung beetle contradicted it, saying that he went by a year ago. So, boys kill the burying beetle but merely turn the dung beetle on its back, because it lied in a good cause.

The Irish traditionally say that the devil's coach horse beetle is putting a curse on you when it raises its tail, and

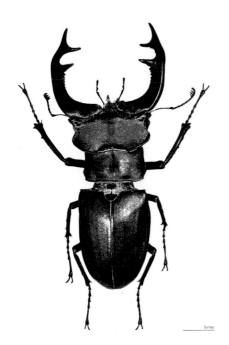

Lucanus cervus **(stag beetle), dorsal side**

there are still people in Britain who are said to be upset by the ominous tapping of the death watch beetle—and not just because such beetles devour wood with an appalling speed.

In Africa, Baronga women threw noxious beetles into a lake, screeching the obscenities which were characteristic of rain-making ceremonies. Arabs used to employ sympathetic magic to recall a runaway slave, tethering a beetle of the sex of the fugitive by a thread to a nail, in the belief that, as it crawled in diminishing circles, the slave would be drawn back. In East Anglia at the end of the nineteenth century a beetle was suspended by a thread round a child's neck to cure whooping cough, on the assumption that, as it decayed, the ailment would disappear.

It has been widely believed that butterflies, being ethereal creatures, were the actual souls of individuals. A myth of the Pima Indians of North America relates that the Creator flew around as a butterfly to find a place for man. On Greek vases the soul was at first represented as a tiny winged human being; later artists depicted it as a butterfly. Among some tribesmen

of northeastern Asia, it was thought that the soul-substance could leave the body during life, so causing illness or unconsciousness. A grey butterfly or moth was tied in a cloth round a patient's neck to restore him.

There was a Gaelic (Scots-Irish) tradition that a butterfly flitting over a corpse was its soul; in Ireland such an event indicated its everlasting bliss. In 1810, an Irish girl was reprimanded for chasing a butterfly because it might be the spirit of her grandmother. According to a Gaelic folktale, a soul in the guise of a butterfly went wandering and was about to enter a sleeping man when it was killed. In Calabria in southern Italy, a white butterfly fluttering around a cradle was called the baby's spirit, while in East Anglia, to see a white butterfly signified that a baby had died.

According to an Australian tale, an aborigine who left his starving son in a shelter of bark and branches while he hunted for food was reassured on finding the larva of a case moth (a species which surrounds itself with a case of bark) clinging to a tree. The boy had evidently been changed into this insect. In the Solomon Islands a man could choose the creature of

his reincarnation and often selected a butterfly. In China and Japan this insect has propitious symbolism. One Japanese Noh play concerns a human soul transformed into a butterfly.

Perhaps the widespread association of butterflies with the disembodied soul has given them a sinister reputation in some areas and in particular circumstances. From Scotland to the Balkans, they were sometimes thought of as witches or as the souls of witches. Romanians said that naughty children became butterflies and that these should therefore be killed. Butterflies have also been believed to be disease-carrying spirits. In some English counties it was the custom to kill the first butterfly seen and in Westphalia children knocked at doors on St. Peter's Day, 22 February, bidding the butterflies go away. The householders themselves might go through the rooms to expel the insects by this sort of ritual which, if omitted, could entail misfortune such as the multiplication of vermin or outbreaks of cattle disease.

Depending to their numbers or their hue, butterflies could have different significance. In Cambridgeshire to see three butterflies was lucky, while

Dung beetle, Etosha National Park, Namibia

MAN, MYTH, AND MAGIC

in other counties this could mean misfortune. In the North of England red butterflies were often killed. A dark butterfly forecast illness in Bulgaria, a white one in Ruthenia in the Russian Ukraine. The death's head hawk moth, because of the similarity of its thorax markings to a skull and its ability to squeak, was also regarded as sinister.

The wormlike appearance of the caterpillar, the larva of the butterfly or moth, is probably the reason for the widespread superstition that it was made by the Devil, or by witches with the help of the Devil. In Switzerland there is a belief that tree spirits are responsible for caterpillars, and that they send them to creep into a man's brain and drive him mad. In Romania they are said to have originated in the Devil's tears, and the Bantu of South Africa believe that the souls of the dead take the form of caterpillars.

The insect has some virtues in folk medicine: according to English lore carrying a caterpillar around will ward off fevers, and in ancient times the bite of a poisonous snake was rubbed with a mixture made from a cabbage caterpillar and oil.

The Devil's Darning Needle

Cicadas and crickets attracted special attention because of their chirping or stridulating calls. Alike in ancient Greece and in Shantung in China they were believed to live on wind and dew. According to Plato's account of the story told by Socrates the Muses live again in these insect songsters. Early Chinese authors wrote enthusiastically about them and the Chinese still keep them in small cages. Aesop's fable of the Ant and the Cicada (or Grasshopper) is very ancient. In Japan the cricket is regarded as giving warning of the approach of winter.

Swallowtail butterfly

In Europe if crickets forsake a house it may be regarded as an evil omen but occasionally one of these insects chirping in a house where they have not been heard before is considered to be an omen of death. These are instances of the tendency for some unusual occurrence to be considered to foretell a calamity.

Magical ceremonies were widely conducted with the aim of destroying or expelling locusts and grasshoppers. An Arab writer mentions a golden locust set up to guard a town from infestation and it is reported that Naples was rid of grasshoppers by means of bronze or copper images of them. In Japan straw images of larvae of a certain species of insect which was damaging the rice fields were paraded around the infested area by villagers bearing torches, ringing bells and beating drums. The images were then thrown into the river or burned. In the Argentine tin cans were beaten to frighten away grasshoppers, as in Europe beekeepers made a similar din to encourage swarming bees to settle.

When locusts or beetles were destroying the crops in Albania the women would go in funeral procession to a stream and drown a few in the hope of eliminating them all. In Mirzapur, India, an insect was caught, its head marked with a red spot and dismissed with a salaam on the assumption that it would lead its fellows away. Among the Wajagga in Africa a locust's legs were tied together and it was let fly in the belief that the horde would accompany it beyond the boundaries of the tribe. In 1590 a plague of locusts in Ethiopia was excommunicated and confidence in the effectiveness of the procedure was reinforced by the outbreak of a storm which destroyed them.

The long, slender bodies of dragon flies have given rise to their being called 'Devil's darning needles'. They have been viewed with suspicion partly

Enallagma cyathigerum **(common blue damselfly) with prey**

because their claspers at the end of the abdomen have been supposed to be stings. It was said that they would sew up the mouths of scolding women and cursing men. In Cambridgeshire an elderly man said recently that it was lucky to see a dragonfly skimming over a pool. He would then cross his fingers and wish, as he had been told to do during his boyhood. In Japan, where the dragonfly is an emblem of summer it is regarded as a lucky talisman. It symbolizes courage and the return of the dead to their homes on Earth. On the South China coast when dragonflies appear in large numbers they are believed to presage a typhoon.

Fleas were said to be generated from dust, filth, or horse urine, whereas lice were believed to appear spontaneously from greasy cloth or 'from the very flesh of man'. In East Anglia infestations of lice were attributed to the malevolence of witches. The remedy was to stick pins into a piece of flannel which had been next to the patient's skin and then burn it at midnight. In Ireland it was thought that strewing foxgloves around would cause fleas to leave and in England until the end of the last century a housewife would rise early on 1 March to brush around the lintel and hinges of the door; it was

assumed that the fleas would know better than to enter or to remain where the lady of the house was so diligent.

It was also believed that one could rid one's person of fleas by leaping across the Midsummer bonfire. The first century writer Pliny advised those

Anax junius **(green darner dragonfly)**

who would banish fleas to scrape up earth from beneath the right foot when the cuckoo was first heard. The ancient Egyptians smeared a slave with asses' milk to attract the insects to him and American farmers brought a sheep or goat into the house for the same purpose. The story of the fox which rids itself of its fleas by wading deep into a pond carrying moss in its mouth, until all the fleas retreat into the moss, and then lets it float away, is generally held to be a fable.

Children's Night-Lights

Luminous insects, such as the firefly and glow worm, are so unusual that myths were devised to explain their origin. Among the tribespeople of Orissa in India a number of such myths are current. It is said that after a battle among the gods many were killed but their eyes remained and became fireflies. Another story relates that sparks from a fire kindled to drive off mos-

Ants on the March

The 'vagrant' calls the ants to arms:
To arms! To arms! The road between
  the blades of grass
Is threatened. Do you hear? The
  cranny from blade to blade,
A span of earth from grass to grass,
  your sacred rights,
The greatest interests of the state,
  the greatest problem in the world,
All is at stake. Ants, to arms!
How could you live, if another
  possessed
The world between two husks.
  If another carried
Ant-baggage into a strange ant-heap.
A hundred thousand lives for these
  two blades of grass
Are too few. I was in the war, oh,
That's a handiwork for insects,
  indeed. Dig trenches,

Root yourself in clay, hurrah, an
  attack in extended order,
At the double over stacks of corpses,
  fix bayonets,
Fifty thousand dead, to capture
Twenty yards of latrines. Hurrah,
  to arms!
The interest of the whole is
  concerned, the heritage of your
  history is concerned,
Nay more, the freedom of your native
  land, nay more, world power,
Nay more, two blades of grass. Such
  a mighty cause
Can be settled only by the dead.
  To arms! To arms!

CHRYSALIS

The whole earth is quivering
Something mighty it is delivering,

I am being born.
To the beating of a drum the troops
  of the ants advance with rifles,
  bayonets, and machine guns, with
  metal helmets on their heads, and
  line up in ranks . . .

VAGRANT

(Passing along the ranks.)
See what good training does.
  Attention! Sound the roll all.
Soldiers, your country is sending
  you to war,
That you may fall. Two blades
  of grass
Are watching you.

Josef and Karel Capek,
The Life of the Insects

quitoes were transformed magically into these insects. Among these tribes, bats were reputed to carry fireflies to their homes because their children could not endure any other light.

In the island of Nias in Indonesia the sorcerer treated a sick person as if his soul had escaped and had become, or taken refuge in, a lanternfly, so he would catch one in a cloth and place it on the patient's forehead. In parts of China, a aluminous insect whose larvae live in decaying vegetable matter appears in swarms in hot weather about the time when the summer festival of the dead was celebrated. At such times illness tends to be moe common than usual and the insects were held responsible. The 'vital spirits' of corpses were believed to give rise to these flies which were said to have appeared as five girls in embroidered garments representing north, south, east, and west and the centre of the universe. If these insects entered a house some calamity might be expected. Burning incense was used to expel them.

In England it was said that glow

worms were born of putrefaction. Possibly this belief was encouraged by observations of luminous fungi. During the Second World War the floor of a London anti-aircraft site was thought to be covered with glow worms but in the morning it was found to be decayed wood infected with a fungus.

The fly had a place in early forms of worship according to Pliny, Pausanius the Greek traveler and geographer, and Aelian the Roman teacher and writer. A Jewish legend relates that Elisha was recognized as a prophet because no fly approached his place at the table. Among the Greeks an ox sacrifice took place annually at the temple of Zeus at Actium to honour him as an averter of flies. Apollonius of Tyana is said to have freed Constantinople from flies by setting up a bronze fly statue. Hera is reputed to have set a gadfly to chase Io because of her amorous relations with Zeus and in Norse mythology Loki transformed himself into a fly to torment his enemies.

In the folktale motif of 'hiding from the Devil' the hero conceals

himself first in a raven's egg, then in a fish and finally in an insect. There are affinities with the Irish myth in which Etain is transformed into a fly. Among Christians, flies were regarded as having devilish affinities but the legend of St. Colman mentions a kindly fly which marked his place in a book when he went to take part in services.

In northern tundra regions mosquitoes and midges may occur in such numbers as to make life difficult. Throughout much of northern Asia and in Mongolia a tale, known in a number of variants, explains how these insects originated. The Ostyaks of western Siberia say that a cannibal demon woman in the far north created them. According to other versions a hero, sometimes said to have been born of a virgin, attacked a man-devouring monster and slew him. From his decaying carcass came clouds of mosquitoes to plague mankind. A different version tells of the monster being reborn again and again until his carcass was burned; then the mosquitoes appeared from the ashes.

Head of a jaguar. Tumba de Chac Mool, Chichén Itzá (Yucatan, Mexico)

Tondo depicting the Lamb of God, fragment of the floor mosaic from the Baptistery of St. Giovanni in Florence, Italy

Jackal

In Indian folktales, a shrewd and cunning animal, like the fox of European folklore which it resembles; as a scavenger and eater of carrion, often associated with death; Anubis, the Egyptian guardian of cemeteries who guided the dead to the judgment of Osiris, was depicted as a jackal or dog: traditionally a timid creature, and Bushmen would not eat the heart of a jackal in case they should become cowardly themselves.

Jaguar

An animal which plays an important part in South American Indian myths, being regarded as a brother-in-law, as man's rival in killing game, and as a rival in sexuality: some tribes believe that the hero who gave them their culture was a jaguar and that a Celestial Jaguar will one day make an end

of the world: in Brazil it is thought that the sun takes the form of a jaguar at night and shamans are possessed by the jaguar spirit, sometimes turning into were-jaguars at death.

Lamb

Often the victim of sacrifice in early times because it seemed to stand for unblemished purity and innocence; in Christian tradition it is a symbol of Christ, who is referred to in the Bible as the Lamb of God; Van Eyck's painting, the *Adoration of the Lamb*, is one of many examples of this concept in art; the term 'flock' is used to denote the members of the Church, when Christ is seen as the Good Shepherd.

Lion

The size, strength, and magnificent appearance of the lion caused it to be associated in ancient times with

divinity and hence with royalty; leonine qualities were attributed to gods and goddesses and this animal is still referred to as the 'King of Beasts'. The Egyptian goddess Sekhmet was represented as lion-headed. At Syracuse in Sicily a lion was led in procession in honour of the Greek huntress goddess Artemis and at Baalbek (in modern Lebanon) chants were sung to a lion apparently regarded as divine, while it ate a calf.

The beast appeared frequently in the role of a guardian, a function which persists to this day. Effigies of the lion guarded temples; a chained lion guards the palace of the Emperor of Ethiopia. Even in China, the guardian lion is a common symbol and at the New Year Festival lion dancers used to gambol in the streets.

In recent times the natural habitat of the lion has become greatly curtailed. Only a few remain in Western India, and south of the Sahara they exist in diminishing numbers, although they are plentiful in the reserves and national parks of East

Guardian lions and Zhaobi outside of Daci temple in Chengdu, Sichuan Province, China

Animals and Animal Symbols in World Culture

Hochdorf Chieftain's Grave, Germany. The Hochdorf Chieftain's Grave is a richly-furnished burial chamber. Regarded as the 'Tutankamon of the Celts', it was discovered in 1977 near Hochdorf an der Enz in Baden-Württemberg, Germany.

and South Africa. The symbolism, mythology, and folklore of the lion differs in various regions, according to the extent to which people are familiar with it. Among those who know the beast only by hearsay or in captivity its characteristics have been exaggerated and embellished, whereas in the lore of African tribes folk accustomed to living among lions, they may be revered or regarded, as in some folktales, as rather stupid and ridiculous animals.

'This Land Is Mine'

African names for the lion and sayings about it may express respect or familiarity but seldom horror or terror. The Arabs of Algeria who used to hunt the lion called him by a name equivalent to 'Mr. John Johnson' while in Botswana his name means 'the Boy with the Beard'. Such names are sometimes given to awe-inspiring animals or beings from fear of invoking their appearance, if the real name were used. An African tribe calls it 'the Owner of the Land' and according to a Swahili saying the beast's roar means, 'Whose

is this land? Mine, mine, mine.'

Among many primitive peoples the distinction between man and animal is blurred; some African tribe's folk believe that a sorcerer can transform himself into a lion and the Bushmen think that a lion can become a man. The Dinka of Sudan regard lions as their totemic ancestors, sleep out in the wilderness without fear and leave portions of the animals they kill for them. On the Congo and Zambezi Rivers the souls of dead chiefs are believed to pass into lions but among the Ngonis of Central Africa this was not thought of as a privilege reserved for chiefs. Some tribes treated a dead lion with ceremonial respect.

In contrast, the lion of folktales may be depicted as easily outwitted by smaller and weaker animals, as in versions of the widespread and universal motif in which the downtrodden get the better of the mighty (as in Cinderella). In the Panchatantra (a Sanskrit book of fables), a Tibetan folktale, and some African stories the lion is tricked by the jackal or the hare. One of these

relates that a lion one day found a hare leaning against a rock. In answer to the lion's inquiry the hare said that the rock was liable to fall. Would the lion kindly help to support it? The lion obligingly put its weight against it while the hare sneaked away, leaving the lion pushing against the perfectly stable rock. This story illustrates the diffusion of folktales for versions of it are told in Georgia and Puerto Rico, as a part of the cultural heritage brought to the New World by slaves. In contrast to this story, the lion in Aesop's fable, 'The Lion's Share', outwits the other animals.

Magnanimous Beast

There are many tales of the magnanimity of the lion, in which the beast spares or befriends human beings. One of the earliest is the story of 'Daniel in the Lion's Den', and the 'Androcles and the Lion' motif is also ancient. A similar story is told of St. Jerome, who is often depicted in art with the lion from whose paw he extracted a thorn. According to another variant, a Christian hermit unable to bury his friend in the hard soil of the desert is surprised and gratified when two lions appear and scrape out a grave with their paws.

Although St. Peter compared the Devil to 'a roaring lion seeking whom he may devour', in Christian thought the lion acquired symbolism connecting it with noble virtues such as courage and generosity. Christ was called the 'Lion of Judah', and because of the animal's friendly associations with the early Christian desert hermits it became symbolic of the contemplative life, wisdom and generosity. As the emblem of St. Mark it became associated with the city of Venice in Italy.

Natural historians of the fifteenth and sixteenth centuries gathered together a great store of fabulous lore concerning the lion, most of it quoted or elaborated from earlier Greek and Latin authorities. Although the greater part of it is fantastic, it includes some grains of truth probably gained from observation; such as, that the lion when gorged will go for two or three days without eating and that it will not kill a man except when in great hunger. Among the fabulous appears the old story that the beast is frightened by the crowing of a cock. We are told that the lion, when ill, may be healed by the blood of an ape, that it charms other animals by circling around them marking a line with its tail, that it is afraid of a mouse or a cartwheel and that clothes wrapped in a lion's skin are safe from moths.

Today the lion remains a symbol of sovereignty and nobility, appearing alike on the British Royal Standard and as a trade mark on articles of merchandise.

Lizard

In the warmer regions of the world, lizards, a group including some 2,500 species, are more numerous and conspicuous than in northern Europe. They vary in size from a few inches to creatures such as the so-called Komodo Dragon ten feet in length. Many of the smaller species bask or run about actively on sun-warmed rocks though the larger lizards and chameleons tend to be sluggish. Some, including the European green lizard, are brightly coloured, others have strange adornments such as skin excrescences or patches of colour which are displayed during courtship. The ability of some species to replace a lost tail is one of their many characteristics that has aroused man's curiosity and wonder.

The sun-loving behaviour of many species has inspired various beliefs that they are associated with the sun. In the ancient Near East they symbolized overpowering heat, and in Egypt they were associated with fecundity, probably because of their increased activity when the Nile floods stimulated the resurgence of life. In Dahomey, the lizard is said to have fetched fire from the sun. The reappearance of lizards after hibernation seemed mysterious and in Europe it was believed that during this period they became blind. It was said that in spring these creatures climb up an eastward-facing wall and look to the east; when the sun rises their sight is restored. European lizards are mostly keen sighted and so the belief arose as long ago as the time of Pliny (1st century AD) that a lizard talisman restored sight to the blind. Lizards appear carved on corbels in medieval cathedrals, such as South well and Wells; they symbolize the life-giving and enlightening power of the gospel.

The idea of the lizard as a god, kin to the gods or their messenger, appears to have been due mainly to its associations with the sun. Such beliefs are particularly characteristic of Polynesia, where lizard cults were observed. The Samoans revered several gods in lizard form. The Maoris considered the green lizard to be an incarnation of Tangaloa, the heaven god, and for the Hervey islanders of Polynesia, Tongaiti, the night heaven god, was a nocturnal spotted lizard. In Africa the Shilluk had a tribal lizard god. The Australian Aranda connected the lizard with their sky and earth myths and believed that the sky would fall if they killed one of these creatures.

Like some other animals this reptile tended to be regarded in some places as evil, in others as beneficent. In the medieval Church it stood for rebirth and resurrection, a significance which it may have owed partly to the influence of the Romans who depicted it on grave monuments as a symbol of hope in life beyond the grave. Among other folk it was associated with death. The Santals of India who believe that the soul may appear as a lizard tell the following tale: as a man lay asleep his soul went off as a lizard to drink from a pitcher but the owner placed a cover on it and the man died. Soon afterward the pitcher was uncovered and the man revived. Such notions arise among peoples who do not distinguish clearly between unconsciousness and death.

Beliefs of a somewhat similar kind linger in Europe. In Austria it is said that a lizard runs out of the mouth of a delinquent child and quickly disappears. In German folklore there are tales of a lizard who is really a bewitched princess, of another appearing as a lizard after death and of witches transforming themselves into these reptiles. There is a belief in Italy that fairies appear as lizards.

Progeny of Devil and Witch

The dualistic ideas associated with lizards are particularly evident where witchcraft and good and bad luck are concerned. Among the Jews, the lizard was considered unclean—a creature born of sexual intercourse between the Devil and a witch. The somewhat handlike feet of the lizard may have

contributed to the notion that it had an uncanny affinity with human beings. In some areas of France and in Schleswig-Holstein a lizard buried alive under the threshold was considered an antidote against witchcraft and in regions of the Near East lizard amulets were worn. From ancient times the lizard figured in sorcery, as used among the ingredients of the witches' brew in Macbeth. A concoction including parts of a lizard was smeared by the door of the person it was hoped to bewitch in some parts of Germany.

Because of their resemblance in some respects to snakes, there was a fairly widespread belief in Europe that lizards could sting. On the other hand, among the Slavs as well as the French and English, the lizard was regarded as a protective spirit against snakes and it was the custom to fix one on the roof of a stable to ward them off. In Périgord in France there was a saying: 'The lizard is man's friend'. In parts of Britain it was believed that if a lizard saw a snake approaching a sleeping man it would awaken him, but that for a lizard to cross the path of a bride was ominous.

In general lizards are considered luck bringers in France and Germany but in the Central Celebes, Indonesia, they are killed to ward off misfortune. When a lizard's tail is seized by a predator it becomes detached and another grows, but an injury at the base may cause an abnormal two-tailed appearance; Italians regard such a two-tailed lizard as particularly lucky. The Latin writer Aelian (170–235 AD), unaware that a lizard after losing its tail could grow another, stated that the body and tail became reunited.

Lizards were regarded as sacred in various parts of the world. Samoans venerated the creature as the son of the High God and the rainbow, possessing power to ask the weather god for propitious weather. According to a local German tradition the lizard licked away Christ's drops of blood and therefore should not be molested. Sicilians say that the little lizards called San Giovanni must not be killed because they are in the presence of the Lord in Heaven and light the lamp to the Lord.

Administered medicinally, potions containing lizard ingredients have been regarded as cures for many kinds of disease varying from running eyes, liver complaints, and syphilis to getting rid of warts. On Easter Eve gypsies in southern Europe placed the dried remains of a lizard, together with herbs, in a specially constructed receptacle. Then all the members of the clan spat on the reptile as it was carried from tent to tent before being thrown into running water. It was believed that in this way the illnesses which might have affected the community during the coming year were banished. In Arabia lizard medicine was prescribed to remedy the impotence of aged men—probably on the assumption that they would acquire some of the vitality of such an active creature. To cure fever a lizard would be buried alive in Madagascar. During the Middle Ages it was believed in England that by licking a lizard a person could acquire the ability to heal wounds and sores by licking them. There was a belief in Germany that rupture in children could be cured by catching a lizard, making the child bite it, and then suspending it on a reed in the smoke of a fire. As the lizard died the rupture would be cured.

Lizard medicine was also administered to remedy the ills of cattle and horses, though, in contrast, Bretons believed the green lizard to be poisonous and blamed it for killing cows by biting them on the nose. In antiquity it was thought that fruit trees could be prevented from bearing unsound fruit by smearing them with the bile of the green lizard. Pliny advocated this procedure and Konrad Gesner, the sixteenth century Swiss biologist, also recommended it. In Silesia the practice continued into the twentieth century.

Magpie & Rook

One of Britain's larger birds, the magpie has a loud and raucous voice; it is exceptional in building a large covered nest, from sticks, and its long tail and black-and-white plumage attract attention. It is wary but also bold, and where it is not persecuted the magpie will frequent houses and even nest in cities. There is some evidence that it moved into parts of Europe in comparatively recent times. The European folklore of the magpie is therefore not of very great antiquity.

The magpie's contrasting plumage contributed to its being regarded as a mysterious, sinister, and oracular bird.

The contrasting colours of the feathers of a magpie have made it the subject of speculation as to its true nature.

Opposite page:
The Fall of Man and The Lamentation,
Hugo van der Goes (c. 1440–1482)

Animals and Animal Symbols in World Culture

93

According to a North of England legend, it was a hybrid between the raven and the dove, the two birds released by Noah from the ark, and therefore had not been baptized in the waters of the Flood. In Germany witches were said to ride on magpies or to appear as these birds, and in Sweden there was a saying that in August the magpies go off to draw the Devil's wagons of hay, hence their neck feathers can be seen to have been rubbed by the yoke. In northeast Scotland the magpie was 'the De'il's bird' and was believed to have a drop of Satan's blood on its tongue. It could acquire human speech if its tongue were scratched and a drop of blood from a human tongue was inserted.

Such beliefs probably arose from the calls uttered by a party of magpies which sounded, to the imaginative, like human chatter; and from the fact that it had been observed that magpies in captivity are able to imitate words. In Brittany it was said to have seven of the Devil's hairs on its head. Because of the bird's sinister and Satanic associations in many areas, it was considered unlucky to kill a magpie, or thought advisable to do so only during certain periods of the year.

Significant Numbers

These associations gave rise to legends in which the bird was represented as anti-Christian. It was said that unlike other birds it did not go into full mourning after the Crucifixion, hence its black-and-white appearance. In France another legend related that the magpies pricked Christ's feet with thorns while he was on the Cross, but the swallows tried to pull them out, acquiring their blood-red breasts as a result. From this time on the magpies were condemned to nest in tall trees whereas the swallows found shelter under the eaves of houses.

As with many creatures and objects which raise doubts in men's minds because of their behaviour and appear-

ance, the magpie is regarded ambivalently in folklore. It may bring good or bad luck according to circumstances, and in a number of country rhymes one may expect propitious or unfortunate events according to the number of birds seen. One of these rhymes, well known and widespread, is:

One for sorrow, two for mirth,
Three for a wedding, four for a birth.

In South Germany a magpie calling near a house was said to portend disaster, but if it merely chattered the arrival of a guest was expected. English folk also regarded the chattering of magpies as predicting the arrival of strangers.

In Norway a pair of magpies nesting close at hand was believed to bring good luck and Shropshire folk would express a wish when a magpie was seen. A Welsh informant tells me that his father, a distinguished physician, would take off his hat on encountering one of these birds.

Because the magpie makes a massive nest with the entrance at the side, it acquired some of the folklore associated with the woodpecker, as this bird also enters its nest in a tree trunk from the side. In France it was believed that the magpie knew a magical herb which she would apply to any barrier placed across the nest entrance, causing it to spring away.

Rooks for a Rainy Day

The rook is so common in Britain and rookeries so obvious in the countryside that it is not surprising that considerable lore should be associated with the bird. The traditions and sayings mainly concern inferences to be drawn, and predictions which can be made concerning the weather and human affairs.

In Yorkshire it was believed that when rooks congregated on dead branches there would be rain before night but that if they perched on live

branches the day would be fine. In Devonshire it is said that if rooks stay at the rookery or return in the middle of the day there will be rain, and similar beliefs are held elsewhere. There is a basis for these ideas to the extent that rooks cover their chicks when it rains. In the Cambridgeshire fens it is also assumed that if rooks fly far away from their nests in the morning there will be no rain. It is said in this area, and indeed elsewhere, that when they make aerial dives and twists bad weather is on the way.

In Shropshire it was believed that rooks never carry sticks to their nests on Ascension Day but perch quietly without doing any work. There was also a saying that if you did not wear something new on Easter Day the rooks would let droppings fall on your clothes. The association of these birds with religious festivals seems to have been an extension of the idea that because their congregations were so vocal, rooks must have some affinity with human beings.

There was a widespread belief that the desertion of a rookery betokens ill for those on whose land they were established, and another that the birds leave before the downfall of the family owning the estate. It was a fenland tradition that rooks always knew when a gamekeeper had died. They would form into a line and fly over his coffin as it was carried to the church for the funeral.

Mice & Rats

Mice are said to embody the soul which may sometimes leave the body during sleep in the form of a mouse; if a mouse was killed (and so did not return) it was believed to be able to bring about the person's death. The Greeks had a mouse god, Apollo Smintheus. The white mice kept at his temple were used to predict the future.

Paintings on ceramic tile from the Chinese Han Dynasty (202 BC–220 AD); these figures, cloaked in Han Chinese robes, represent guardian spirits of certain divisions of day and night.

In Germany mice are thought to be the inventions of witches who make mice out of pieces of cloth. In Rhineland legend it is said that in AD 997 Widrerolf, bishop of Strasbourg, was devoured by mice after he suppressed the convent of Selzen, and that in 1112 Bishop Adolf of Colgen was devoured by mice or rats. When a death is imminent mice will, it is said, leave a house. Mouse colour is signficant: a black mouse is thought to be stained by sin, while a red one has a pure soul.

On the water, superstitious fisherfolk will always steer clear of saying 'mouse' and 'rat', for fear of ill luck or even death. On land or sea the gnawing of rats and mice is believed to be a predictor of death. In his Natural History of AD 77, Pliny the Elder attributed the death of the general Carbo to the fact that mice had eaten away the fastenings of his shoes, while St. Augustine of Hippo proclaimed that

when your clothes are torn by mice you must 'dread more the omen of a future evil than the actual damage'. To rid a house of mice an old remedy in Europe is to write on a piece of paper a dire warning to mice not to return, which is then hung up before sunrise in an infested place.

Proverbial deserters of sinking ships, rats are reviled for their fecundity, their destructive habits and their ability to carry disease. Yet rats were deified by the Egyptians who believed they symbolized both wise judgement and total destruction. At Deshonk in Rajasthan, India, a temple was built in the sixteenth century to the goddess Shri Karniji who shares her symbolism with the rat. Here some 10,000 protected rats still live and are fed by pilgrims. To the Romans a white rat was a sign of good fortune. To dream of a rat is said to betray the fact that you have powerful enemies; if you kill

a rat in your dream these enemies will be defeated. In Robert Browning's 1888 poem, *The Pied Piper of Hamelin,* both rats and children are led from the rodent-run town by the piper's music but the children were stolen and never returned.

The Greek god Apollo was known as the rat killer after he sent a swarm of rats in pursuit of his neglectful priest Crinis. Seeing the animals approaching, the priest repented and was pardoned. Apollo then destroyed the rats with his long-range arrows.

In Chinese astrology those born in the year of the rat (1936, 1948, 1960, etc., by increments of twelve years) are ambitious and hardworking leaders, often charming to the opposite sex and enjoy gossiping.

Monkey & Ape

The monkey is sacred in India, probably because of its resemblance to humans; there are several famous monkey chieftains of Indian legend, including Hanuman. There is an African belief that apes can speak but refrain from doing so because by speaking they would be made to work. In Egypt the baboon was sacred to the god Thoth, deity of wisdom, learning and creativity. In one tale, Thoth disguises himself as a baboon in order to rescue Tefnut, daughter of the supreme god Ra, who has transformed herself into a lioness. As a reward Ra appointed Thoth his earthly representative.

A typical Creole folktale tells of Mr. Monkey who fell in love with a beautiful young girl. He dressed as a man and called on her. One day he took his best friend with him, who hinted to the girl's father that there was a secret abroad. On Mr. Monkey's wedding night the friend sang a song that made all monkeys dance, inducing Mr. Monkey. He jumped about so wildly that his tail came out of his clothes, revealing his identity. The father understood the secret, and beat the bridegroom, but the friend ran off, dancing and singing.

In Bolivia, the Yuracare Indians sprinkle the bodies of apes they have killed with chicha, a fermented maize-based drink. In the Celebes, people of the northwest believe that they are descendants of monkeys; food is put on bamboo rafts and floated down streams to sustain their ancestors.

The Three Wise Monkeys originated as images carved above the portico of the Sacred Stable of the Nikko Toshogu Shrine, a seventeenth-century Japanese temple. Their associated motto, literally translated, reads 'don't see, don't hear, don't speak' and is popularly rendered as 'see no evil, hear no evil, speak no evil'.

Monkey appears in the Chinese zodiac for the sequence of years 1932, 1944, 1956, etc., by increments of twelve years. To be born in these years is to be brilliant, curious, and a good problem solver with an excellent memory but impatience for rapid results.

Nightingale

The song of the nightingale has been more generally admired and praised than the song of any other European bird. The male sings by night as well as by day, so that even those with little interest in birds cannot fail to notice and appreciate its characteristic song.

Among Greek and Roman writers who commented on this song were Aristophanes, who tried to reproduce the sound verbally in his play *The Birds*, and Pliny, who departed from his usual matter-of-fact style to describe it enthusiastically. It was the Greek myth of Philomela, however, which was responsible for the prominence of the bird in Latin literature and eventually in our own.

According to the story, Procne, the wife of Tereus, king of Thrace, asked

The nightingale, a tiny bird, has a song that lives in legend and poetry.

him to bring her sister Philomela to stay with her but when Tereus laid eyes on his sister-in-law, he fell violently in love with her. On the journey home, he ravished her and cut out her tongue so that his crime might not be known. He kept her hidden, but Philomela was able to inform her sister by weaving an account of what had happened into a cloak which she sent to her.

Procne took terrible revenge on Tereus, killing their son Itys, and serving him to her husband for dinner. The sisters fled from the tyrant king, and when he pursued them Zeus turned Procne into a nightingale, Philomela into a swallow, and Tereus into a hoopoe. Latin poets misread the story and made Philomela the nightingale, so that English poets, following them, wrote of Philomel as the nightingale. This tragic myth was mainly responsible for the bird's song being interpreted by many poets as melancholy. In Shakespeare's *Rape of Lucrece* he wrote:

> Come Philomel, that sing'st of
>   ravishment
> Make thy sad grove in my
>   dishevell'd hair.

Keats, in the most famous tribute of all, *To a Nightingale*, refers to its

'plaintive anthem', and suggests that it is the 'selfsame song that found a path through the sad heart of Ruth, when sick for home'. Chaucer however, had referred to the 'merry nightingale' and Coleridge denied in verse that the song was melancholy.

According to a belief which can be traced back to the sixteenth century the nightingale sings with its breast pressed against a thorn. Shakespeare, again in Lucrece, wrote:

> And whiles against a thorn thou
>   bear'st thy part
> To keep thy sharp woes waking.

It is said that the thorn was a protection against the snake and served to keep the bird awake and alert.

Singing Praise to God

The song of nightingales has not always been admired. A hermit in a Sussex forest was so disturbed by their singing that, so it was said, he laid a curse upon them so that they never again appeared in the neighbourhood. St. Francis, on the other hand, is said to have competed with a nightingale in singing his praises to God—and to have admitted himself defeated.

A nightingale in full song can indeed sing around the clock with a few intermissions. Country people, noticing this, associated the bird with insomnia and drew the conclusion that organs of the nightingale could be used to produce sleeplessness, on the magical principle of 'like producing like'. The eyes and heart, if placed close to a person in bed would keep him awake—and if they were dissolved surreptitiously in his drink he would certainly die of insomnia. In England rustic rhymes commented on the date of the bird's arrival in spring and it was believed to be a good omen if the nightingale's song was heard before the cuckoo called.

Depiction of an ostrich in a mosaic on the Northern Aisle floor of the Byzantine Church of Petra, Jordan

Ostrich

It was probably as a source of food that the ostrich first aroused man's interest, for its eggs have been eaten since very early times. A North African rock engraving of the Stone Age depicts a hunter aiming an arrow at an ostrich, while frescoes in Egyptian tombs show the bird's plumes being used for personal decoration. Greek and Roman writers refer to the ostrich, but in Europe traditional lore concerning it mainly sprang from the biblical allusions which credited it with being forgetful, stupid, and cruel (Job 39.13–17; Lamentations 4.3). As few Europeans until recent times had opportunities to observe the behaviour of the bird in the wild, there was ample opportunities for the little that was recorded to be misunderstood.

Biblical writers incorrectly inferred that the ostrich neglected its young, partly from the bird's habit of retreating when approached, and also because ostriches in the Near East sometimes left their eggs covered with sand to be kept warm by the sun's heat. The notion that the bird did not brood, which dates from at least as far back as the second century, led to the belief that it hatched its eggs by gazing at them intently. This belief was repeated by writers down the centuries, including Vincent of Beauvais and Montaigne, and the ostrich egg thus became a symbol of single-minded devotion. In present-day Greek churches an ostrich egg suspended in a conspicuous position is a reminder to the worshipper to focus his thoughts and prayers. The moral was drawn that as the ostrich leaves the eggs so the hermit retires from worldly involvements.

The belief that the bird consumes hard, inedible objects is also of long standing. Pliny said the ostrich could digest anything, but Aelian, who was better informed, stated that it kept pebbles in its gizzard. Rabbinic writers commented that it ate glass. An early Christian document (Physiologus) remarks that the ostrich eats glowing iron because 'his nature is very cold', and the poet John Skelton (c. 1460–1529) mentions that the bird will eat a horseshoe. In *Henry VI, Part 2*, Jack Cade blusters: 'I'll make thee eat iron like an ostrich.' Living in unnatural conditions ostriches will indeed swallow incongruous objects; thus observed fact was exaggerated into fantasy.

Among the fanciful ideas about ostriches given currency by writers of the fifteenth and sixteenth centuries were that these birds terrified horses by flapping their wings, and that underneath the wings there was a small bone with which they pricked themselves when provoked to anger. Such ideas may have arisen from observations of these strange birds flapping their short wings as they ran away.

For some reason the idea arose that the ostrich is deaf as well as silly. In Philemon Holland's translation of Pliny, *Historia Naturalis* (1602), we read: 'But the veriest fools they be of all others;—for as high as the rest of their body is, yet if they thrust their head and neck once into any shrub or bush, and get it hidden, they think then they are safe enough, and that no man seeth them.' Hence the proverbial ostrich, symbolical of stupidity and an inability to face realities. No doubt the belief arose from ostriches being seen with heads down feeding before they became alarmed.

The belief, mentioned by Aristotle, that ostriches lay more eggs than any other bird was based on the finding of large clutches. As many as sixty have been recorded but the ostrich is polygamous and several may lay in one nest.

Silver *tetradrachm* issued by Athens (c. 450 BC). Reverse: owl, olive spray, and crescent moon, with the inscription ΑΘΕ (Athens). The bird is the animal symbol for the goddess Athena.

Owl

Almost everywhere owls have been associated with strange powers, especially the forces of evil and misfortune. The lore concerning owls has such basic similarities throughout most of the world that it would seem to have arisen from a deep-seated and disquieting emotional response, evoked by a creature having characteristics interpreted as partly human. Thus, an owl with large eyes set in a flattish 'face' stares like a human being. Moreover, many species utter hoots, halloos or screams which sound like human calls. To hear a screeching at night in a tropical forest as of a woman in agony is a spine-chilling experience—until it is realized that the call is being uttered by an owl. The nocturnal habits of owls contribute to their sinister reputation, especially as their silent flight enables them to appear with alarming unexpectedness from the darkness. Furthermore, as owls often roost by day in holes and crevices in abandoned, dilapidated buildings, they are often regarded as embodiments of spirits or evil presences.

As early as the Old Stone Age we have evidence of the interest aroused by this bird, for a pair of nesting snowy owls with their chick is engraved on a rock face in a cave in southern France. On a Sumerian tablet dating from 2300–2000 BC a nude goddess is depicted flanked on either side by an owl. She is believed to be the goddess of death. A number of biblical references associate the owl with misery and desolation, and the bird is mentioned in connection with 'dragons' and wild beasts and also with mourning. Greek and Latin writers refer to the owl as a bird of ill omen. Ovid, Pliny, and other authors associ-

ate the birds with death and their calls are mentioned as sinister. When an owl appeared in the Capitol at Rome it occasioned such alarm that the place was cleansed with water and sulphur to expel any evil influences it might have brought.

As is not uncommon with creatures or objects regarded as mysterious and arousing a strong emotional response, owls may sometimes be regarded as having properties contrary to those generally attributed to them. Something which is apt to frighten people may come to be considered effective as a deterrent against that which they fear; the evil thing may be enlisted as an ally. In ancient China, where owl sacrifices were offered, ornaments called 'owl corners' were placed on buildings in the belief that they protected them from fire. In Semitic countries the owl is usually regarded as ominous and in Persia is spoken of as 'the angel of death', yet in Israel little grey owls are considered good omens when they appear near the crops. Perhaps the belief originated from the observation that these birds prey on birds and mammals which damage crops. In ancient Athens the little owl was associated with Athene, probably as goddess of night, but being a common bird it was regarded in a friendly way and became the emblem of the city. 'There goes an owl' was the Athenian saying indicating signs of victory.

Latin writers early in our era alluded to the custom of hanging up owls in order to deflect storms and

Owl-Egg Soup

In North America notions concerning owls varied. While the Pawnees thought of them as giving protection, the Ojibwas believed in an evil spirit which appeared in the guise of an owl. In California the white owl was thought to be an evil spirit and its feathers were worn as a counter-charm.

it was believed that an owl nailed up with wings outspread would avert hail and lightning. The custom of nailing owls to barn doors persisted into the nineteenth century in England. The Romans used representations of owls to combat the Evil Eye. Among the tribes of northern Asia owls were regarded as able to counteract evil powers. An owl might be placed over a child's cot to frighten away evil spirits. In India owl feathers were placed under the pillow of a restless child in order to induce sleep. The Ainu people of Japan made wooden images of owls and nailed them to their houses at times of famine or pestilence.

In Great Britain, as in most of Europe, the owl has been, and to some extent still is, regarded as ominous. Chaucer wrote of the owl as the bringer of death, and Shakespeare in *Julius Caesar* (Act I, Sc. 3) mentioned it among other evil omens:

> *Yesterday the bird of night did sit*
> *Even at noon-day upon the*
> *market place*
> *Hooting and shrieking . . .*

In Africa owls are commonly associated with sorcery. When an owl perched on a dwelling in Bechuanaland the witch-doctor was called in to perform purificatory rites. The souls of sorcerers were called 'owls' in Madagascar. The Yoruba of Nigeria believe that wizards send out owls as their emissaries to kill people. In certain regions of Nigeria the natives avoid naming the owl, referring to it as 'the bird that makes you afraid'.

Since owls were regarded as embodying weird powers they were associated in Germany and elsewhere with witchcraft. The witches in *Macbeth* (Act IV Sc. 1) included in their brew 'Lizard's leg and howlet's wing': Pliny stated that an owl's heart placed on a woman's breast would force her to divulge secrets. This was repeated by Albertus Magnus and reappeared as recently as 1863 in a book published in Pennsylvania. Among the Greeks magical and medicinal virtues were attributed to owls' eggs. Given to a child they would ensure his life-long temperance. Owl-egg soup was a remedy for epilepsy and treatment of grey hair with the contents of an owl's egg would darken it. As the egg had to be one from which a male chick would have emerged, any failures could be easily explained.

The owl figures in a number of fables and legends. The story of 'The War of the Owls and Crows' may have symbolized the opposition between the moon and the sun. It came into Greek literature from India. According to a legend from Normandy the owl is disliked and mobbed by other birds because when the wren burned its feathers in trying to fetch fire from heaven the owl refused to help by contributing some of its own to clothe the wren. The owl's reputation as a bird of wisdom may have arisen through its association with Athene, the goddess of counsel.

FURTHER READING: E. A. Armstrong. The Folklore of Birds. (Collins, 1958).

Ox

Before coins were invented, the ox was used for material exchange, hence its use as a symbol of wealth. In Christianity the winged ox is the emblem of St. Luke. The evangelist and the animal are linked because the ox was a sacrificial animal and Luke wrote of the sacrifice of Christ. The ox was one of the cherubim seen in his vision by the prophet Ezekiel and subsequently one of the four beasts in Revelation that stood around the throne of the Lamb. In the Chinese calendar, those born under the sign of the ox (years 1937, 1949, 1961 etc) are said to be responsible and hard working but also stubborn and bigoted.

Panther

Due to the attractive sweetness of its breath, which made it a friend of all other creatures except the dragon, the panther gained a place in the bestiaries of ancient times as an emblem of Christ. By the sixteenth century, however, its true nature had become appreciated, transforming it into a symbol of both evil and hypocrisy. The skin of the panther was used as clothing by the god Dionysus. To the Yuchi people of the southeastern United States, Panther is a creator who, when Chipmunk made the night, was so angry that he inflicted the stripes which his victim wears to this day.

Peacock

The peacock is native to southern Asia and beliefs about it are widespread in that region, especially in India where, since 1963, it has been recognized as the national bird. As far back as the Rig-Veda, the Hindu collection of sacred writings dated c. 1200 BC, it was recorded that the steeds of the god Indra possessed hair like peacock's feathers. The peacock has an important place in Hinduism and the national epic, the Ramayana, relates that when the gods transformed themselves into animal forms in order to escape the demon Ravana, Indra, the god of thunder, rains and war, became a peacock. In recompense the bird was endowed with 1,000 eyes in its feathers, the capacity to rejoice when the rains came and the power to kill snakes; obviously it had been observed that the bird attacks serpents, and displays and calls noisily at the beginning of the rainy season.

Various names signify that the peacock dances joyfully on seeing clouds or hearing thunder. The term for one of the 108 postures of the classical Hindu dance signifies 'sportive like the peacock'. A number of divinities are portrayed mounted on the bird—in India Brahma and his wife Sarasvati, in Indo-China the warrior god Skanda, and in Japan Kujaku-myoo (Mahamayuri), who protects from calamity and is besought to send rain.

The association of the peacock with rain also spread throughout Europe, where as far west as Ireland its calls are believed to forecast rain. The fifteenth century Hortus Sanitatis declares that it is a sign of rain when the peacock 'mounts on high' and Michael Drayton (1563–1631) wrote of 'the strutting peacock yawling 'gainst the rain'.

Protective Powers

From the knowledge that the peacock kills snakes there developed in India the belief that its bile and blood acted as an antidote against poison; smoke from its burning plumes was held to dispel venom and, in the Punjab, those bitten by snakes smoked its feathers. Travelers were recommended to carry a peacock to ward off snakes. In England during the fifteenth century the Eastern notion of the antipathy between the peacock and snakes became elaborated into the assumption that the bird's raucous call frightens away serpents and all venomous creatures.

Besides providing antidotes to poison, various parts of the bird were regarded as effective in curing many diseases and disabilities ranging from tuberculosis, forms of paralysis, asthma, catarrh, and headaches to barrenness. Among Hindus and

Muslems peacock feathers are believed to ward off evil, especially evil spirits. Umbrellas of the plumes were carried by persons associated with royalty and one is still held over the pope on important occasions. In India the mere sight of the bird is believed to bring good luck and to bestow peace of mind.

In Chinese and Japanese art the peacock has decorative and symbolical significance; it is often depicted together with the peony. A defeated Chinese general of the Chin dynasty who took refuge from his enemies in a forest is said to have been so grateful to the peacocks for not betraying him that he conferred peacock feathers on those showing special bravery in battle.

The Bird of Hera

The reference in the Old Testament to 'apes and peacocks' sent to Solomon (I Kings 10.22) cannot be taken seriously, as the translation is guesswork. However, peacocks are known to have been kept in Babylon. Aristotle mentions the peacock which, like the cock, was called 'the Persian bird', and a reference in a play by Aristophanes may imply that a Persian ambassador brought a gift of peacocks. Alexander the Great imposed heavy penalties on those who killed Indian peacocks.

The birds were depicted on Greek coins. They were sacred to Hera, and a myth relates how the goddess set the hundred-eyed giant Argus to guard her husband's mistress, Io; when Zeus sent Hermes to charm and kill Argus, Hera used the giant's eyes to ornament the peacock's tail.

Pelican

The lore of the pelican has so little relevance to the actual behaviour of the bird that it might refer to a mythical species. Its chief interest is in illustrating the origin of an important symbol

from confused ideas. The pelican was familiar in Egypt as a large bird opening its wide gape to enable the young to feed from the fish brought in its pouch; but the symbolical pelican's significance was mainly borrowed from the vulture. In the Bible vultures are not clearly distinguished from eagles. Thus in Exodus 19.4 we should read: 'I bore you on vultures' wings' rather than 'on eagles' wings' and in Deuteronomy 32.11: 'Like a vulture . . . that flutters over its young, spreading out its wings.' As the Hebrew words for 'vulture' and 'compassion' are very similar, an association was established between large birds and parental care which was apparently transferred to the pelican. The notion that the pelican feeds or revives its young with its own blood may perhaps be traced to vultures being seen to bring bloody morsels to their chicks.

The Physiologies, an early Christian compilation which wove together biblical ideas with Egyptian mythology concerning animals, contained two stories elaborated from these notions. One relates that the pelican loves its young very much but they, when they are large enough, strike at their parents. The old birds retaliate and kill the chicks; but soon they are overcome with compassion and the mother comes on the third day, opens her side and sheds blood on them, restoring them to life. It is also stated that in order to foil the snake the pelican makes its nest in a lofty situation and builds a hedge around it. The snake, representing the Devil, puffs his venom on the nest and kills the young. When the pelican returns she flaps her wings against her sides, drawing blood which rains down on the chicks and resuscitates them.

Christian writers used these stories to illustrate their teaching. St. Jerome interpreted them as showing how those dead in sin were made alive through Christ's bloodshed on the

---

Opposite page:
Hindu deity Karktikeya, or Murugan, with his consorts on his Vahana peacock

cross, and down the centuries emphasis was laid on the parental affection of the pelican. The representation in carved wood or stone and in stained glass windows of the bird pecking her breast to supply her young with blood became frequent in the Middle Ages as a symbol of Christ and the Eucharist. Such symbolism had special importance during centuries when few could read but the pelican also acquired considerable prominence in literature. In the thirteenth century St. Thomas Aquinas wrote:

Pelican of piety, Jesus, Lord and God, Cleanse thou me, unclean, in thy most precious blood.

John Skelton (c 1460–1529) also made use of the symbolic pelican in his verse:

Then said the pelican, When my birds be slain, With my blood I them revive. Scripture doth record The same did our Lord, And rose from death to life.

Shakespeare could assume that his audiences would understand allusions to the symbolic pelican. King Lear, for instance, recalling the story of the bird's ungrateful young, refers to Regan and Goneril as 'pelican daughters'. But for centuries the 'pelican in her piety', as the heraldic representation of the bird was called, continued to be a symbol of the noble virtue of heroic self-sacrifice.

Pig

Since it provides the staple food of many people's but is the tabooed flesh of others, the pig occupies the paradoxical position of being both loved and loathed at the same time, if not in the same place. It was first domesticated by the Chinese and later at

A pelican feeding her young

an unknown date by the English and other European communities. The European variety is descended from the wild boar, modified by crossing with Asiatic breeds, and has inherited some of the occult qualities of its turbulent ancestor.

The domestic pig has never ranked very highly in popular esteem, for not only is it the Buddhist symbol of indolence and the European symbol of license, but to the ordinary mind it represents gluttony and obstinacy. Yet the pig is undoubtedly a noble animal and was deservedly an object of worship in Crete, while in Greece it was sacrificed to the gods at the time of the planting of the corn.

In ancient Egypt the pig represented the spirit of Osiris at sowing time and the spirit of Seth at the harvest. It was regarded as unclean, and the swineherds who attended it were not allowed to enter a temple and not permitted to marry outside their own ranks. Pig meat was eaten by the Egyptians only at the Midwinter feast, and the pig could only be sacrificed at the full moon. As a possible relic of this tradition there are those who still

believe that a pig must be slaughtered when the moon is waxing or otherwise it will shrink in the pot.

The eating of pig is taboo to both Jew and Muslim and it was also long out of favour in Scotland and in parts of northern Ireland. One possible explanation for this custom is that the pig had originally been the symbol of a social group—its totem—and was regarded as the tribal ancestor: thus to eat a sacred pig could be fatal to the interests of the tribe. A further reason for the prohibition of certain kinds of food is the belief that one becomes what one eats. The fastidious individual who accepts the doctrine that one assimilates the habits of the pig by eating pork is naturally disinclined to adopt this type of diet.

In the past, both Hebrew and Arab have been prepared to accept martyrdom rather than eat pork and in sixteenth century Spain anyone with a distaste for this meat stood in permanent danger of arrest by the Spanish Inquisition as a secret adherent of Judaism. His Catholic Majesty Philip II of Spain gave signal proof of Christian orthodoxy during the period he lived in England by consuming vast quantities of bacon, as a result of which he became ill.

To the Celts and Teutonic peoples pork was the food of kingly hospitality and other-world feasts. Both the Anglo-Saxons and the conquering Norman aristocrats enjoyed pork; evidence of the popularity of the pig as food among all English classes in the past. But never has the pig had more eloquent a champion than the writer Charles Lamb who declared in his Essays of Elia: 'There is no flavour comparable I will contend to that of the crisp, tawny, well watched not over roasted crackling'. Pork was customarily served at Christmas time in England in the past. At Queen's College, Oxford, a boar's head with an orange in its mouth is traditionally brought to the table with great ceremony at the season of goodwill. A similar custom is observed in Scandinavia at Yule, when a loaf made from the last sheaf of the harvest is baked in the shape of a boar.

Hunted and Tortured

Christian teaching has allocated a conflicting role for the pig, in that it represents the principles of both good and evil. St. Anthony was the patron saint of swineherds: to him young pigs were sometimes dedicated, and even today the smallest pig of the litter is called a 'Tantony pig'. On the other hand the pig has become a token of evil largely due to the accounts in the New Testament of demons expelled by Christ from their human abode immediately entering the bodies of the Gadarene swine. The whole situation remains complex, because the pig could be either the personification of Satan or, alternatively, his victim. The Black Boar, one of the less familiar of the Devil's guises, occurs in the folklore of New England and Ireland.

Demon pigs were familiar to English peasant life; the two best-known examples being the Winwick and Burnley pigs of Lancashire, whose effigies may be seen carved on the walls of the respective parish churches. The pig

Aeneas lands on the shores of Latium with his son Ascanius behind him; on the left, a sow tells him where to found his city.

alive in Huntingdon in 1833, and in Lincolnshire it was once the custom to score the back of a living pig with a red-hot poker to preserve the remainder of the litter.

The pig fared equally badly at the hands of medieval lawyers. Inspired by the Law of Moses which decreed: 'When an ox gores a man or a woman to death, the ox shall be stoned and its flesh shall not be eaten', a sow and her young pigs were condemned to death in 1457, the piglets receiving a last minute pardon 'due to their extreme youth'.

The pig also fell victim to the huntsman. Until disafforestation caused their extinction, wild boars were hunted for sport by the nobles. Among the English agricultural class pig racing was long in vogue, and involved a wild chase through the countryside after a pig whose tail had been coated with soap.

Before the publication of George Orwell's *Animal Farm*, it was only in the fairground that the intellectual

was extremely vulnerable to the Evil Eye and it was as the victim of diabolical assault that it occupied a place in the annals of English witchcraft. Arising from some confusion of the old idea of torturing a witch by remote control through her victim, and the doctrine that by sacrificing a living animal it would be possible to save the others, a sick pig was actually burned

From Middle Sepik, New Guinea, a pig mask. Currently in the Ethnological Museum in Berlin.

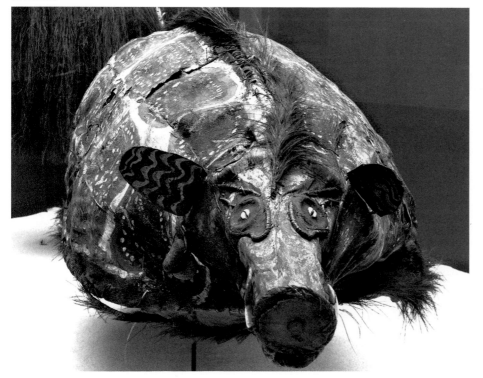

A Gift for the Beast

A group of boys stranded on an island sense an unknown menace and offer a pig's head to it:

He paused and stood up, looking at the shadows under the trees. His voice was lower when he spoke again.

'But we'll leave part of the kill for . . .'

He knelt down again and was busy with his knife. The boys crowded round him. He spoke over his shoulder to Roger.

'Sharpen a stick at both ends.'

Presently he stood up, holding the dripping sow's head in his hands.

'Where's that stick?'

'Here.'

'Ram one end in the earth. Oh—it's rock. Jam it in that crack. There.'

Jack held up the head and jammed the soft throat down on the pointed end of the stick which pierced through into the mouth. He stood back and the head hung there, a little blood dribbling down the stick.

Instinctively the boys drew back too; and the forest was very still. They listened, and the loudest noise was the buzzing of flies over the spilled guts.

Jack spoke in a whisper.

'Pick up the pig.'

Maurice and Robert skewered the carcass, lifted the dead weight, and stood ready. In the silence, and standing over the dry blood, they looked suddenly furtive.

Jack spoke loudly.

'This head is for the beast. It's a gift.'

The silence accepted the gift and awed them. The head remained there, dim-eyed, grinning faintly, blood blackening between the teeth. All at once they were running away, as fast as they could, through the forest toward the open beach.

William Golding, *Lord of the Flies*

superiority of the pig was recognized. A learned pig was exhibited at St. Bartholomew's Fair in the early eighteenth century, advertised as 'The pig of knowledge, being the only one ever taught in England'.

In China and in Europe the pig is a good luck talisman, yet among many fishing communities the animal itself is regarded as extremely unlucky, and even the use of its name is taboo. There are occasional reports of fairy pigs emanating from the Isle of Man, and at Andover in Hampshire a spectral pig is said to be seen on New Year's Eve.

The long-standing association between the pig and the wind is confirmed by the countryman's superstition that a pig has the power either to see or smell the wind and is thus a useful weather prophet. In parts of the United States hogs are supposed to detect the approach of a tornado. It was long a custom in Ireland to drive a pig into the house on May morning for luck, yet oddly enough a pig that enters a house at any other time is an omen of poverty.

Power Animals in Shamanism

Power animals are helping spirits in animal form who guard and protect the shaman in the physical world and in the spirit world. Though it is not possible to define any helping spirit in an absolute sense, a power animal is best understood as the spirit of a species of animal, e.g., bear, giraffe, or anaconda. Power animal spirits are one source of the type of power the shaman draws on from helping spirits to use in healing. Power animals serve as conduits for wisdom, guidance, and information from the spirit world. When the shaman uses an embodiment trance for healing or conducting ritual, it is often the power animal that works through the shaman. In many cultures the shaman develops a deep relationship with one particular animal that then summons other helping spirits or allies as they are needed to perform aspects of the shaman's work. The shaman knows that there could be no power for healing without the spirits of animals, plants, and Nature.

Shamans believe that the animals are manifestations of a natural power that is stronger and wiser than human beings. However, shamans do not lift animal spirits up to the status of deities, nor do they lower them to the status of a mere psychological metaphor. The shaman is empowered by his or her relationship with the power animals. Their relationship is a partnership. The partnership with the power animals is not easily forged. The shaman must prove himself worthy of the power the animal spirit offers and then learn from the animal spirit how to use that power. In many cultures, strict taboos must also be observed by the shaman to maintain the relationship with the power animals, such as not eating the flesh of the animals that help them. In all cultures, offering gratitude and respect for the power animal's help in human matters is fundamental to maintaining the working relationship.

Ancient cave paintings reflect the use of ritual by humans to evoke the mysterious sacred powers of different animals. Gaining access to the special qualities of the animal spirits is one facet of the extraordinary relationship between the shaman and the power animals. The power animals are also teachers. They may teach the shaman

Medicine Man, Performing His Mysteries over a Dying Man, George Catlin (1796–1872)

power songs and/or give the shaman the words to invoke power (to call power in) or to cast power (to send power out). Still other shamans learn the language of the animals and at times speak that language while in trance. In some Australian tribes acquiring the power to speak to birds and animals is one mark of shamanic abilities. Totem spirits, who are inherited through a family line, and tutelary spirits are specific types of power animals. Power animals are also referred to as guardian spirits, allies, and spirit helpers. The fact that an individual has a relationship with a power animal does not make them a shaman. Most children have guardian spirits and, in many cultures, all adults must connect with a helping spirit as an aspect of their initiation into adulthood.

FURTHER READING: Eliade, Mircea. Shamanism: Archaic Techniques of Ecstasy. *(Princeton, NJ: Princeton University Press, 1964). Harner, Michael J.* The Way of the Shaman. *(San Francisco: Harper-Collins, 1990.) Redmond, L.* When the Drummers Were Women: A Spiritual History of Rhythm. *(New York. Three Rivers Press, 1997).*

Ram

The ram, because of its vigorous coupling and the imagery of its horns, is a symbol of fertility in the Egyptian, Greek, and Roman traditions. Its power was personified in the Egyptian god Ammon and the Greek god Zeus, both of which sported rams' horns. Because it was sacred to Zeus, and to Jupiter, the ram was often used in sacrifices, and to be baptized with a ram's blood was to acquire the animal's vital force. In Mesopotamian myth the ram in the sky—the sign of Aries in the zodiac—was believed to hold within it the stars of the winter solstice.

Raven

A large black bird of the crow family, the raven is possessed of a harsh croaking voice and an appetite for carrion, and generally is of disturbing and sinister character in folk belief. The raven is an important figure in the mythology of American Indians of the North Pacific coast where he is both a creator, who released the sun and moon into their positions in the sky, and a destroyer, who not only tricks others but is tricked himself. In many tales he is led into adventures both violent and amorous by virtue of his voracious appetites.

The raven is frequently associated with battlefields, corpses, and death. In Europe a raven croaking between 10 pm and midnight presages death while a raven circling over a house means that a death is imminent. To the Blackfoot Indians a raven circling over the camp signified the arrival of a messenger from afar. Two ravens acted as the spies of the god Odin, and Alexander the Great is said to have been guided across the desert by a pair of ravens. British legend relates that should the ravens resident at the Tower of London ever depart then the kingdom will fall.

Rhinoceros

According to legend of the Kalahari bushmen of Naron, the rhinoceros is instrumental in determining the pattern of night and day because at sunset the sun turns into a rhinoceros which is killed and eaten by the people of the west who, after their meal, throw a shoulder blade toward the east where it is reincarnated as the creature each morning. Elsewhere, myths about the rhinoceros focus on the animal's horn which is widely regarded as a symbol of sexuality and, when ingested, a powerful aphrodisiac. In Greek mythology it was thought that rhino horn could purify water, while the ancient Persians believed that rhino horn vessels could be used to detect poisoned liquids.

The Garden of Earthly Delights **(detail), Hieronymus Bosch (c. 1450–1516)**

Robin

The robin enjoys greater popularity in the British Isles than in any other part of the world. Although it has ancient folklore associations, its fame rests largely on the importance it attained in English prose and poetry a few centuries ago. Every Christmas the robin appears on many Christmas cards and until recently it would have been difficult to find a child who could not answer the nursery rhyme query, 'Who killed Cock Robin?'

The bird owes its popularity to the bright colour of its breast and its confiding behaviour. In most European languages it is called by the equivalent of 'Redbreast' and its folklore owes much to this. Bright-eyed and alert it follows the gardener around, watching for worms and grubs uncovered by his spade, or perches singing on a twig close by.

The first mention of a tame robin is in the biography of the sixth century Scottish saint, Kentigern. His teacher had a pet robin which came daily to perch on his head or shoulder and feed from his hand. According to the legend, mischievous boys handled it so roughly that it died, but St. Kentigern restored it to life. The biography was not written until the twelfth century but used a much earlier source. St. Kentigern's robin is depicted in the coat of arms of the City of Glasgow. More than a century after this saint's biography appeared, the biographer of St. Francis of Assisi, the most famous saint associated with compassion for animals, related how he fed and tamed a pair of robins and their brood which came to the brethren's table at mealtimes. In Italy, where robins have long been persecuted, such tameness could be regarded as almost miraculous.

The robin's red breast inspired associations with fire and blood. According to a Welsh legend, the robin flies to a land of woe and fire with a drop of water and tries to quench the flames, but gets its feathers scorched so that it is called Bronrhuddyn, 'scorched breast'. When it returns it feels the cold more than other birds and should be given crumbs. In France, where it is said that the wren fetched fire from heaven, the robin went too close to it when its feathers were in flames and so its own breast was signed. What appears to be a degraded version of these stories is told in Guernsey. The robin brought fire to the island but scorched its plumage on the way. According to a legend current in the Inner Hebrides, when the Christ child was born the fire in the stable almost went out but the robin fanned the embers into flame, burning its breast feathers. Mary blessed it and when the feathers grew again they were red instead of brown. In western France on Candlemas Day a peculiar ritual was performed. A robin's body was spitted on a hazel twig and set before the fire. As the hazel was a magical tree among the Celts, this hints at some pre-Christian belief. In Germany it was commonly held that the presence of a robin averted lightning.

A Drop of God's Blood

The similarity between the colour of the robin's breast and bloodstains linked the bird with death and religious beliefs. The old Scottish saying

European robin. The name robin is given to several species of birds, on different continents, that have a red breast.

that the robin should not be killed because it has a drop of God's blood may be a reminiscence of strange, ancient ideas. According to a Breton legend, while Christ was hanging on the cross a robin plucked a thorn from his crown and in so doing pierced its own breast. As a reward it was given power to enrich one young girl every year.

In the sixteenth century the robin acquired a reputation for covering dead bodies with moss. A person finding one near a corpse in a wood could suppose that it was about to perform this kindly office, especially if it held nesting material in its bill. The origin of the Babes in the Wood story may be ascribed to the sixteenth century, although the complete version dates from the late seventeenth century.

No burial this pretty pair
From any man receives,
Till robin redbreast piously
Did cover them with leaves.

The most famous allusion is Shakespeare's. In *Cymbeline*, Arviragus says:

With fairest flowers,
Whilst summer lasts, and I live
*   here, Fidele,*
I'll sweeten thy sad grave: thou shalt
*   not lack*
The flower that's like thy face, pale
*   primrose; nor*
The azured harebell, like thy veins;
*   no nor*
The leaf of eglantine, whom not to
*   slander,*
Out-sweeten'd not thy breath: the
*   ruddo would,*
With charitable bill,—O bill,
*   sore-shaming*
Those rich-left heirs that let their
*   fathers lie*
Without a monument!—bring thee
*   all this;*
Yea, and furr'd moss besides, when
*   flowers are none,*
To winter-ground they corse.

John Webster in *The White Devil* (c. 1612) associated the wren with this ritual:

Call for the robin redbreast
*   and the wren,*
Since o'er shady groves they hover,
And with leaves and flowers
*   do cover*
The friendless bodies of
*   unburied men.*

Thus in the course of time, an incident such as seeing a robin carrying moss for its nest near a corpse became embellished by poets. Possibly, too, observations of robins perching near places where graves were being dug added to the bird's associations with funeral rites. But the tradition of birds taking part in church services goes back beyond the thirteenth century.

From such antecedents originated what has been styled the best known poem in the language, '*The Death and Burial of Cock Robin*':

Who killed Cock Robin?
I said the Sparrow
With my bow and arrow
I killed Cock Robin.

Although the oldest printed example is in an eighteenth century chapbook, it evidently evolved from earlier ideas. Suggestions that it was originally a political satire or an allusion to the death of Balder are mere speculation. Late in the eighteenth century it was printed together with another set of verses, '*The Marriage of Cock Robin and Jenny Wren*'. In it the birds act various roles:

Then on her finger fair
Cock Robin put the ring.
'You're married now,' says
*   Parson Rook;*
While the Lark amen did sing.

It is more likely that the notion of robin and wren being male and female

of the same species arose because of associations created by the poets than that country folk made this mistake. The belief is not entirely extinct. There was a saying:

The robin redbreast and the wren
Are God Almighty's cock and hen.

Sentiment, religious associations, and tradition combined to create friendly feelings for the robin, sometimes resulting in beliefs that various ills would befall those who injured it or disturbed the nest. In England, Scotland, and Germany it was believed that the cows belonging to a man who killed a robin would yield bloody milk. In Suffolk and Bohemia you would suffer from trembling of your hands if you robbed a nest, and the belief is still current in Wales that a broken limb may be the penalty.

As we might expect, a bird around which so many associations have gathered has been regarded as having oracular powers. There is a Suffolk rhyme:

If the robin sings in the bush,
Then the weather will be coarse;
But if the robin sings on the barn,
Then the weather will be warm.

This may have arisen from the observation that in autumn the bird sings softly, perched fairly low in trees and bushes, whereas when the temperature is rising during the spring and the male is defending his territory he often sings from higher perches. In Germany it is considered a good omen when a bridal pair sees a robin on their way from the church.

E.A.ARMSTRONG

FURTHER READING: David Lack. Robin Redbreast. (Oxford Univ. Press, 1950); I. and P. Opie. The Oxford Dictionary of Nursery Rhymes. (Oxford Univ. Press, 1951).

Salmon

In both its natural and supernatural aspects the salmon has always been a fish of mystery. Until comparatively recently all that was known about its habits was that it hatches out in rivers and makes its way to the sea; that it later returns to the river as a grilse and spawns there, after which it is known as a kelt. Salmon are found in the rivers and seas on either side of the Atlantic and in parts of North America they inhabit certain landlocked lakes.

Salmon lore is essentially a part of the folklore of fish in general and, in common with all other fish, the salmon is symbolically speaking a 'psychic being'. Extremely prolific, it was a symbol of abundance; and it represented philosophical retirement because of its mysterious journeyings to the sea. It also symbolized prowess in battle, a result of its ability to overcome adversity in leaping up seemingly impassable rapids. But the salmon is primarily the 'fish of wisdom', and it crops up in this guise time and time again, in ancient and modern traditions. All communities dependent upon salmon for their livelihood have created special ceremonies associated with the fish harvest, varying from individual acts, such as spitting on the fishhook, to collective rites in which the sea is formally blessed.

A number of extremely interesting customs, usually ecclesiastical in character, are connected with the first fish of the season as with the first fruits on land. At Christchurch in Hampshire the Church retains the right to the first salmon, but the more interesting customs of this type are found further north, where salmon fishing continues to be a major industry. In Norham, on the river Tweed in Northumberland, the nets were blessed by the vicar, after which the first of the catch was handed over to him as rent. Tea parties, known as salmon kettles, are held at Tweedsmouth, the border town opposite Berwick-on-Tweed, a custom replacing the trade fair that was formerly held to celebrate the season's first fish. A Salmon Queen is now elected, instead of the ancient Master of Revels.

A salmon is incorporated in the arms of the city of Glasgow and in certain ecclesiastical seals. The fish's religious associations are also reflected in a legend of St. Kentigern, patron saint of Glasgow, who recovered a lady's lost ring from the belly of a salmon. The fish and ring theme is widespread.

References to mystical salmon are found in Welsh mythology, where it assumes its traditional role of fish of wisdom. According to one anecdote, a salmon is said to have become notorious for winking at married women who gathered on the banks of the sacred stream Alum. The salmon of the Dwyfach and Dwyfer in Merionethshire voluntarily surrendered to the fishermen every Christmas morning, freely permitting themselves to be removed from the water.

The salmon was known as the food of kings among the ancient Irish and it was forbidden to those not of royal birth. The fish is prominent in Celtic lore as Eo Feasa, the fish of knowledge, and it was said to confer prescience

The Glasgow coat of arms includes several salmon in its design.

5602. Salmon Leaping Falls, Ketchikan, Alaska.

Salmon swimming upstream to spawn

when even a thumb was laid upon it. As such it became the emblem of the Irish folk hero Finn, who, after being presented with a specimen, ate its flesh and acquired not only foreknowledge but 'magic counsel'; and, in allusion to the courage of the salmon, his physical powers were said to have been supernaturally strengthened.

The European fishing communities of the North American continent brought some of their native customs to the land of their adoption, but the more ancient forms of salmon legend are to be found in the traditions of the North American Indians. The Kwakiutl tribes of British Columbia believe that twins are transformed salmon and will never permit them to venture near the river in case they should become fish again. Like twins all over the world, they are credited with supernatural qualities, in this case the ability to summon salmon into the nets of the waiting fishermen by the power of their voices. This has much in common with the Indian custom of 'preaching to the fish', which was a form of magical incantation.

Welcoming the Salmon

The salmon harvest was of enormous importance to Indian tribal economy and was associated with elaborate ceremonies. The Karoks of California had their own special salmon dance to ensure a good catch, and in the north the Alaskan Indians engaged in magical practices in connection with the first fish of the season. In British Columbia, in the middle of the nineteenth century, crowds of Indians would assemble for a great festival in anticipation of the arrival of the first fish in the Columbia River in early June. At the sentries' cry of 'salmon' the community would abandon its merrymaking and hasten to the river banks to capture the fish, which were cured as fast as they were landed.

The Indians of this territory invented an intriguing 'fairy tale' to account for the presence of the huge rapids that the fish have to climb in order to attain the river's upper reaches. It relates how in the remote past an evil spirit, seeking to injure their people, caused an earthquake which obstructed the salmon by blocking the course of the river. The Indians, not to be outwitted, constructed a salmon ladder which the fish climbed in their ascent, resting on the ledges to recover from their exhaustion. These ledges were set with salmon traps by the Indians who were able to triumph over the wily evil spirit in this way.

Scorpion

The scorpion is classified, not with the insects, but with the spiders. The virulence of its venom has been exaggerated, though there are a few records

from the Near East of people dying after being stung. Species living in the Sahara and Mexico are more dangerous. No species is found in the British Isles, but it is familiar by name to most people because of references to it in European literature and the Bible.

The Judean wilderness is mentioned as a place of scorpions, and throughout the Bible these creatures are regarded as malignant (Deuteronomy 8.15; Ezekiel 2.6; Revelation 9.5,10). They are associated with drought, wretchedness and pain. King Rehoboam is reported

as saying: 'My father chastised you with whips, but I will chastise you with scorpions' (1 Kings 12.11). The allusion may be to whips armed with spines. Such references contributed to the scorpion becoming symbolic of that which is hurtful and unpleasant.

Although these creatures were familiar to people living in southern Europe, medieval writers and illustrators depicted them in highly imaginative ways. The scorpion was said to have a face like a woman and in a twelfth-century manuscript in the British Museum it is shown with a human head and four legs, and with a body impaled on the spearlike sting. In the Ancren Riwle, a work of devotional instruction dating from about the same period, the scorpion is described as 'a kind of serpent that has a face like that of a woman and puts on a pleasant countenance'. The same notion appears in the works of Elizabethan writers.

Apollonius of Tyana was reputed to have cleared Antioch of scorpions by burying a bronze image of one in the centre of the city. Pliny, in his Natural History, was responsible for a number of odd ideas about scorpions becoming current in later literature. He says that the scorpion provides a cure for its own poison: 'It is thought good . . . to lay to the sore the same scorpion that did the harm; or to eat him roasted, and last of all to drink it in two cups of pure wine of the grape.'

Scorpion lore illustrates both the extent to which Pliny's statements influenced successive writers for many centuries and the ingenuity with which these writers elaborated and embellished such notions without any attempt to find out the facts. The Jacobean dramatists Beaumont and Fletcher wrote in *Philaster:* 'Now your tongues like scorpions both heal

and poison.' And in *Rosalynde* (1590) Thomas Lodge remarked: 'They that are stung by the scorpion cannot be recovered but by the scorpion.' Although these ideas are fantastic, ever since the discoveries of Edward Jenner it has been recognized that immunity from certain diseases may be attained by administering small doses of toxin.

Lupton, a writer of the sixteenth century, commented that eating basil counteracts a scorpion's sting. He gave this recipe: 'One handful of basil with ten sea crabs, stamped or beaten together, doth make all the scorpions to come to that place that are nigh to the same.' Presumably this was based on the magical concept that 'like attracts like', there being a vague similarity between crabs and scorpions. Topsell, in the seventeenth century, had fanciful notions: 'The sea crab with basil in her mouth destroyeth the scorpion.' He describes vividly how scorpions, in order to reach a sleeping man, form a chain from the ceiling, each giving place to another after it has stung him.

Seal

The folklore of the seal owes much to the animal's resemblance, in some respects, to a human being. The round head with its large, staring eyes, appearing suddenly out of the water near a boat or an observer on the rocks, tends to arouse the sense of mystery associated with semihuman creatures.

Seal at the National Seal Sanctuary at Gweek in the Helford Estuary, Cornwall, England

The curiosity of seals induces them to swim close to where there are sounds of talking or music, and some of their calls, especially when heard echoing in sea caves, have a weird human timbre. Even on shore some of the movements made by a seal's flippers bear a grotesque resemblance to human gestures. It must also be remembered that people living near great rivers, lakes, or the sea have commonly supposed the water to be inhabited by strange beings with partly human, partly animal, characteristics.

Beliefs and customs concerning seals have naturally been most detailed and numerous where acquaintance with these mammals is greatest—among those who depend on them for food, clothing and light. The Inuit attitude toward seals is similar to that of other primitive hunting peoples to their quarry. In Baffin Land, and around Hudson Bay, a man who killed a seal was regarded as committing an offence for which he must make atonement. The taboos he had to observe after such a transgression were basically similar to those imposed for killing a man. He must not scrape frost from a window, clean drips from his lamp, shake his bed, scrape hair from skins or work in wood, stone, or ivory. A woman was forbidden to comb her hair or wash her face.

The scrupulous observation of these rules was essential; otherwise the goddess Sedna's fingers would give her

A sea lion pup poses for the camera in the Sea of Cortez, Mexico. The pups kept giving their watchful mother the slip.

pain, for seals were believed to have originated from her severed fingers. Thus, there was no clear distinction between men and animals, and divine beings were believed to have some affinity with both. Almost all observances were designed to retain Sedna's goodwill or appease her wrath. She was the mythical mother of the marine mammals which lived in the lower world and controlled the destinies of men. Human motherhood was also her concern. If a woman concealed the fact that she had given birth prematurely, people who came near her would be adversely affected so that the seals would avoid them, and the offence would be attached to the souls of the animals, who would carry information of it down to Sedna.

When a seal was killed, its soul had to wait three days before returning to her, so the men responsible rested for three days after the animal's death. Unless the taboos were scrupulously observed the seals would evade their hunters. These procedures helped to conserve the food supply by preventing ruthless exploitation. Greenlanders avoided breaking the skulls of seals but kept them intact by the door so that the souls of the animals might not be offended and frighten other seals away.

In Kamchatka, Siberia, mimetic ceremonies were performed before sealing expeditions in order to further their success. Packets of herbs were placed to represent seals and miniature replicas of boats were drawn along the sand. The Eskimo of Bering Strait preserved the swim bladders of seals as the repositories of the beasts' souls, offering them food. The bladders were suspended and made to dance by pulling a string while the people flopped around in a dance imitating the movements of the animals. The shaman, bearing a huge torch, ran to the ice, with the men following, carrying the bladders on their harpoons. The bladders were then thrust below the ice, so that the souls of the dead animals could be reborn, and then the participants purified themselves by leaping over a fire.

In certain areas where the caribou were hunted, Sedna was believed to dislike these beasts and certain rules had to be observed lest she should be annoyed. This likely indicated when the Inuit moved south and were able to augment their resources by hunting caribou as well as seals this new activity was not readily assimilated into their culture.

In the west of Ireland, the islands

north of the Scottish mainland, and the Faroes, certain families or persons are said to be descended from seals. The sept (division of a clan) of the Mackays in Sutherland are known as 'the descendants of the seal'. The laird of Borgie in Sutherland saw a mermaid seeking a place to land. He stole her cowl (or cap), which gave him power over her and she became his wife. She told him her life was bound up with the cowl. The laird hid it in the middle of a haystack, but eventually his servants found it and showed it to the mermaid. She took it and, leaving her baby son in his cot, plunged into the sea. From time to time she came close inshore to see her son, weeping that she could not take him with her. He and his descendants became famous swimmers and it was said that they could not drown.

A similar story is told of the Mac-Codrums of North Uist. In Colonsay in Argyllshire, the McPhees were held to be descendants of a drowned maiden whose sealskin the clan chief had found by the shore. It is said that people belonging to such families must not kill seals. The Coneelys in

the west of Ireland were said to have been seals—hence their name, which has that meaning. According to the tale it became changed to Connelly. Comparable stories were told of the O'Sullivans and O'Flahertys of Kerry, the Macnamaras of Clare, and the Achill Islanders. In them we have the vestiges of very ancient beliefs in which a clear distinction between men and animals was not recognized.

It is debatable whether these beliefs have been influenced by notions once prevalent in the Arctic and sub-Arctic where men, by means of mimetic performances and wearing or wielding skins or parts of animals, identified themselves with seals. They must be viewed in relation to the widespread swan maiden theme, according to which birds are seen to alight, doff their feather garments and reveal themselves as women to a watching man who, stealing a robe, makes one of the maidens his wife. The basic motif is certainly of great antiquity.

The earliest literary references to seal people are by Greek writers—Hesiod, Pindar, Apollodorus—but oral traditions may date from much earlier. The

Phocians of Central Greece were said to be descended from seals. According to myth, Phocus (the name still used in the scientific classifications of seals) was a son of the Nereid or sea nymph Psamathe, who had been pursued by Aeacus and, in spite of transforming herself into a seal, was forced to submit to his embraces. If, as has been suggested by Robert Graves, the dance of the fifty Nereids on the shore at the wedding of Thetis, and her return to the sea after the birth of Achilles, was a fragment of the same myth this would increase the story's resemblance to northern versions.

One such story told in the Faroes is about a young man who stole a seal maiden's skin while the seal people danced on the shore. This legend has a tragic ending as, in spite of the warning given by the seal maiden in a dream, men kill her seal husband and children and a curse comes upon the islanders so that many are killed on the cliffs or drowned at sea. The theme of kinship with man which underlies many of the seal traditions has not prevented their ruthless exploitation: nine species are thought in danger of becoming extinct.

In 1616 a Scottish woman was brought before a court on a charge of offering a man's finger bone to be used in order to cause butter to come more readily in the churn. She was convicted although she said that the bone came from a seal. It is doubtful, however, whether seals have ever been connected with witchcraft.

A story said to have been current in nineteenth-century Greece seems to be a recent fabrication. A swimmer, too far out at sea, might be strangled by a seal. The creature would then carry the corpse to shore and weep over it. Thus arose a saying that when a woman wept false tears she 'cried like a seal'.

Scandinavian seal sculpture

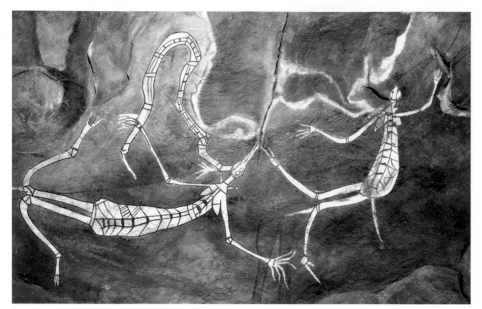

Australian Aboriginal art: Namaroto spirits and the Rainbow Serpent Burlung (Borlung)

Serpent

There is probably no creature which is found more widely distributed in the mythologies of the world than the serpent. Snakes occur even in the myths of lands where there are no snakes—such as among the Eskimo of the far north, perhaps recalling long-past days in warmer regions. St. Patrick may have driven the snakes out of Ireland but could not cleanse the isle of snake legends, including his own.

In the modern West most people, especially those who share the widespread abhorrence for this creature, might instantly think of the mythical serpent in its biblical role, as the tempter of Eve, and as the embodiment of evil whose head is to be forever bruised by mankind. But in the older mythologies the serpent is not always an evil being. It is, however, invariably one thing—an unswervingly, chthonic being, as C. G. Jung makes clear, a being of the primordial, dark, earthbound, underworld ways. As such, in the religions of man, it may pre-date even the primeval cults of the Earth Mother; certainly it has some connections with those cults, but with its own fertility and phallic implications.

At the dawn of history, or at least in its early morning, the age-old chthonic religions faced invasions by new cultures worshipping sky gods, gods of light. As the two groups of people met and fought, so their religions came into conflict as well. In India one outcome of such a conflict was that prehistoric snake cults were not entirely lost but were assimilated into the religion of the invading Aryans and survived in the later Hindu myths of semidivine beings with serpent bodies, called the Nagas.

In many folktales the Nagas are not evil but act beneficently, and a female Naga or Nagini may often marry a mortal. But they are vengeful and terrible if harmed, and so exhibit a considerable share of demonic aspects. Hindu gods and heroes, including Krishna, often come into conflict with them; but elsewhere, Nagas play valuable parts in the mythic structure. Much outright snake worship remains in parts of India, including that of the snake goddess Manasa in Bengal, who is identified as a most high-ranking Nagini.

Ousted by Apollo

In Western myth, the clash between old chthonic gods and incoming sky gods appears, predictably, as a straightforward battle. It is especially so in Greek mythology where in two crucial instances the serpent motif appears on the side of the old gods. Apollo, the brilliant new sky god of the Hellenes, displaces a pre-Hellenic worship (probably a snake cult) in the myth of his combat with Python, a serpent monster. The god killed the serpent on the slopes of Parnassus, in its lair at Delphi. There his temple was established; there the Delphic oracle under his patronage grew to its later position of considerable power in the Greek world. And the priestess who delivered the oracles when possessed with the god was called the Pythia.

In Egypt the god Seth at a late stage of development took on the attributes of an evil god and was identified with another serpent monster of Greek myth, Typhon, who was defeated in a great battle by Zeus. This creature was the last of the fearsome old gods, children of Mother Earth, who resisted the incursion of the gods of Olympus. In some versions of the myth of Apollo's battle the consonants of his enemy's name are reversed, and Python is called Typhaon. The etymological similarities are clear. Typhon, in the Zeus myth, was formed of coiled serpents from the thighs down, with arms and hands composed of hundreds of snakes. Zeus, the supreme sky god, fought this chthonic horror and was finally victorious.

Superman against Serpents

These battles against snake creatures are myths of central importance, signaling major religious upheavals and transitions. But they are also representatives of one of the most widespread hero myths. It seems that every hero in myth and legend must at some time confront a monster which is usually reptilian, though not always a snake. Hercules, for example, strangled two serpents while he was still an infant, and later killed the hundred-headed water serpent Hydra). Krishna also killed snakes in his infancy; Japan's hero Susanoo fought a multiheaded serpent. Perseus slew his share of serpents, including those on the head of Medusa. Sigurd of Scandinavian myth fought the giant serpent Fafnir, and Maui of Polynesian legend did battle with a monster eel. And in Norse myth Thor fought with the world-encircling Midgard serpent.

Thor's combat may be another instance of the displacement of an older, chthonic divinity, but it also overlaps with another mythological motif of great antiquity, that of the 'cosmic snake'. The Midgard serpent may be the best known, but there is also the great Naga lord of Hindu myth, the many-headed serpent Sesha, who supports the world and on whom Vishnu sleeps during peaceful epochs.

None of these cosmic snakes is evil—not even the Midgard, in its world-girdling aspect, though it may be seen as malevolent in its role as offspring of Loki and adversary of Thor. No one would deny that in myth, the snake has been used often enough as a handy container for evil forces. But it is clear that world mythology does not regard the serpent motif as invariably a symbol of evil.

The younger cultures, like that of the Hellenes seem to have justified their conquests by projecting an evil image onto the displaced gods. And because so many of the displaced were snakes, that creature acquired more than its share of evil. Perhaps the bluntest, most explicit image of this defeat occurs in the *Iliad* of Homer, when the combatants look up and see an eagle carrying in its claws a wounded snake—a terrible omen, symbolizing the victory of the Achaeans over the old earth-oriented Asian ways.

Devil's sermask with serpents from Erogaricuaro, Michoacan, on display at the Museum of Artes Populares in Mexico City

Union of Earth and Sky

The Nagas of India show that the confrontation of dark against light, earth against sky, need not always mean total war and the triumph of the latter. It can lead to a peaceful blending or assimilation, a reconciliation of opposites. And this notion even managed to creep into Greek mythology. There, as elsewhere, its usual symbolism makes use of a combination of the bird and snake motifs.

The combining of earth and sky motifs occurs in the myth of the Olympian god Hermes; with his winged sandals and snake-entwined caduceus, he was the intermediary between heaven and the underworld, and acted as guide to the souls of the dead. Similarly, in the myth of the Greco-Roman god Asclepios, founder of medicine; as the son of Apollo he shared the god's association with the sky, yet his symbol was the snake. The symbol may have come from another pre-Hellenic snake cult and oracle (a minor version of Delphi) taken over by the Asclepian cult. It would be reinforced by the symbolism of renewal in the snake, which casts its skin each year. Of more importance, the priests of Asclepios performed diagnoses and cures by a technique that began with dreaming. The Greeks saw dreams as issuing from the underworld (a concept not unlike that of the unconscious mind) and so the snake, as inhabitant and symbol of that region, naturally became the symbol of the god who healed by dreams. And the snake still appears as the chief emblem of the medical profession today.

In his *Footprint East Africa Handbook, 7th edition*, Michael Hodd identifies the building housing these paintings as an 'Iqa-bet, a two-story stone storage building, which contains religious artifacts.' The building is next to the Church of Abba Afse, Yeha, Tigray Region, northern Ethiopia.

A more striking instance of the reconciliation between earth and sky can be found in a great mythological motif held in common by all the principal religions of Central America, Mexico and even the southwest of the United States. This is the concept of the plumed serpent, the androgynous combination of bird and snake. It can be seen in a major divinity of the Maya, the feathered serpent god Kukulcan. But it can best be seen in the glory of the Toltec deity Quetzalcoatl. He was a sky god, sometimes identified with the wind and at other times with the morning star. But he rose to dominate the Toltec religion as a sun divinity, a major creator, a divine king. His rule, and his manifestation as the plumed serpent, spoke of reconciliation, harmony, and peace.

This theme, the reconciliation between underworld and heaven, occurs also in the image of the rainbow, traditionally and obviously seen as a bridge between earth and sky. But in myth and symbol rainbows are also often considered to be snakes. The concept can be found in ancient Persian myth, in folktales of Brittany, in Australian aborigine myth, in West African myth, in North and South American Indian myth, and elsewhere. In Australia the rainbow snake is an especially important deity, a culture hero and creator with wide fertility implications.

One of the most remarkable of the world's serpent deities is the god Da or Dan of Dahomey in West Africa. He is usually seen as a snake with tail in mouth and therefore resembling a cosmic snake like that of Midgard, but also a rainbow and water snake with fertility associations; he has another role again in oracular divination. Da was exported with West African slaves and became gradually translated into Dam-balla, one of the principal deities of the New World's vodun or Voodoo religion. Yet even there he retains the Dahomean form of rainbow snake, intermediary between heaven and Earth.

Similarly, the rainbow is a water serpent in Arawak myth in South America, and is an earth or underworld spirit gone to drink at the sky in Malayan and in Yoruba myth. In the arid southwest of the United States the water snake motif diminishes somewhat, but the earth-sky reconciliation remains: the Mohave of southern California tell of a giant rattlesnake who is a sky spirit. And an important Pueblo snake god (who is also sometimes a plumed serpent) figures in a major Hopi ritual that is a rain-making weather magic.

The Mystical Power of Serpents

The Hopi shamans underline their appeal to the rain by holding venomous snakes in their mouths while performing; again the underworld snake becomes a sky symbol. The performers are members of the snake clan, and are confident that they will not be bitten. Similar dances occur among the Comanche; and most southwestern Indians have some form of traditional magic that protects against snakebite and that involves the handling of rattlesnakes by the medicine men. Californian tribal shamans have been said to invite rattlers to bite them, during snake-handling rites, in order to prove their resistance or their curative powers.

The white man, too, has his version of these ancient rites, such as the ecstatic snake-handling Christian sects of the United States, in Tennessee and elsewhere. Faith, apparently, is supposed to protect these poisonous snakes which unwillingly join in the worship. Perhaps it could be said that the snakes, in turn, symbolize the handlers' achievement of a higher spiritual plane.

Other North American Indians include snake gods in their pantheons, but these are generally lesser Nature spirits, no more important than other animal gods. Even so, they will have their own celebrations, usually in mimetic dances—follow-the-leader chain dances or open-ended round dances—which emulate the sinuous movement of a snake. The Iroquois and Cherokee, among others, had this form of snake dance; and indeed it was once traditional, and may still occasionally be encountered, among North American college students at football rallies and other open air festivities.

Among lesser snake gods in the mythologies of the world are Urcaguay, the Inca snake god who guarded treasure just as dragons do in European folktale; the Icelandic Nidhug or Nidhoggr, predominant among the countless serpents who gnaw the roots of the world tree yggdrasill, the snake-legged Cernunnos, horned and carrying a ram-headed serpent.

The snake appears in magic as prominently as in myth. A major mystic symbol is the ourobouros, the snake with its tail in its mouth like the cosmic snakes, strengthening the serpentine role in the 'reconciliation of opposites' by being half dark and half light, like the yin and yang symbol that has the same function in oriental belief. Alchemy has its share of encircling serpents; and it depicts the vital spirit-substance Mercury as a winged serpent, reflecting the Roman god of the same name, and the Greek Hermes, with winged sandals and snake-encircled caduceus. So the snake retains in magic and mysticism its symbolic role as an underground being who may nevertheless mediate with heaven. But then magic in Christian times also places the mantle of evil on the serpent—as when a fifteenth century cabalist named Joseph della Rayna conjured up two devils, who appeared as serpents. And Aleister Crowley wrote about a devil whom he summoned up, who appeared in various forms including that of a snake.

Snake Skin for Rheumatism

Predictably, evil is also ascribed to snakes in the homelier magic of popular superstition; if a pregnant woman is frightened by a snake her child is expected to have a snakelike constricted throat, and in Britain a live adder on the doorstep is a death omen. American superstition includes the delightful fantasy of the 'hoop snake', which takes its tail in its mouth like a kind of crazed ourobouros and rolls with great speed at its enemies. Folklore universally insists that all poisonous snakes can spit their venom, all snakes have hypnotic powers, and the poison is injected into a bite by the snake's tongue.

None of these beliefs have forestalled the wide use of snakes, or their parts, in folk medicine. The powdered rattles of a rattlesnake, in a drink, according to American backwoods belief, would assist a mother in a difficult birth. Kentuckians believed that the rattles worn as a hair ornament prevented headache, and rattlesnake skin worn round the affected part could cure rheumatism, as could adder skin in Britain. Even more positively, the dried skin of a snake hung over the hearth was said, in Britain, to protect the house from fire and to bring good fortune to the family who lived there.

This bit of homespun magic parallels the more generous view of snakes held in places like Lithuania and Armenia, and among ancient Teutonic peoples, where a family might have its own 'house snake' as both a useful rat-catcher and a minor guardian house spirit. In this way European folklore bypasses the Christian projections of evil onto the serpent to retain the older, and somehow far more satisfying idea of it as a chthonic earth spirit, which is deserving of our veneration.

Sheep

In prehistoric times sheep were already domesticated; it may be assumed that they practically domesticated themselves, because a newly born lamb has so strong and undifferentiated an instinct to follow a large moving object that it may become attached to man. As in the nursery rhyme:

> Mary had a little lamb,
> Its fleece was white as snow,
> And everywhere that Mary went,
> The lamb was sure to go.

No doubt a few such lambs, led or brought back to human settlements, constituted an asset as a ready supply of milk, butter, meat, and clothing.

An early example of a lamb becoming a pet is provided by the parable of the rich man and the poor man told to David by Nathan, reproving him for bringing about Uriah's death in order to enjoy his wife Bathsheba (2 Samuel, chapter 12). The little ewe lamb grew up in the poor man's house with his children, 'it used to eat of his morsel, and drink from his cup and lie in his bosom, and it was like a daughter to him'. So docile and profitable an animal naturally became highly important in the economy of pastoral peoples over much of Asia, Europe, and Africa.

At an early period the sheep became associated with religious and magical ideas and customs. Its remains in Neolithic graves indicate that it served as a burial offering. Khnemu, the great god of Elephantine in Egypt, was represented originally as a ram but in historical times as a ram-headed human figure. From the 16th century BC he became combined with the sun god Re and was worshipped throughout southern Egypt as Khnemu-Re, ram-headed and wearing a solar-disc, indicating his connection with the sun. The provincial god of Thebes, Amun, became more important with the rise of Theban power. As Amun-Re, with a ram's head or horns, he became king of the gods of all Egypt.

The Bans treated rams as sacred, but once a year they killed, flayed and cut up one and draped the statue of the god with it. They ran around the temple mourning the animal's death and then buried it in a sacred sarcophagus.

According to the myth of the Golden Fleece, Pelias, king of Iolcus in Thessaly, urged Jason to set forth to Colchis to fetch the Fleece in which, according to one version, Zeus had climbed to the sky. After achieving a number of prodigious feats, he managed to seize it, having lulled to sleep the dragon which was guarding it, by means of a potion provided by Medea.

Other myths, Greek, Etruscan, and Italian, connected prosperity with a

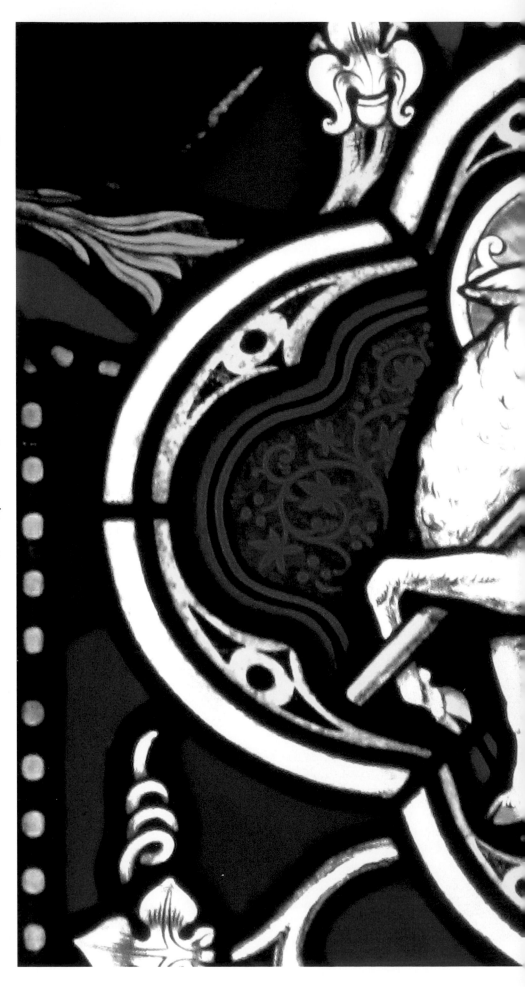

Parish church of St. Peter, Jersey, England

ram bearing a golden or purple fleece. At the season when the dog star rose and heat was greatest, youths clad in skins from newly slaughtered rams ascended Mt. Pelion in Greece. Thus as a ram god Zeus was a solar deity and connected with the powers of growth and fertility. In Crete Pythagoras submitted to a purificatory ceremony, lying by the sea during the day and by the river at night, with the fleece of a black lamb wrapped around him. Then he descended to the reputed tomb of Zeus clad in black wool. The wearing of a sheep's fleece may have meant that the man so clothed was regarded as a sacrificial substitute for a sheep. Although the records are fragmentary, this view accords with what is known of a ritual observed at Hierapolis in Egypt during which the sacrificer ate some sheep's flesh and laid the skin on the ground, kneeling on it with the feet and head over his own head. Thus, pleading with the god, he made a vicarious sacrifice.

The Lamb of God

The ram was widely regarded as a sacrificial animal. Genesis 22.1–18 relates how Abraham was prevented from sacrificing his son Isaac and how he substituted a ram. This is generally regarded as indicating that, among the Hebrew and other Semitic peoples, animals at some early period were substituted for human sacrifices. After childbirth a Hebrew mother made an offering of a yearling lamb (Leviticus 12.6) and a leper's sacrifice was two yearling rams and one yearling ewe lamb (Leviticus 14 .10). The custom of slaying the Passover lamb, traced back to the delivery of the Israelites from bondage in Egypt but apparently an adaptation of an earlier custom, continued as a Jewish observance which influenced Christian doctrine and imagery.

As lambs, unblemished and representing innocence, figured in Jewish thought as sacrificial objects it was natural that this imagery should be transferred to Christ. John the Baptist is reported as saying, when Jesus came to him: 'Behold the Lamb of God, who takes away the sin of the world' (John 1.29). When Philip met the Queen of Ethiopia's official on the road to Jerusalem, he read to him a passage from Isaiah identifying Jesus with the sacrificial lamb (Acts 8.32). In Revelation 7.9–17 Christ is again referred to as the 'Lamb of God'. According to a widespread English folk tradition current into the late-nineteenth century, a person mounting a hilltop at dawn on Easter morning would see the symbol of the Lamb of God, bearing a banner marked with a red cross, on the sun's disc.

The concept of the Church as Christ's flock has exercised a powerful influence on Christian thought. During the first centuries of the Christian era the figure of the Good Shepherd was the most important Christian symbol. In biblical times the shepherd did not drive but led his flock; and the crook or crozier carried by a bishop is symbolic of his pastoral office as shepherd of Christ's flock.

Festivals and Celebrations

Another line of tradition, long established in Europe, has contributed to the folklore and customs connected with sheep. The Roman sheep festival known as the Parilia was honoured by shepherds and herdsmen, and considered highly important for the maintenance of the health and increase of their animals. The festival took place on 21 April and was celebrated in both town and country, but obviously its origins were rural. People who went to the temple of Vesta were given ashes, blood, and bean straw to use in a cleansing rite during which they fumigated themselves and also, probably, their beasts. The blood was from the tail of a horse sacrificed in October and the ashes were those of unborn calves taken from the womb on 15 April.

It was believed that the rites quickened the wombs not only of cows and ewes but also of women. The sheepfold was decorated with boughs and a wreath hung on the door. The flocks were purified by being driven through bonfires of pine wood, laurel, branches of the male olive, and grass. They were also fumigated with burning sulphur.

Sixth century Byzantine mosaic in the apse of the basilica of Sant'Apollinare in Classe, Ravenna, Italy

The shepherds provided offerings for the deity, including pails of milk and cakes of millet, praying as they faced toward the east that the sheep might be preserved from witchcraft and wolves, that fodder might be plentiful, and the animals prolific. Then the shepherds washed their hands in the morning dew, drank a bowl of milk and wine, and jumped over bonfires. Their petitions were not only for the material well-being of their flocks. They sought pardon from the nymphs for the disturbance of the pools by their animals and for trespassing unwittingly in sacred groves.

Many festivals exhibiting features similar to those of the Parilia were celebrated elsewhere in Europe. Some of these still survive. Usually the procedure is observed on 23 April, St. George's Day, when the cattle are driven out to pasture. In the Carpathian mountains the Huzuls kindle a fire of dung on St. George's Eve, fumigate the animals, and decorate the gateposts with boughs of the silver poplar, considered effective in repelling evil spirits. Before the cattle are turned out on St. George's Day the Ruthenians fumigate them with smoke from a burning snakeskin or rub their horns and udders with serpent's fat. The widespread observance of comparable ceremonies at the same time of year indicates their antiquity.

Later in the year, the sheep-shearing celebrations were the counterpart of the harvest festivities among agriculturalists. Shepherds and their families and friends gathered to the shearing and there was feasting and merriment. Among the Romans it was a very convivial occasion. In southern England the sheep-shearing festivities were more elaborate than in the northern counties. A good dinner was provided for the shearers, their relatives and friends and also for the young people of the village.

Divination by Sheep's Bones

The sheep was regarded as having oracular significance. Virgil (Aeneid, book 7) refers to priestesses sleeping on fleeces in order to hold converse with the gods. In England and Germany it was considered lucky to meet a flock on setting forth from your house. Good fortune could be expected if, on seeing the first lamb in spring, its head was turned away from you. In Germany if a sheep bore three black lambs it was feared that someone belonging to the household would die.

A girl, anxious about when she would get married, would go to the sheep stall at night on Christmas Eve and grab an animal. If it turned out to be a ram, this was propitious, but if she found herself holding a ewe she would remain unmarried in that year. In England it was believed that you could forecast the weather by observing the sheep. If they were quiet, fine weather might be expected, but a restless flock betokened wind and rain.

Divination by means of sheep bones, especially the shoulder blade, was widespread and probably dates from very early times. Such oracular practices have been noted among the Icelanders, Scots, Southern Slavs, Bedouin, and Mongolians of inner Asia. English maidens believed that a faithless lover could be recalled by piercing a sheep's shoulder blade with a knife and repeating this charm:

It's not this bone I wish to stick
But—'s heart I wish to prick.
Whether he be asleep or awake
I'd have him come to me and speak.

For divinatory use in Scotland the shoulder blade of a black sheep was scraped, avoiding the use of iron. On Lewis the seer held it lengthwise in the direction of the island's greatest length. In some areas of the Highlands two persons cooperated, one holding the bone over his left shoulder while the other inspected the broad end and interpreted what it revealed, according to the lines and shades.

The ram was involved in magical ceremonies in many parts of the world. The Tibetans, who feared earth demons, regarded the goddess Khon-ma as their leader. Dressed in golden robes and holding a golden noose, she rode on a ram. In order to deter her host of fiends an elaborate structure containing a ram's skull as well as precious objects of turquoise and silver was placed above the door of the house.

In South Africa the Ba-Thonga attribute drought to the concealment of miscarriages by women and perform rain making ceremonies involving the pouring of water after a completely black ram has been killed.

Various members and organs of the sheep were used to cure all sorts of ills in ways which often savoured more of magic than of medicine. The dung was applied to heal wounds and even eaten as a tonic. It was believed that a child suffering from whooping cough could be cured by taking it to the sheepfold at dawn, allowing a sheep to breathe on it and then placing it on the spot which the animal had vacated. The underlying assumption seems to have been that as sheep bleat in a hoarse way the child's cough would transfer itself to the animal

EDWARD A. ARMSTRONG

Snail

Used for magical healing in the past, especially in wart cures; one method was to rub the warts with a snail and then impale the snail on a thorn, so that as it slowly died the warts would fade away: snail slime was considered effective against consumption and other diseases: shut in a box or dish on Halloween, a snail would trace the initials of your future lover in slime during the night.

Snake

Appears in the myths and religious beliefs of almost all societies, playing many different roles: associated with rejuvenation, immortality, longevity, and wisdom, because it sloughs its skin, and with sexuality because of its phallic shape: snakes which live under rocks or in holes in the ground are connected with the underworld, the dead, fertility, the unconscious mind: in Christianity, linked with evil and sex, because of its role in tempting Eve.

Head of a snake, amusement park of the Prater, Vienna, Austria

Snake-Handling Cults

The snake is a powerful symbol in many different religious traditions. In Judaism and Christianity it has generally represented the power of evil and, perhaps because the snake resembles the phallus, it is frequently identified with unbridled sexual desire.

In Judaism snake imagery is plentiful, and circumcision, as a symbolic act that implies the regulation and social control of sexuality, also suggests the transcendence of the people, through a covenant with God, above the sinfulness of sexual behaviour into which Eve was led by the snake. Christianity employed snake imagery much less. In the gospel of St. Mark, however, it is promised that signs shall follow them that believe, one of which is that 'they shall pick up serpents'.

It is this promise that is invoked to justify the snake-handling cult that has arisen in parts of the United States, and which today is practiced in probably thirty or so different congregations by fundamentalists who accept Holiness teachings; they often regard themselves as anointed saints who have experienced the second blessing of the Holy

Ghost that confers upon them entire sanctification. Their services commonly include a variety of dramatic practices: speaking in unknown tongues; shaking, jerking and ecstatic dancing; faith healing; and foot-washing. These independent congregations are locally controlled and served, by lay, or self-ordained evangelists. They do not constitute an organized, centrally administered movement, and they are linked, if at all, only by itinerant evangelists. Some of these evangelists have been responsible for introducing snake-handling to congregations which already worship in an ecstatic manner.

Snake-handling appears to have begun in 1909. In that year, George Went Hensley decided that the scriptures commanded that the faithful should handle serpents; and he introduced the practice in churches in Tennessee and Kentucky. The cult spread to neighbouring states, particularly to North Carolina, Virginia, and West Virginia, and in more recent years has been encountered in Georgia, Florida, and California. Despite legislation introduced in some states to prohibit the cult, it has not been eliminated by being made illegal.

The practice appears to have arisen spontaneously in Holiness churches.

It is true that some North American Indian tribes practiced a snake dance, and that snakes were strongly associated with rain-making by many primitive peoples, but this idea has no echo in modern Christian tradition. Indeed the populations among whom snake-handling has arisen in the twentieth century have had little, if any, recent contact with Indians. Their interpretation of the practice conforms to their general literal belief in the Bible: it is done in obedience to scripture. Its ultimate rationale may be beyond man's comprehending: just as God chose to give men the gift of unknown tongues so that they might worship him in ways that transcended their understanding, so, in his wisdom, the Lord decided that the truly faithful should handle serpents.

The snakes used in services are obtained some time beforehand, and the usual types are rattlesnakes, water moccasins, and copperheads—all poisonous snakes. They are kept in a box while hymns are sung, spontaneous preaching occurs, healings are attempted and ecstatic emotions expressed. They are then taken out and handed from one believer to another. Great prestige is attached to those who first handle the snakes. In some services handfuls of snakes are taken up, thrown about, caressed. Believers readily wrap them around their heads or push them under their shirts, or even kiss them. They admit that they fear snakes, but they handle them when the Lord anoints them to do so; and they see their activity both as a proof of their own sanctified condition, and as a demonstration of faith and a glorification of God.

The snakes are actually handled for about fifteen or twenty minutes, a period which forms the high point of the service, which may last altogether about four hours. There is no question of these poisonous snakes having had their fangs drawn beforehand. Usually snakes are kept for only a few services and are then released, and new ones captured. Votaries of the cult are frequently bitten, but most of those who are bitten recover. There have, however, been a considerable number of fatalities in the course of half a century and most of these have been given widespread and adverse publicity. In 1955, Hensley himself, then aged seventy, received a fatal bite while practicing in Florida. Adepts regard recovery from a bite as a miracle wrought by God, but they also profess their willingness to die when the Lord decides, since they believe that the true saint is then brought to God's throne.

The cult has been prohibited in Kentucky, Tennessee, and Virginia, and also by some municipal authorities in North Carolina, but adherents are prepared to travel long distances to services in states where the practice is not forbidden. Some of the leading evangelists have been arrested at services, and police raids have occurred periodi-

cally. The notoriety that such attention from the police engenders appears to be not unwelcome. Insurance companies some years ago decided to refuse to regard death from snakebite at church meetings as accidental but this has apparently not affected the practice of the cult.

Excitement in a Grey World

The congregations which practice snake handling are all located in relatively remote country areas, particularly in the Appalachian Mountains. There, Holiness religion of the more extreme type flourishes, and many sects indulge in ecstatic manifestations of Holy Ghost power, with free expression of their emotions, and sometimes with tongues, jerks, and rolling. This is a typical economically depressed area, and among the snake cultists even the younger members are usually unemployed. Although rural, these areas are not farming districts, and many of the population live on government relief. Snake handlers tend to come from the poorest section of the population, and their members have little education.

Holiness religion appears to have an important function in these culturally retarded areas in asserting that, despite poverty, its adepts are more worthy than the affluent and socially

A Rattler Round the Neck
Snake-handling at Dolley Pond Church, Tennessee

The climax comes when the power is strong within the congregation, heightened by the clichéd preaching of the minister. A rope is stretched out by a member to separate the audience from the snake-handling devout, and visitors are warned that the snakes are about to be produced. This precaution may be barely accomplished before an impatient believer snatches up a snake from the angry knot in the opened box. Removing a snake from the box is regarded as a supreme test of faith, for the constantly jolted reptiles are by then thoroughly aroused and it is believed that they are most likely to strike when they are first touched. The box has been kicked, in a kind of half-jocular sin-baiting, because the snake represents the Devil, whom the spirit of God allows the true believer to overcome . . .

The snake may be held in various ways . . . Sister Minnie Parker, a buxom elderly gap-toothed woman—who walked barefoot among seventeen buzzing rattlesnakes in a homecoming service in the summer of 1946—held a beautiful large timber rattler around her neck like a necklace, with the free neck and head of the snake along the outside of her left forearm, while cooing with closed eyes and a delighted expression on her face.

Weston La Barre,
They Shall Take Up Serpents

Church leader Dewey Chafin (L) with Ray Christian (3R) handling timber rattlesnakes while trio of musicians play and sing behind them during worship service at the Church of the Lord Jesus.

respected. Their sense of superiority is powerfully reinforced by what they regard as the tangible spiritual power evident in the emotional vigour of their services, and in their ability and daring in handling snakes. The cult offers the intense excitement of real danger for people who have fewer inner resources and little creativity, and whose daily lives are marked by boredom and lack of cultural interests. Their normal social relations are emotionally impoverished, and they live in areas characterized by frustration, cynicism, and repression. The element of fatalism in the cult may also serve to absolve its members from blame as social failures.

Psychoanalytic interpretation of the cult might suggest that since the snake generally symbolizes the phallus, the manipulation of snakes represents the ability to handle phallic power: the cult thus appears as a significant and ambivalent undercurrent in response to the rigourous sexual morality that is demanded in Holiness religion. In his book *They Shall Take Up Serpents*, Weston La Barre considers that 'to dominate the snake is to dominate the guilty and dangerous sexual desire'. It may also be a curious sublimation of sexual desire, as indicated by episodes in which women have gained immense elation from repeatedly kissing the snake over its whole body despite being struck repeatedly by it. Psychological tests do not suggest much abnormality in snake handlers; the older members show more cheerfulness and fortitude in the face of old age and death than do members of conventional Churches. Nor have the young proved to be particularly maladjusted. Relations of young and old in these churches appear to be more harmonious than among the general population of people in similar social circumstances. Older people are accorded respect by the young for the greater frequency with which they

handle snakes and for their greater knowledge of the Bible. These results may, however, reflect the amount of authoritarianism in the belief system of Holiness Churches.

FURTHER READING: Weston La Barre. They Shall Take Up Serpents. *(Oxford Univ. Press, 1961); Harold Preece and Celia Kraft.* Dew on Jordan. *(New York: Dutton, 1946); W. D. Weatherford and E. D. C. Brewer.* Life and Religion in Southern Appalachia. *(New York: Friendship Press, 1962).*

Spider

'"Will you come into my parlour"? said the spider to the fly'. The spider inevitably suggests an evil arch-intriguer, weaving a web of duplicity in which fragile innocence is entrapped, or a bloodsucking moneylender who entangles the unwary borrower in his toils. In fact, the spider is as much preyed on as predator, providing food for lizards, wasps, and other foes, and it is ironic that the fly, a creature of disease, should be equated with the innocent victim who is ensnared.

Some people have a deep loathing of spiders and could not bear to touch one, but although the spider can be a type of evil and betrayal, and so of Satan, it has also been seen as a model of industry and wisdom, and a spider motif engraved on a precious stone makes a talisman which is supposed to confer foresight on the wearer.

Attitudes to spiders vary considerably, in fact. In West African and West Indian folklore, there is a great body of stories about Ananse, or Anansi, a spider who is a hero and trickster of infinite cunning and resource, and in some cases the Creator of the world. In European lore the spider spun a web to conceal the child Jesus from his enemies, and spiders also saved the lives of Mohammed and Frederick the Great.

The famous story of Robert the Bruce and the spider points to the moral that faith and persistence can bring victory out of defeat. Or the spider's web can be regarded as the home of the eternal weaver of illusions, and the spider which spins and kills, creates and destroys, can symbolize the perpetual alternation of forces on which life depends for its precarious balance.

The cross on the back of the common garden spider has helped to preserve it from the hostility of mankind, and the spider, like the toad, has played an important part in the folklore of medicine, since both creatures were believed to contain within their bodies a powerful health-giving stone. The seventeenth century antiquarian Elias Ashmole claimed to have cured himself of the ague by suspending three spiders around his neck. To relieve whooping cough it was once customary to wrap a spider in raisin or butter, or shut one in a walnut shell, the malady fading away as the spider died. Spiders were was used as a bandage for wounds and were supposed to cure warts.

On the other hand, in Suffolk in 1645, an accused witch named Mirabel Bedford admitted possessing a familiar imp in the form of a spider called Joan. In another trial, one of the accused defended himself with such eloquence as almost to sway the court in his favour, until the prosecutor noticed a spider crawling close to the prisoner's lips and cried out warningly, 'See who prompts him'. The prisoner was sentenced to death.

Spider's venom was once in demand as poison, and in Shakespeare's *The Winter's Tale,* Leontes remarks, 'There may be in the cup a spider steeped'. The bite or sting of the tarantula spider was supposed to cause Tarantism, a hysterical disease characterized by an extreme impulse to dance, and the Italian Tarantella was a wild dance which was thought to be the only cure for it.

Warrior Minamoto Raiko and the Earth Spider

The golden money spider, the living symbol of a gold coin, confers riches on anyone upon whose body it runs, and if caught and put in the pocket ensures plenty of ready cash, or a new suit of clothes. The superstition is current in Norfolk that a money spider suspended over the head is a charm for winning the football pools.

'If you would live and thrive, let a spider run alive' is an old saying. In Britain to kill a spider brings unwanted rain, and in Scotland and the West Indies the spider-killer is sure to break his crockery or his wine glasses before the day is out. The appearance of numerous spiders is a sign of much rain. A long thread of spider's web hanging from a tree or a beam symbolizes the ladder or rope by which you can ascend to heaven, and if you should find a web inscribed with your initials near the door of your house, it will bring you luck as long as you live there.

Stag

Animals with horns or antlers are depicted in paintings and carvings executed by men of the Old Stone Age; and the 'Horned Sorcerer', a painting of a man wearing antlers, in the cave of Les Trois Frères in southern France, suggests that such beasts were of ritual importance. Among the Hittites a god whose sacred animal was the stag was worshipped. His cult, which dates back to the 3rd millennium BC, was widespread, and models of stags have been recovered from tombs. A god of the countryside, he is represented standing on a stag, holding a falcon and a hare, and it is possible that, before the Hittite city states arose, he may have presided over the chase.

The Celtic divinity Cernunnos was depicted wearing antlers and, usually, in a squatting posture, as on the Gundestrup cauldron found in Jutland, where he is shown surrounded by animals and may have been regarded as a Lord of Beasts. A rock carving in Val Canonica in northern Italy shows a phallic figure apparently worshipping before a horned god who wears a torque (metal ornament). The god was probably regarded as a source of fertility and power. Evidence from the Near East indicates that horns represented supernatural power.

At Syracuse in Sicily women singers wore garlands and antlers on their

Actaeon, turned into a stag, is attacked by his dogs

heads, and at a festival in honour of Artemis men were similarly adorned. In another such ritual men postured like women. There was yet another ceremony in which men wore phalluses, and one in which women wore imitations of the male organ. There were evidently ambivalent ideas concerning Artemis, the huntress goddess, who was represented in art with one or more stags. Animals, and even human beings, were sacrificed to her. Actaeon, the young hunter who inadvertently interrupted her bathing, was transformed into a stag and torn to pieces by his own hounds.

There is a curious connection between the stag and precious metals. The hinds captured by Artemis and harnessed to her golden chariot bore horns. Hercules's third labour involved capturing the Ceryneian hind which had brazen hooves and golden horns, and was sacred to Artemis, and bringing it to Mycene. The Ramayana, an Indian epic, mentions a golden-antlered stag whose coat was flecked with silver, and in China deer are associated with places where precious metals are mined. Silver models of deer were placed in Christian sanctuaries because the stag was regarded as a symbol of Christ; when confronted with a serpent it represented the Christian overcoming evil.

A ritual stag hunt took place on Mt. Lycaeum at the beginning of the Christian era, and as late as the 5th century AD stag mummers danced in the south of France. In North America deer dances were performed increase fertility by causing rain to fall, and to encourage the growth of wild crops. Men wearing antlers still perform a dance in September every year at Abbots Bromley in Staffordshire.

Deer Women

The abundance of legendary lore concerning deer where Celtic culture and languages survive confirms that the stag was regarded as a supernatural animal. In the Scottish Highlands and islands the deer is associated with supernatural beings, always female, and there are many tales of deer-human transformations. These fabulous creatures are seldom malicious, but they are sometimes thought of as being gigantic. There was one, for instance, who was so colossal that when she waded across the Sound of Mull the water came only up to her knees.

A Gaelic tale relates that after a tragedy in which her baby was killed, a woman took to the hills where she lived with the deer and eluded her husband's attempts to capture her. After seven years he decided to marry again, but when the day for the wedding arrived his wife appeared at the church and took her place by his side; she was covered in fine fur like that of a red deer fawn. In other tales a hunter sees a deer turn into a woman and falls in love with her. He arranges to meet her at a church where they are to be married, but their plans are foiled by a witch. After many adventures they meet on a distant island and marry.

According to another Celtic legend Ossian hurled his spear at, but missed, a beautiful white deer, who turned out to be his mother. She led him to a rock in which a door mysteriously opened, and closed after them, and then revealed herself as a lovely woman. Yet another story describes how a hunter wounded a deer which managed to escape. Later she appeared to him in a

dream, in human form, and returned the arrow with which he had shot her.

The ghosts of deer were thought to change into supernatural women. In some areas the lore concerning deer suggests that they were connected with the underworld but there are also signs that they were solar animals; a rock engraving in Scandinavia shows stags drawing the disc of the sun.

Fairies' Cattle

Folklore in Scotland and elsewhere refers so frequently to deer serving mankind in various ways that it has been suspected that red deer were domesticated at some time in the remote past. However, with the exception of the reindeer, there is little firm evidence of their having been tamed in ancient times. In Scotland they were said to be the fairies' cattle, and tales of benevolent deer go back to ancient times. Telephus, Hercules's son by the virgin priestess of Athens, was abandoned

in a forest, and was said to have been suckled by a doe. Stories of Christian saints and hermits similarly describe their receiving sustenance from these creatures. Hermits gave sanctuary to hunted deer, who aided them in various ways, by carrying baggage, or providing an antler book rest or antler candlesticks.

The antlers of deer have often been regarded as having special powers, often magical. Picks made from deer horn, and a chalk phallus, which were found at the end of a worked-out seam in a Neolithic flint mine at Grimes Graves in Norfolk may have been placed there in the hope that the mine could be made more productive. Practically every part of the deer has been believed to have medicinal qualities, in one part of Europe or another, while in China powdered antlers was thought to be an aphrodisiac. In some areas antlers are hung up on buildings to ward off evil influences.

Abbots Bromley Horn Dance above Blithfield Reservoir

Stork

Two species of stork, the white and the black, breed in Europe, but folklore is concerned mainly with the white species, which is more conspicuous and bolder. In many parts of Europe, and in North Africa, it has adapted itself to living in close proximity to man and chooses to nest on houses, church towers and, in some places, cartwheels that have been specially fixed on tall poles or heavily pruned tree trunks.

Although the white stork is practically voiceless, the clattering of its mandibles as it arches its neck over its back attracts attention. Ovid, Petronius, and Dante are among the writers who mention this characteristic. The regularity of the bird's appearance in spring was noted in ancient times. Jeremiah commented: 'Even the stork in the heavens knows her times' (Jeremiah 8.7); while the Roman writer Pliny remarked that the birds' comings and goings were mysterious.

Legends tell of storks being transformed into human beings, possibly because the large size and upright posture suggest an affinity with mankind. Typical versions occur in Germany, where it is also said that a wounded stork weeps human tears and there are modern Greek and Arab stories relating that in the distant lands to which the birds go in autumn they live as men. As early as the thirteenth century, Gervase of Tilbury mentioned people who at times became transformed into storks. There is an Eastern legend of a man who managed to turn himself into a stork, and who found the birds' conversation so amusing that he forgot the formula by which to regain human form.

Filial Duty

During the Middle Ages writers quoted Aristotle to the effect that the male stork kills his mate if she is unfaithful, and Chaucer referred to it as 'the avenger of adultery'. In the 3rd century AD Aelian embroidered on this belief in a story about a stork who blinded a human adulterer in gratitude to the husband who had allowed it to nest on his house. From classical times the stork has had a reputation for filial piety. The young were said to care for their parents in old age. The English poet Michael Drayton (1563–1631) referred to the 'careful stork . . . in filial duty as instructing man'. In a Russian folktale an old man pleads with a stork to be his son.

The fable that the stork brings babies seems to be a fairly recent one and is most detailed in Germany. Bavarians say that baby boys of good disposition ride on the bird's back while naughty boys are carried in its bill. In some localities, if a Christmas mummer dressed as a stork nudges a woman or girl it is said that she will soon be pregnant. In Holland and Germany children sing to the stork to bring them a little brother or sister.

An Allegory of Destiny, Georg Schöbel

A number of ancient ideas may have contributed to the development of the baby-bringing theme. Its association with water connects the stork with fertility, it was the messenger of Athene, who in some places was associated with childbirth, and its old Germanic name, Adebar, means 'luck bringer'.

The stork's bill is red and, in common with a number of other birds with red markings, it is associated with fire. A stork's nest on the house protects it from fire, although if its young are stolen it may set the building alight. Although it is generally regarded as a bringer of good fortune, there are localities where it is held to be an evil portent if a stork alights on a house. In other regions a wedding may be expected if this occurs.

A Welcome Guest

As an ambassador of spring the stork's arrival is greeted with a great variety of welcoming calls and songs. Predictions may be made from the birds' behaviour; for example, that when they arrive late in spring the season will be unfavourable. To see a white stork foretells a dry year, whereas a black one indicates that the coming months will be wet. An exceptional saying is that if storks circle over a group of people one of them will die shortly.

The kindliness with which the bird is generally viewed is probably due in part to the fact that certain types of storks kill small snakes. This is given as the reason why it was held in such great honour in ancient Thessaly that a man who killed a stork was treated as a murderer.

The stork has long been regarded as possessing valuable medicinal qualities. The bird's stomach was a remedy against murrain, an infectious disease in cattle. Its sinews were used to bind up a foot afflicted with gout, on the principle that a bird with legs so long and healthy must be capable of alleviating pain in human limbs. According

Illustration in Hans Andersen's fairy tales (1913), Constable, London, England

to Jewish folk traditions, its gall may be used to cure scorpion stings.

The stork appears in Aesop's Fables, where we are told that the wolf swallowed a bone which stuck in its throat. He roamed around howling with pain and offering a generous reward to anyone who would help him. At last the stork undertook the task. Poking his long bill into the wolf's throat he extracted the bone. When he asked for the promised reward the wolf laughed and said: 'You should count yourself lucky that I did not bite your head off when it was in my mouth.' The moral is that kindness is not always requited.

In another fable a farmer catches a stork in a net with cranes and geese.

The stork pleads that he only happened to be in the company of the other birds and was not stealing grain as they were, but the farmer tells him that as he was with thieves he must suffer the same punishment. In other words, be careful what company you keep.

Swallow

When man began to erect solid buildings the swallows found that the eaves provided sheltered niches for their nests. An ancient Egyptian papyrus refers to a lovesick girl hearing the swallows early in the morning inviting her into the countryside. Greek writers often mentioned the bird which, in common with other European peoples, they looked upon as a harbinger of spring. And it was a Greek writer, Aristotle, who first wrote: 'One swallow does not make a summer.' A black-figured Greek vase now in the Vatican depicts an elderly man, a youth and a boy greeting the first swallow to appear in spring. The youth shouts 'Look, there's a swallow!,' the man cries 'By Heracles, so there is.' The boy exclaims 'There she goes,' and then, 'Spring has come.' In the 2nd century AD boys went from house to house on Rhodes singing:

> *The swallow is here and a new*
> *   year he brings,*
> *As he lengthens the days with*
> *   the beats of his wings,*
> *White and black*
> *Are his belly and back.*
> *Pay his tribute once more*
> *With cheese in its basket,*
> *And pork from your store,*
> *And wine from its flasket,*
> *And eggs from your casket,*
> *   and bread when we ask it.*

A springtime swallow song is still sung in some areas of Greece. The Greeks had a low opinion of the swallow's song which they likened to a chattering in barbarous tongues. In spite of its joyous spring associations, the swallow became associated with wretchedness in the story of Philomela and Procne. In this myth, Tereus cut out the tongue of his wife Procne lest she should divulge that he had violated her sister Philomela. Whereupon the gods transformed all three into birds: Tereus was turned into a hoopoe, Procne into a nightingale, and Philomela into a swallow. Ever since, the swallow has only been able to utter incoherent twitterings.

Augurs claimed that they could interpret the bird's call, and inferences were drawn from its behaviour. The

Painting above the main entrance of 'televerket', the old telegraph house in Göteborg

fluttering of a swallow around the head of Alexander the Great was regarded as a portent of tragedy, but returning swallows were considered to predict the safe return of Dionysus. Greek and Latin writers mention that weather was forecast from the swallow's flight; and throughout Europe low-flying swallows are still regarded, with some justification, as an indication of bad weather.

Observations of swallows flying low over lakes and rivers may have inspired the Chinese to throw swallows into water when they prayed for rain. The associations between swallows, rain and springtime growth were responsible for offerings being made to the

genius of the house on the day when the swallows returned. According to one poem, heaven decreed that the swallow should give birth to the Shang Dynasty. Its egg was said to have caused the pregnancy of the ancestress of the Shang line.

The swallow has long been associated with gifts of healing. The white or red swallow stones which were believed to be secreted in the bellies of the nestlings had medicinal value. During the Middle Ages, this belief became elaborated into the notion that the swallow fetches a pebble from the seashore to restore the sight of its fledglings. Confusion apparently arose between the swallow stone legend and the ancient belief that the swallow brings to its nest a herb which cures the young swallows of their blindness. Parts of the bird were widely believed to cure various diseases: snake bite, epilepsy, rabies, and so on. Its droppings cured diphtheria and turned hair grey; and mud from its nest was a remedy for erysipelas (a fever accompanied by inflammation of the skin).

A Drop of Devil's Blood

In general the swallow has been viewed as a helpful, propitious bird, but as is often the case with other lucky birds, it has in some localities been regarded with suspicion. In regions of France and Hungary it was said that if a swallow flew under a cow's belly it would give bloody milk, and in Scotland it was reputed to have a drop of the Devil's blood in its veins. Yorkshire folk considered it a death omen when a swallow came down the chimney. If the first swallow seen by a girl in Czechoslovakia was alone she would be married within the year but if she caught sight of a pair she would remain unmarried.

It is widely believed that swallows should be kindly treated, and that ill luck befalls those who harm them. The Tyrolese say that if you destroy a swallow's nest your own house will be burned down. In France it was believed that if a man robbed a swallow's nest his horse would go lame. The Chinese revere the bird, and although they use most organisms as food or medicine, they do not molest the swallows nesting under the low eaves in city streets.

The helpful swallow plays a prominent part in Christian legends. The Swedes say that it hovered over the Cross crying 'Svala! Svala!', 'Cheer up! Cheer up!'. The Norwegian version is that it twittered 'Console him!'. In France it is said that the swallow picked off the Crown of Thorns ignoring the wounds made in her breast by

the spines. Ever since, the swallow has borne stains of blood on her breast. Similar stories are told of the robin and crossbill, both of which have red breasts. According to another French legend, magpies pricked Christ's feet and head with thorns while he was resting in a wood, but swallows came and extracted them. Because of this the magpie has been hated and forced to build its nest in tall trees, but the swallow breeds in safety in man's dwellings.

In English folk rhymes the swallow is included among sacred birds:

The robin and the wren
Are God Almighty's cock and hen;
The martin and the swallow
Are the two next birds that follow.

The disappearance of swallows in autumn and their reappearance in spring caused speculation and gave rise to one of the oldest ornithological fallacies, that they had hibernated in crevices or even under water. Aristotle mentions this belief which was substantiated by natural historians up to the nineteenth century.

Swan

Several characteristics account for the swan's importance in mythology and folklore: they are among the largest birds of the Northern Hemisphere and, except for the Australian black swan, all swans have conspicuous white plumage. Moreover, except for the mute swan, which makes a remarkable musical sound with its wings as it flies, the other species—the whooper, trumpeter, and bewick—utter loud vocal calls.

Aphrodite on a swan. Tondo from an Attic white-ground red-figured kylix. From tomb F43 in Kameiros (Rhodes)

Engravings and designs from the Old Stone Age onward of long-necked birds resembling the goose or swan indicate that such species had a magico-religious significance in various ancient cultures. The Middle Bronze Age Urnfield folk of Central Europe and other later cultures incorporated such long-necked birds in designs which included a sun disc, showing that these birds were associated with solar beliefs. As swans and geese fly high and also frequent water they became linked as well with ideas about growth and fertility. Swans appeared over northern tundra areas when the days were lengthening, the sun's path in the heavens was getting higher, and the snows were melting, and the flowers appearing. Thus swans are thought not only to accompany spring but to help usher it in. Even now, some of the inhabitants of the woodlands of northern Asia erect poles with wooden effigies of flying swans near sacrificial platforms; below they place carved wooden models of fish, symbolizing the powers of sky, earth, and water.

Since myths in which people are transformed into swans are ancient and widespread, they evidently hark back to primitive modes of thought in which the distinctions between gods, men, and animals were blurred. Aeschylus, the Greek playwright, mentions swan maidens; Aphrodite was represented in art riding on a swan or goose, and Ovid tells of Cycnus being turned into a swan by his father Apollo. Both Apollo and Venus rode in chariots drawn by swans. Zeus was said to have turned himself into a swan to couple with Leda. The sacred character of the swan is indicated by the belief held in areas as far apart as Siberia and Ireland that to kill a swan brings misfortune or death. In County Mayo the souls of virtuous maidens were said to dwell in swans.

Porcelain figurine of Leda with the swan-form of Zeus

For Love of a Swan Maiden

The most widespread swan transformation myth tells of a man who sees a flock of swans alight by the water, and watches them discard their feather garments, revealing themselves as beautiful maidens. He steals the robes of one of the swan maidens and lives happily with her until one day she finds the garments, puts them on and disappears. In an Irish account dating from the eighth century, Angus, the son of the Dagda, 'the good god', falls in love with the swan maiden Caer who appears to him in a dream. On visiting Loch Bel Dracon at the time of the great Celtic festival of Samain (1 November), he sees a flock of 150 swans, each pair linked with a silver chain, and among them his beloved Caer wearing a golden chain and coronet. When he calls to her she leaves the flock and he, too, takes swan form. Together they circle the loch three times and, chanting magical music which puts to sleep all who hear it for three days and nights, they fly to the royal palace. Among the Buriats of Siberia who regard the eagle as their paternal forbear and the swan as the mother of their race, a swan maiden tale is told which has close affinities with Irish stories. There are also Indian versions, and in Malaya and Siam the theme forms the basis of a dramatic performance. It appears to have inspired the Japanese Noh play, *The Robe of Feathers*.

Christian elements introduced into swan transformation stories are obviously later embellishments; this confirms that these stories date from pre-Christian times. In a Russian ballad, a swan maiden declares that she will not marry the hero until he has been baptized, and a version of the beautiful Irish tale of the Children of Lir relates that after centuries had elapsed during which Fionnuala and her brothers, transformed into swans, swam the Irish sea, they were restored to human form in a very weak condition, and were baptized just before they died.

The belief that the swan sings while dying has a long history. Although Pliny contradicted this tradition it has been transmitted down the ages, and has been endorsed by poets almost up to our own times. This story may also have originated in the North. Although dying swans do not sing, a flock of bewick swans in full cry produces a resonant, mysterious, melodious tumult which seems to pervade the whole landscape. Chaucer refers in *The Parliament of Fowles* to 'swan song'. Shakespeare wrote in *Othello* 'I will play the swan, and die in music', and in *The Merchant of Venice* 'He makes a swanlike end, fading in music'. Drayton in *Polyolbion* referred to 'swans who only sing in death' and Byron made the sad request:

> *Place me on Sunium's marbled steep,*
> *Where nothing but the waves and I*
> *May hear our mutual murmurs*
>   *sweep;*
> *There swanlike, let me sing and die.*

Yet another poet to make use of

this familiar theme was Alfred Lord Tennyson, in *The Dying Swan*. The notion that swans are linked together or wear chains is also ancient. In Shakespere's *As You Like It* Celia says:

> *And whereso'er we went, like*
>   *Juno's swans,*
> *Still we went coupled*
>   *and inseparable.*

In Greek art, swans are depicted harnessed; a French medieval legend refers to six brothers and sisters whose transformation into swans depends on the possession of golden chains, and in Grimm's tale *The Six Swans*, a golden chain is placed around the neck of the swan maiden. After Edward I

had knighted his son at Westminster, two swans with trappings of gold were brought into the palace. The stories of the Knight of the Swan both in France and in Germany also embody such traditions.

Tiger

Feared as a man-eater and shape-shifter, the tiger is often regarded as a sensitive creature which must be treated with formal respect. In Sumatra apologies are offered to a man-eating tiger, and its forgiveness asked, before it is killed. It is also deemed unlucky to walk along a tiger trail that has not been used for some time for fear of trespassing, to travel bare-

Goddess Durga, fighting Mahishasura, the buffalo demon (Hindu mythology)

The tiger at Dragon and Tiger Pagodas, Kaohsiung, Taiwan

headed, which is disrespectful, or to look behind you in case the tiger takes offence. Bengalis believe that should a man kill a tiger without divine permission he himself will be killed in return.

In Malaya tiger claws and whiskers are valued as charms against illness and evil and tigers are said to live in houses in their own village, where the roofs are thatched with human hair. Where tiger meat is consumed, as by the Miris of Assam, it is reputed to give men courage and strength. Women are discouraged from eating it for fear they will become too strong willed. Ground tiger bones, taken with wine, are a recipe for strength in Korea; in China the creature's gall bladder is regarded as most power-giving.

The Tiger is a creature of the Chinese zodiac. People born under the sign of the Tiger (1938, 1950, 1962, etc., in increments of twelve years) are charismatic and courageous deep thinkers who can also be indecisive, sensitive, and apt to show off.

Toad

The importance of the toad in world folklore seems to derive more from its basic characteristics than from any diffusion of notions about it from one area to another. Being associated with water, toads and frogs are involved in rainmaking and other fertility rites. Moreover, the fact that toads resemble grotesque, miniature human beings arouses the ambivalent feelings so often inspired by mysterious and possibly sinister creatures. Not only are the faces of toads reminiscent of a very wide-mouthed human face but their attitudes while swimming and copulating bear some resemblance to human postures and human movements.

The toad is rightly regarded as venomous. If irritated, toads exude a substance from glands on the skin, which carries two separate poisons sufficiently violent to cause dogs to foam at the mouth and become feverish. During the Middle Ages, bandits sometimes forced a toad into the mouth of one of their victims. Thus there are adequate grounds for regarding toads with repugnance.

Opposite page:
Tenjiku Tokubei riding a giant toad. Tenjiku Tokubei is the main character of the kabuki play. He is a magician and he evokes his magic by making a magic sign with his fingers.

天竺德兵衛

一勇斎国芳画

In England, particularly in East Anglia, the toad had an evil reputation. A toad might be a witch's familiar and she was said to make a magic lotion of toad spittle and the sap of the sow-thistle. With this concoction, she outlined a crooked cross on her body, and so could make herself invisible. In parts of central Europe, toads were believed to be witches and in many areas their evil repute was such that they were killed, but in Romania a toad killer was believed capable of murdering his mother and therefore they remained unmolested.

In Cambridgeshire certain men, called toadmen, were believed to have special power over horses, and to be able to make them stand still despite all efforts to get them to move. They could also render horses uncontrollable. Such a person might be regarded as in league with the Devil and viewed with some anxiety. A man wishing to acquire this power had to skin a toad, or peg it to an anthill until its bones were picked clean. He then carried the bones in his pocket until they were dry, and at midnight, when there was a full moon, he floated the bones on a stream. They would screech and one bone would set off upstream. If he secured this bone, he gained the powers of a toadman. Such men were said to be found in Cambridgeshire up to 1938. It is difficult to decide the extent to which this ritual was actually carried out or taken seriously.

Also in Cambridgeshire, toads were regarded as predicting storms. It was believed that they could hear distant thunder, inaudible to human ears, and could then be seen making their way to water. The origin of this belief may be that toads move from their winter quarters to their breeding place with remarkable unanimity within a period of a few days, and thunderstorms may occur around this time.

Toads, or parts of them, were considered efficacious as charms. A

Herefordshire man declared that he could steal as much as he liked, and would never be found out, because he wore a toad's heart around his neck. In Devonshire, toads were burned because they were believed to be in league with the Devil. Perhaps on the principle 'Set a thief to catch a thief, the toad was reputed to be able to drive away noxious things. In a book on gardening which appeared in 1593, Thomas Hyll recommended that before sowing seeds a toad should be drawn around the garden, then placed in an earthenware pot and buried in the centre of a flower bed. He advised that after the seeds had been sown the toad should be dug up, otherwise the vegetables growing round about would acquire a bitter taste. Having taken these precautions, the gardener could feel confident that no creeping thing would injure his crops. This appears to be a version of an ancient belief: the Greek writer Apuleius and the Roman writer Pliny advocated placing a toad in an earthenware pot in a field to avert storms, and two years after Hyll's book appeared another writer repeated this time worn recipe for protecting the fields.

There was said to be enmity between toads and spiders. Toads do indeed eat spiders, and possibly by an extension of this observed fact the creatures were credited with being able to repel evil.

Jewelled Head

A toadstone (in practice, any stone that resembled the toad or frog in shape or colour) was believed to have the power of curing bites and stings, when applied to the affected part. You could always tell whether such a stone was genuine by holding it in front of a toad; if the toad jumped forward to snatch it from you the stone was no counterfeit.

During the Middle Ages and later, it was believed that the toad

concealed a precious jewel in its head. In Shakespeare's *As You Like It*, the Duke remarks:

Sweet are the uses of adversity;
Which like the toad, ugly and
*   venomous,*
Wears yet a precious jewel in
*   his head.*

Earlier writers also refer to this belief. One, in 1569, commented: 'There is to be found in the heads of old and great toads a stone they call borax or stelon, which being used in a ring gives a forewarning against venom.' The fear of assassination by poison was very real among the upper classes in some countries during the medieval period and the Renaissance. Lyly, the Elizabethan playwright, wrote in Euphues: 'The fayrer the stone is in the toades head the more pestilent the poyson is in hir bowelles.' Thus association proceeded from the fact that the toad produces a poisonous secretion to the supposition that it carries within itself an antidote.

The belief in the toadstone's efficacy against poison dates from at least as far back as the twelfth century. But the poisonous characteristics of the toad were recognized much earlier. Pliny said that the creature was full of poison and Aelian (3rd century AD) added his own touch of exaggeration, remarking that people had been killed instantly by drinking wine to which the blood of a toad had been added. Milton, influenced by his classical learning, relates in *Paradise Lost* that Satan transformed himself into a toad in order to squat by Eve's ear and inject poison into her blood.

Probably because the toad and the fabulous basilisk were both reputed to be venomous, they were brought into association during the Middle Ages.

The basilisk was said to kill shrubs by touching them and smash stones by breathing on them. Writers of the twelfth and thirteenth centuries stated that it was born from an egg laid by a cock in old age and hatched by a serpent or toad.

In general, and especially in ecclesiastical circles, the toad was regarded during the medieval period as a revolting, Satanic creature. A story was told of a monk who, during Lent, caught a cock in order to cook and eat it. When he put in his hand to extract the entrails he pulled out a toad. Another tale relates that as an extremely avaricious moneylender lay dying he begged his wife to place a purse full of money in his tomb. This she did, as stealthily as possible, but the secret leaked out. Searching for the money, some people went to the grave and opened it. They saw there two toads, one in the opening of the purse and the other on the man's breast. 'One with its mouth was extracting coins from the purse, the other taking those that had been extracted and putting them into his heart. It was as if they said: "We will satisfy that insatiable heart with money."' Those who concocted such stories were not interested in natural history but in edification, so they associated a revolting creature with self-indulgence and greed. A sculpture at Strasbourg entitled *The Seducer of Unfaithful Virgins* depicts snakes and toads climbing up a handsome youth's back while he holds forth an apple.

The fact that one of the Zoroastrian sacred books states that toads are evil creatures and should be killed, shows that the dislike of toads is not confined to Christendom and confirms that their appearance and characteristics awaken a deep-seated and repugnance.

St. Zeno monastery church in Bad Reichenhall. Tomb of prior Wolfgang Lueger (1515) as *memento mori*. Detail shows toad nagging at the intestines

Such feelings may account for the toad being among the animals which in various parts of the world are treated as scapegoats. In Togoland the Hos enacted an elaborate ceremony annually to expel noxious things and influences from their midst. After they had besought evil spirits and witches to enter into bundles of creepers, which they carried out of town, they swept their houses and yards, and washed their faces with magical medicine. At night, a toad, tied to a palm leaf, was drawn through the streets. Among the shamanistic Gilyaks of Northern Asia the toad also figured as a scapegoat. After bears had been ritually sacrificed, the figure of a toad, made of birch bark, was placed peering in through a window while inside the house a dummy bear, dressed in Gilyak costume, occupied a bench of honour. The guilt of slaying the bear was laid upon the toad.

Turtle & Tortoise

It is the shelled back of the turtle and tortoise, into which these animals can retreat, that defines their role in mythology, and in many accounts the two are interchangeable. The turtle is a symbol of steadfastness and tranquility, which can also be evil, carrying unsuspecting people out to sea where they are condemned to drown; the tortoise is the essence of wisdom and self defence. The Iroquois and other native Americans believe that, since he was the only creature who could keep the planet stable, the Earth rests on the turtle's back. In Mohawk mythology earthquakes are a sign that this World Turtle is trembling or stretching beneath the great weight she carries. The turtle also features in the creation myths of Polynesia, in which humans are believed to be born from eggs laid by the World Turtle. In Tahiti the turtle is lord of the oceans.

In Hindu mythology the four elephants on which the world rests stand on shell of a turtle and the tortoise named Akupara carries both land and sea on his back. In order to give succour to the pious, and to destroy evil doers, the Hindu god Vishnu assumed ten different physical forms or avatars; the second of these was the giant tortoise Kurma. This incarnation was necessitated when the gods were in danger of losing their authority over the demons. In their distress they applied to Vishnu for help, who told them to churn the sea of milk so that they might procure the Amrita, or water of life, by which they would be made strong, promising to become himself the tortoise on which the churning stick should rest. In Hindu symbolism, described in the sacred Vedic text the Shatapatha Brahmana, the earth is the pastron or underside of the tortoise shell, the atmosphere its soft body and the heavens its hard carapace.

For the Chinese, the tortoise is sacred and symbolizes longevity, power, and tenacity. It is said that the tortoise helped the hairy giant Pangu create the world. According to the ancient Chinese Book of Rites the tortoise, along with the dragon, unicorn, and phoenix, is one of the four benevolent spiritual animals. Tortoise shells were used for divination and, as vehicles for the earliest writing, revered as the source of the Chinese script.

In Africa, the tortoise is said to be responsible for the hippo's habit of coming on land at night and is explained in the Nigerian folktale of the Isantim and his seven large, fat wives. Although Isantim regularly held feasts for the other animals none of them knew what the hippopotamus was called. While the hippo and his wives were bathing the tortoise overheard one of the wives calling his name. At the next feast he revealed his knowledge; the hippopotamus, shamed by the discovery, went down to the water and stayed there as long as the sun was up, forever needing darkness to hide his nightly activities.

Patriarch's Basilica, Aquileia. Mosaic (fourth century)

The slow but sure progress of the tortoise over the speedy but boastful hare makes it the winner in Aesop's fable of the Tortoise and the Hare whose moral is that slow and steady wins the race.

Whale

The ancestors of the whale were probably land mammals, whose structure became adapted to living in the sea. Because of its immense size and energy, the whale has attracted a wealth of superstition and folklore. In medieval times, for instance, it was regarded as an aggressive creature armed with huge tusks, a misconception that probably arose from a confusion between the whale and the walrus.

The whale is called 'Fastitocalon' in an Anglo-Saxon bestiary and is described as a deceptive floater on ocean streams, upon which men build a fire and sink to the hall of death; in other words, when the immense bulk of a whale was at rest on the ocean's surface it would occasionally be mistaken for an island by naive sailors who, in attempting to land upon it, would be suddenly plunged to a watery grave. A similar story is told about the kraken. Perhaps because ambergris was an ingredient in perfume the whale was said to have so sweet a breath that fish were lured into its wide-open jaws. As a result of this mistaken belief the creature became the symbol of deceitfulness. It also stood for unintelligent immensity, violent passion, and lust.

The whale was worshipped as Mama-cocha, or 'Mother Sea', among the Indians on the east coast of Central America. The Arabians believed that a fabulous whale, Bahamut, provided the base upon which the whole world rested, and that earthquakes were the result of its movements. (The beast referred to in Job 40:15–24, by the similar name of Behemoth, is now considered to have been the hippopotamus.) The whale that swallowed Jonah, and in whose belly the prophet spent three days and three nights, is one of the ten animals that have been allowed to enter paradise, according to Mohammedan legend.

In Christian thought the whale became an allegory of evil, the emblem of the Devil, the archetypal snare, baited with sweet aromas, which lured the unwary to eternal damnation. The whale's mouth has often been depicted as the gateway to the otherworld, while its belly has been said to symbolize the infernal regions.

Among some Indian tribes on the western coast of America, the whale was regarded as a totem animal, and was thought to have the power to sink enemy canoes. Whales' teeth and whalebone are both supposed to be extremely effective as amulets; in fact, the teeth have been used for that purpose since Neolithic times. Chieftains of Tonga, Soma, and Fiji wore necklaces of whales' teeth, shaped like curved claws, as signs of high rank. Pieces of whalebone were highly valued as charms since they were supposed to confer some of the physical powers of the whale upon the owners.

Ambergris, a grey waxy substance found in the intestines of the sperm whale, is supposed to be a powerful aphrodisiac. According to Boswell, the biographer of Dr. Johnson, it produces 'a greater activity in the intellectual faculties, a disposition to cheerfulness, and venereal desires'.

Primitive whale hunts were associated with a number of specially devised magic rituals which were thought to be necessary because of the dangers involved in hunting. Among the Eskimo, the hereditary role of

Stained glass study of Jonah and the whale, at Saint Aignan, Chartres, France

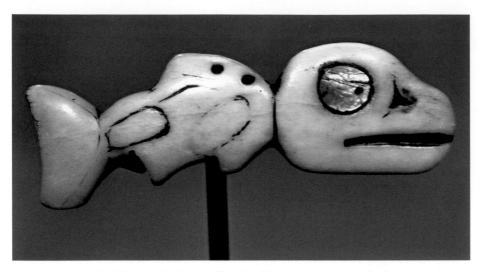

Amulet in form of a killer whale, Alaska, Tlingit culture, eighteenth or nineteenth century. Made from walrus tooth and haliotis mother of pearl

whaler verged on shamanism, and the whaler was skilled in the art of psychic mimicry and the imposition of taboos. Ritual purity was essential among Greenland hunters if the chase was to be successful, and anyone who wore soiled garments, or who had been in physical contact with a corpse, was excluded from the party. Chastity on the part of the tribal chief was obligatory in many communities. Siberian whale hunters sought to pacify the mother whale, whose offspring they proposed to kill, with prayers for forgiveness.

Among the Indians of the Bering Straits all work was suspended for four days after a whale had been slaughtered, in the belief that its ghost lingered in the vicinity of its body for this length of time. The Annamese, of what is now Vietnam, regarded even a dead whale washed up on the beach with considerable awe, and always buried the body with elaborate ceremonies which included burning incense and lighting firecrackers.

Shape shifting between the whale and other creatures of land and sea was not unknown. An Icelandic myth tells of a godless youth who was condemned to assume the shape of a whale as a punishment, and who was killed when he attempted to swim up a waterfall. North American Indians have legends of a terrible killer whale which approaches the shore and assumes the shape of a ravening wolf. In 887 AD a snow-white mermaid, 190 feet long, was reported and was said to be the metamorphosis of a white whale.

The whale represents one of the great cosmic forces of the universe. This symbolism is found in Herman Melville's *Moby Dick*, which tells how Captain Ahab pursues, and finally destroys, the great white whale. This has been interpreted as the eternal conflict between good (Ahab) and evil (the whale), as the war in heaven which led to the downfall of Lucifer. On the other hand, some have maintained that the white whale is the spirit of absolute goodness, while the proud Ahab is evil.

Wings

Perhaps because man's body, wingless and earthbound, has never normally been able to levitate, let alone fly, the ability to take off and soar freely away from terra firma, as demonstrated by birds, has aroused man's awe and longing. Ancient man peopled the mysterious upper and lower regions of his world with imagined creatures of unhampered mobility, often with winged appendages, whether for flight or not, as a symbol of extraterrestrial power.

In some ancient myths, the sky itself was depicted as a winged vulture, and the Egyptian sun god Re, when he was disenchanted with human beings, was advised to mount the Heavenly Cow, rise up and become the sky itself. The Mesopotamian god Anum created a winged bull, called the Bull of Heaven, and sent it to earth to redress a slight to his daughter Ishtar (the wings, however, did not prevent the bull from being slain).

In Greek myths Hermes, messenger of the god Zeus, wore winged sandals and a winged hat to make him invincibly swift and mobile. Eros, a beautiful winged youth, sped where he willed to shoot his victims with arrows of love. The Sphinx, a woman-fronted lion with an impressive wing spread, killed people who could not answer her riddles, epitomizing the evil use of supernatural flight.

The Fall of Icarus

Of several winged horses in ancient myth, Pegasus, steadfast and courageous, traveled the air faster than the wind, attained the heights of Olympus and drew the thunder chariots of Zeus across the heavens. Al Borak ('Lightning'), milk white and with the wings of an eagle, carried Mohammed to the seventh heaven.

Less appealing, the winged Harpies, which were partly women but had eagle's claws and beaks, swooped down viciously to seize man's food and depart, leaving a terrible stench. The griffin (or gryphon) had the head, wings, and feet of an eagle and the hind part of a lion. Only the female was winged; the male counterpart had protruding spikes instead. Aeschylus called griffins 'the hounds of Zeus, who never bark, with beaks like birds', and they were considered fierce guardians against theft. Nemesis, avenger of wrongdoing, was a winged woman carrying a

Ceiling detail from Saint-Pierre-le-Jeune, Strasbourgrus tooth and haliotis mother of pearl

sword or whip, who traveled the air in a griffin-drawn chariot. The hippogriff was a variant of the griffin, with the body of a horse, the forefront of a griffin, and an eagle's wings and claws.

The terrifying dragons that appear in many legends are a compound of many creatures, including serpent, lion, antelope, fish, and eagle. Although some alternately ran and flew, many seem to have been able to fly a considerable distance, and most were depicted with wings, signifying the ultimate in supernatural endowment. The wings of the Roc (or Rukh), according to Marco Polo, who had heard of it from many sources, had a span of 'thirty paces', and the wing feathers were 'twelve paces long'. It could rise

to great heights, swoop down on an elephant, bear it far up, then drop it and smash it, and, of course, descend to eat it.

A moral lay in the experience of Daedalus, architect of the labyrinth for the Minotaur in Crete. Daedalus did not have wings at all, but when King Minos imprisoned him and his son Icarus in the labyrinth, Daedalus fashioned some with wax and glue, and he and Icarus took to the one available escape route, the air. Icarus, however, intoxicated by his newfound freedom and power, did not heed his father's warning to fly a middle course between the sun and the sea. He flew too near the sun and his beautiful wings melted. He fell into the sea and drowned. His sorrowful father flew safely on to Sicily.

In later folklore (and theology), both angels and devils had the power of flight, and angels were generally

Peter Pan

The human child's longing for wings, or their equivalent for flight, is never more vividly portrayed or more happily fulfilled than in J. M. Barrie's *Peter Pan*. Peter, the boy who refused to grow up, knew how to fly. He taught the Darling children how to do it by simply believing they could, and then taking a huge jump from their beds into the air. Suddenly, as if wing-borne, they lifted up and followed him out of the window, gliding with speed and exhilarating ease to Never-Never Land'. That their escape from adulthood had sad repercussions did not linger in children's minds as much as the identification with Peter's magic ability.

illustrated with feathered wings, which they apparently did not need to flap to encompass distance; angels' thoughts and desires sped them without this effort.

By the seventeenth century, it was generally believed that angels ruled all spheres above the moon, and devils all below. The seraphim, highest order of angels, had no less than six wings. The main business of angels was the salvation of men's souls, and of devils the damnation of them. By purity of character, men might themselves become angels when they died, thus finally acquiring the supremacy of wings.

Fairies were considered nearer to devils than angels. Supposedly composed of condensed or congealed air, they took countless shapes, and were more often Earth-oriented than celestial, though some were said to have been descended from gods. How, when and why they first acquired wings is uncertain, though probably the form of angels was an influence.

Though fairies are frequently without them, their ability to become invisible in one place and visible in another, to steal in and out of shapes and sizes, has the same supernatural freedom of movement. In Shakespeare's *Midsummer Night's Dream*, Oberon has just arrived from India, and Puck takes but a few minutes to travel from England to Athens and back. Oberon summarizes the fairies' eerie form of flight when he says to Titania:

Then my queen in silence sad,
Trip we after the night's shade;
We the globe can compass soon,
Swifter than the wandering moon.

The art of flying, with or without wings, has been accomplished in one sense—man can and does fly in his dreams. In dreams man may have the pleasure of being conscious that he has risen out of his body's limited sphere. He may ascend only a short way,

looking down at his still reclining and inert body, or rise high into the sky and fly across an ocean. Techniques range from a rapid flapping with the elbows, a forward thrust and outspread of arms that now act as wings, to a controlled tilting and angling of the body to balance it in relation to the air. Flying dreams of any kind are primarily satisfying and delightful; whether man merely rises above his normal confinement, or right out of it, the added dimension of levitation and flight removes frustrating barriers to the supernatural.

Scientists are not sure how real wings were evolved, and it is now believed that they may not be appendages at all, but the extension of the chitin, the outer integument or body wall. In any case, the outstretched human arm is just similar enough to the wing structure of birds to tantalize man with the possibility of developing flight power. Man has spent untold amounts of time strengthening appropriate muscles and appending strange devices to his person, to no avail. In vicarious achievement of his desire, he has flown kites and balloons, invented metal wings and even rocket propulsion. He has become airborne, but still cannot elevate himself more than a few feet off the earth, and this for but a fleeing moment. Until he can do so, man will continue to be fascinated with the supernatural connotations of wings and flight.

Wolf

Few European mammals equal or surpass the wolf in the richness of its folklore, though in the British Isles wolf lore is much scantier than on the European Continent, where in some mountainous forested regions the animals are still to be found. By the mid-thirteenth century there can have been few wolves left in England but

not until the eighteenth were the last wolves killed in Ireland and Scotland.

Much European wolf lore is pervaded by a fearsome awe, less apparent in North American wolf traditions. But although fear of wolves is a natural human reaction, the friendly wolf appears fairly frequently in myths and legends, indicating that the animal awakens ambivalent responses. The Rig-Veda tells of Rijrasva, whom his father blinded because with misplaced generosity he gave 101 sheep to a bitch wolf: the wolf prayed for her benefactor, to the Asvins, benevolent deities, and they restored his sight. On the other hand, according to ancient Iranian doctrines the wolf was created by the evil spirit Ahriman. A similar belief is still current among the Voguls of Siberia.

The associations of Greek gods and goddesses with wolves hint at older traditions beneath the mythology of the anthropomorphic divinities. It was said that the priest of Zeus could take the form of a wolf. Hecate could also take wolf shape. Leto, the mother of Apollo and Artemis, appeared as a she-wolf and a wolf was emblazoned on the shield of Artemis, the huntress. Apollo was said to have expelled wolves from Athens and any citizen who killed one had to bury it by public subscription. Sophocles called Apollo 'the wolf slayer', yet a number of myths describe how his children by mortal girls were fostered by wolves. This motif of children tended by a she-wolf reappears in the story of Romulus and Remus and in later legends. Despite this myth of the kindly wolf the Romans associated the animal with Mars, the god of war.

Opposite page:
St. Francis of Assisi with a wolf

In Scandinavian mythology the Fenris wolf is one of the three children of Loki, the others being the Midgard serpent and Hel (Death). Fenris, whose jaws stretched from heaven to earth, created much trouble among the gods until they managed to bind him with a magic cord. However, as the representative of Fate he bides his time, until at the end of the world he swallows up the sun.

The wolf has innumerable associations with the Devil, especially in Germany. According to one saying the Devil squats between the beast's eyes, according to another he appears as a black wolf. A legend relates that the Devil made the wolf out of mixed constituents—his head from a stump of wood, his heart from stone, his breast from roots, and so forth. The Devil of the witches sometimes took wolf shape. The cross drives away all such diabolical lupine apparitions, and although great ferocity is attributed to the animal it is said to have been cowardly ever since Christ struck it with his staff.

Because wolves were seen on battlefields feeding on corpses, the animals were transformed by imagination into sinister supernatural creatures. They were thought of as corpse demons, connected with Odin and the fierce Norns or Fates. In Normandy horrible spirits disguised as wolves were said to haunt cemeteries in order to devour corpses. In Finland it was said that unbaptized children wandered around in the shape of wolves.

Little Red Riding Hood and the wolf

In Sheep's Clothing

Wolves have ancient associations with witchcraft. The Latin term of *opprobrium lupula* (little wolf) signifies 'witch'. Thessalian witches were said to howl like wolves and to use portions of the animals in their charms, as Shakespeare recalled when he included a wolf's tooth in the witches' brew in *Macbeth*. In Europe, gypsies would say on hearing a wolf howling, 'Take care, it may be a witch.' In Germany witches were said to ride wolves and in Lorraine the 'witch-master' turned into a wolf to go to the witches' sabbath. It was also thought that witches could transform themselves and other people into wolves. A priest who was turned into a wolf remained identifiable by his white collar. In the seventeenth century men and women were hanged for ravages believed to have been committed by them as wolves, although a century earlier Reginald Scot in his *Discoverie of Witchcraft* had ridiculed such ideas. The Navaho and other American Indians believe that a man disguised as a wolf goes around practising witchcraft.

The New Testament reference to false prophets as wolves dressed up in sheep's clothing (Matthew 7.15) embodies the belief that wolves are crafty as well as malicious, and the allusion served to perpetuate these ideas. In a beast fable the crafty wolf sings Psalm 23, the Shepherd Psalm.

On the principle that evil combats evil and what frightens a man also terrifies evil spirits, parts of wolves were used to scare such beings. A pierced wolfs tooth was sometimes worn as a protective charm, and a tooth placed under a pillow was thought to enable the dreamer to identify a robber. In Spain and Sicily a scrap of the animal's skin was believed to avert the Evil Eye, and in some localities was even thought to be effective in keeping flies out of the house. A wolfs hair placed in the rafters was a protection against fire and a wolf bite made a person immune to witchcraft. According to an ancient tradition if a man came upon a wolf and the wolf saw him first he would be struck dumb.

So prominent a place in the imagination of the people was occupied by the wolf that it entered into expressions describing the time of day and the weather. In France dusk is commonly described poetically as 'between the dog and the wolf'—the one being thought of as a creature of the day, the other as nocturnal. Elsewhere, when the wind whistles, 'the wolf sharpens his teeth', and a strong, destructive wind is 'the wolf. If the sun shines when it is raining, it is 'the wolves' wedding'. Around Dusseldorf, when the sky is filled with woolly clouds they say, 'today little sheep, tomorrow wolves'.

From the Babylonian epic of Gilgamesh to medieval tales of wolves invading monasteries and devouring heretical monks, the wolf has been represented as much more dangerous to man than it is. It was, and still is, a menace to domestic animals, but there are hardly any authenticated accounts of a wolf attacking an able-bodied man. It is possible that during times of famine in the Middle Ages wolves broke into flimsy dwellings and seized children or invalids, but stories of packs pursuing travelers on sledges in Russian forests do not deserve credence. They are the inventions of myth makers in comparatively recent times.

Woodpecker

Most woodpeckers assert their possession of a nesting territory not by song, but by a rattling noise or 'drumming' made by striking the bill rapidly on a branch—a distinctive drum roll quite different from the sound made by a woodpecker when pecking at a branch to extract an insect or make a hole for its nest. This drumming was of great significance to our ancestors who, living mainly outdoors and dependent for their well-being on propitious weather, paid much attention to birds which seemed to them to be not only weather wise but actually able to influence the weather, especially the amount of rainfall.

Listening to the woodpecker drumming in a tree high up toward the sky, they assumed that he was making miniature thunder, calling for and bringing down rain. Such a bird, in league with the higher powers, deserved respect and could teach men how to act when they needed rain for their crops. It is a widespread practice for people anx-

Opposite page:
A green woodpecker, *Picus viridis*, photographed in Carol Park, Bucharest, Romania

iously desiring rain to make imitation thunder by drumming, the underlying idea being that like would attract like. In Estonia, during times of drought, a man used to climb a tree in a sacred grove, carrying a small cask or kettle, and rattle a stick in it: he acted the part of a woodpecker making thunder.

It is still believed in the English countryside that the loud and frequent calling of the green woodpecker foretells rain, although observation shows that this has no foundation in fact. In Scandinavia, also, the woodpecker is considered a weather prophet. Frenchmen call the bird 'the miller's advocate', because in times of drought it is thought to plead insistently for water to turn the mill wheel.

The red crowns of European woodpeckers have also played a part in gaining them their status as thunderbirds and rain birds. Species with conspicuous red markings tend to be associated with fire, and so the woodpecker came to be connected not only with thunder but also with the lightning which accompanies it.

Perhaps the first hint in literature that the woodpecker was considered a rainmaker and thunderbird is its name in Babylonian, meaning 'the axe of Ishtar', for Ishtar was a fertility goddess. The earliest written evidence of the bird's exalted status is a reference by Aristophanes: 'Zeus won't in a hurry the scepter restore to the woodpecker tapping the oak.' There appears to have been a belief that the bird once occupied the throne of the High God and received reverence such as Zeus received in Aristophanes's time.

There is definite evidence that the woodpecker was consulted as an oracle, if not actually worshipped. An account survives of an oracle connected with Mars in the Apennine Mountains, where an image of a woodpecker was placed on a wooden pillar; engraved gems show a warrior consulting such an oracle. Mars was

originally associated with fertility as much as with war, which perhaps explains his association with the fertility-bringing woodpecker.

The First Ploughman

There is further evidence that the woodpecker is a bird of fertility. Greek myth relates that Celeus, whose name means 'green woodpecker', attempted to steal the honey which nourished Zeus while he was an infant. As a punishment the angry god turned Celeus into a green woodpecker. Celeus was the father of Triptolemus, the inventor of the plough—a king or chieftain instructed by Demeter, the Earth Mother, in the ritual which procured the fertility of the soil.

The significance of all this is obscure until we realize that the green woodpecker often feeds on the ground, picking up ants, and that its beak could be regarded as serving the same purpose as the primitive plough, which was not much more than a single prong drawn through the soil. The story says in effect that the green woodpecker was the first ploughman.

More recent legends confirm the woodpecker's connection with ploughing. According to a tale of the Letts, a people of the eastern Baltic, God and the Devil engaged in a ploughing match. God had a woodpecker to draw his plough, but the Devil had horses and quickly ploughed a whole field, while the woodpecker was making little progress. During the night God borrowed the horses and ploughed a field. The Devil was so impressed next day that he stupidly exchanged his horses for the woodpecker. When the bird lagged behind he angrily struck it on the head and this is why the woodpecker has a blood-coloured crown. In a veiled way this story tells of the suppression of ancient beliefs.

There are plenty of other indications of the association between the

woodpecker, rain, and fertility. In France, Germany, Austria, and Denmark it is given names equivalent to the English local name 'rain bird'. In Italy there is a saying, 'When the woodpecker pecks, expect rain or storm.' In France the story goes that at the Creation, when God had made the earth, he called on the birds to help by hollowing out places which could be filled with water and so become seas, lakes and ponds. Only the woodpecker refused to join in. A German version says that it was because she would not dirty her fine plumage. So the bird was condemned to peck wood and to drink nothing but rain. That is why she clings to the tree trunk with beak upward calling, 'Rain, Rain'.

It was at one time believed, or half believed, that the mysterious herb springwort, with which doors and locks could be opened, could be obtained by blocking the woodpecker's nesting hole. The bird would fetch the herb and apply it to the blocked entrance. If a strip of red cloth was placed below the nest, the bird, mistaking it for fire, would drop the sprig on it. Another plan was to watch where the woodpecker went to fetch the plant.

The legend seems to be an Eastern tale in Western dress. A version was current in Greece but the bird concerned was the hoopoe. It had its nest in a wall, but three times the owner plastered it up and three times the bird removed the plaster by applying the springwort. The tale as told in Germany is similar to a version quoted by Pliny.

It probably passed from Greek literature into Latin and is not, as might at first appear, the concoction of simple countryfolk. What may be an embellished and distorted version was current in a region of Germany. It was said that a princess incarcerated in the Markgrabenstein could be released by the man who went to the

A group of mummers in Ireland celebrate St. Stephen's Day or 'Wren's Day' on 26 December by processing from house to house with their instruments, and are rewarded with a glass of porter (c. 1955).

place at midnight on a Friday carrying a white woodpecker.

FURTHER READING: E. A. Armstrong. The Folklore of Birds. *(New York: Dover, 1970).*

Wren

Although it is nearly our smallest bird, inconspicuously coloured and unlikely to call attention to itself, except when it utters its relatively loud song, the wren is a familiar bird to most people because it is common, and besides inhabiting woods is to be seen in hedgerows and gardens. The folklore of the wren is of exceptional interest as it is the only bird associated with a fairly elaborate ritual in the British Isles, besides being represented in legends and oral traditions.

Wren ritual is performed throughout most of Ireland and to a limited extent in the Isle of Man. It seems to have disappeared in Wales, as it has in England, but scraps of evidence and local traditions indicate that it persisted until not very long ago, in one form or another, in many of the southern countries. It was never established in Ulster or Scotland.

The Wren Hunt and Procession as performed in Ireland may be briefly described. In those localities where an actual wren figures in the ceremonial it may be caught by beating the hedgerows or captured in its roost.

Troglodytes troglodytes (wren), Denmark

On St. Stephen's Day (26 December) a number of lyoung men form a party and visit the houses in neighbouring villages, carrying the corpse of the bird with them, or more often now a toy bird or some other object representing a wren. Girls occasionally take part, another indication that the custom has deteriorated. The 'Wren Boys' dress up for the occasion in odds and ends such as pyjama jackets and fantastic headgear. When they call at a cottage they sing a Wren Song in English or Irish, seeking a contribution from the householder. When the Wren Boys have finished their calls they hold a celebration, paid for by the collections made during the day.

French wren ceremonies were enacted in an area stretching from Marseilles northwestward up to Brittany. They were more elaborate than in Ireland, probably indicating that the cult was carried to the British Isles from France and lost some of its characteristics on the way. At Carcassonne, the Wren Boys of the Rue St. Jean assembled toward the end of the year and went into the countryside to beat the bushes and obtain a wren. The first lad to kill one was proclaimed King and to him fell the duty of carrying the bird back to town on a pole. The King proceeded through the streets on the last day of the year with all who had participated in the Hunt, accompanied by a drum and fife band and carrying torches. Here and there they would halt and a lad would chalk on a house 'Vive le Roi' and the number of the New Year. On Twelfth Day, the King arrayed himself in a blue robe and, wearing a crown and carrying a scepter, went to High Mass at the parish church; he was preceded by a man carrying the wren fastened to the top of a pole, which was decorated with a wreath of olive leaves, oak or mistletoe cut from an oak. After the service the King, together with his retinue, paid visits to the bishop, the mayor, the magistrates, and other notable citizens. Money was given to the participants, a banquet was held in the evening, and the celebrations concluded with a dance. Unfortunately this picturesque ceremony was suppressed in 1830. In some places in France and the Isle of Man the wren was solemnly buried in a churchyard.

The ceremonies are certainly very ancient and probably date from the Bronze Age. Unfortunately, documentary evidence earlier than the nineteenth century is practically nonexistent, so we have to piece together an interpretation from a variety of scattered clues. The geographical distribution of the ritual is significant. It would seem that the people amongst whom wren ceremonies were important reached southern France from elsewhere in the Mediterranean and carried elements of their culture northwestward, eventually reaching the British Isles. There are grounds for believing that these same folk may have been the builders of some of the megalithic monuments which are found in areas where the wren ritual was practiced.

Through the Keyhole of Hell

The date of the custom provides a valuable clue to its meaning. Midwinter was for our ancestors a crucial turning point of the year and many ceremonies performed at this time were intended to combat or chase away the powers of darkness and cooperate with the sun in restoring light, warmth and growth to the world. The wren frequents thickets and penetrates holes, crevices, and other dark places, as its scientific name *Troglodytes troglodytes*, 'dweller in caves', indicates. It was therefore a suitable representative of the powers opposed to or complementary to the sun.

This view is borne out by the well-known fable of the competition between the eagle and the wren to decide which could fly highest. The wren defeated the eagle—the bird of the sun—by trickery. In many languages the wren is called 'king', suggesting that long ago it was regarded as allied with mysterious powers; these may have been the dark potencies believed to reside in the Earth. An ancient Irish document refers to the wren as a bird with oracular powers.

As heat proceeds from the sun, it was natural that birds, being creatures of the sky, should be regarded as fire bringers. Such birds were commonly identified by the red badge of fire on their plumage. The robin was one of

these and in France the wren was also a fire bringer, perhaps because when it is in its full spring plumage some of its feathers have a ruddy tinge. It was said that when the wren fetched fire from heaven most of its plumage was scorched away. The other birds compassionately donated some of their feathers, but the robin came too close and its breast feathers were burned. Another French version relates that as the wren was flying to Earth with the fire its wings burst into flame; it passed the brand to the robin, whose breast feathers also became alight. The highflying lark then came to the rescue and brought the precious burden to mankind. The Bretons explain that

The robin redbreast and the wren Are God Almighty's cock and hen.

the wren fetched fire, not from heaven but from hell. Her plumage became scorched as she escaped the infernal regions through the keyhole.

So closely were the robin and wren associated in folklore that they were regarded as male and female of the same species—a notion which has lingered to the present time in some localities.

A Scots ballad refers to their marriage tiff over who ate the porridge:

The robin redbreast and the wran
Coost out about the parritch pan;
And ere the robin got a spune
The wran she had the parritch dune.

Although in many localities the wren was hunted and killed at the winter solstice, this does not imply that it was generally regarded as in any sense an evil creature. On the contrary, it was usual for birds and beasts held

in high respect to be sacrificed on some special occasion during the year. In France it was said that the crime of robbing a wren's nest would entail the destruction by fire of the culprit's house, or that his fingers would shrivel and drop off.

An indication of the affection in which the wren was held in France is provided by its appearance in legends connected with various saints. A delightful story records that St. Malo, finding that a wren had built a nest in his habit, which he had laid on a bush while working in the monastery vineyard, went without the garment until the bird had reared its young. St. Dol, noticing that the monks at his monastery were distracted during their devotions by the calls of the birds in the neighbouring woods, ordered the birds to depart. He made an exception of the wren, because its sparkling song cheered the brethren without interfering with their concentration on prayer and praise.

FURTHER READING: E. A. Armstrong. The Wren. (Collins, 1955).

Wryneck

The wryneck is a rather inconspicuous, slim, greyish-brown bird with mottled and streaked plumage, which lives in woodlands and is related to the woodpeckers. Both its common name and its specific scientific name, torquilla, refer to the way in which the bird twists and turns its neck when disturbed at the nest or handled.

Today the wryneck is more common in Europe and attracted the attention of the Greeks in classical times. Aristotle gives an excellent description of it in his Natural History. Among the Greeks it had importance in ritual as well as mythology. It seems that the

bird was spread out on a wheel with four spokes, which was then rotated as part of a magical procedure, probably as a love charm. In all probability this custom, in which the wryneck was associated with a revolving wheel, arose from observation of the peculiar manner in which it rotates its neck. Until recently the wheel had many magical associations, arising in large part from its movement seeming to resemble the curved path of the sun and moon across the sky.

As the rotating wheel had magical power, it was assumed that the bird which rotated its head and arrived from abroad when the sun was rising higher in the sky also had magical significance. Thus it became involved with a complex of ideas—fire and fertility, sun and moon, witchcraft and love, gods and goddesses. On a Greek vase Adonis is depicted holding out a wryneck to the goddess of love, Aphrodite. On another, Cupid, winged and nude, revolves a wheel in front of Adonis while a female figure holds out a wryneck.

When the bird was commoner in England country folk noticed that it returned in spring about the same time as the cuckoo or a little before it; hence it was called in Norfolk 'cuckoo's leader', in Gloucestershire 'cuckoo's footman' and in East Anglia 'cuckoo's mate'. Other names are derived from peculiarities in its behaviour—'turkey bird' because of the way it ruffles its neck feathers when disturbed, 'writhe neck' and 'snake bird' from its neck-twisting and 'tongue bird' because of its long tongue.

The wryneck has been part of cultural lore since the time of the ancient Greeks.

Glossary

Abhorrence Considering something as disgusting or vile.

Adroitness Showing skill and ability.

Amulet An ornament or piece of jewellery believed to have magical powers of protection.

Apocryphal Something reported to exist or be true, but is lost or cannot be proven.

Ascertain To find out definitely by inspecting a given matter.

Assailed To attack aggressively, physically or verbally.

Aurochs An extinct wild, large, oxlike animal that was the ancestor to modern-day cattle.

Auspicious Indicating success; promising good things to come.

Berserkers Norse or Germanic warriors of the past who battled in a wild, frenzied almost uncontrollable manner.

Catacombs Cemeteries under cities (Rome especially) made of lengthy tunnels with carved-out pockets in the walls designed to hold bodies.

Cuckoldry Making a fool of a spouse by being unfaithful to him or her, usually used when the wife is the culprit.

Decretals A letter or proclamation about canon law that comes directly from the pope.

Effigies A model or sculpture made in the likeness of a person or animal, which, oddly, is then either ridiculed and destroyed, or saved in a place to be revered.

Emissaries People who are sent by a leader or government and speak on their behalf.

Expiate To atone or make amends for wrong-doing or a crime.

Fallacies Invalid or mistaken information that can be disproved by fact and logic.

Harbinger A creature or person that signals an arrival or upcoming event.

Hermitage A secluded place or sanctuary for someone seeking solitude.

Heterogeneous Composed of assorted, different, varied parts.

Indiscriminate Done randomly, without any logical pattern or reason.

Lechery Unrestrained and inappropriate sexual desire and behaviour.

Metamorphosed To have totally changed from one being or state into another.

Necropolis An elaborate, usually ancient, burial ground; city of the dead.

Omnivorous Having a diet made up of both vegetables and animals.

Oracular Prophetic, foretelling by communication with spirits.

Portents A sign or omen that something—usually bad—is going to happen.

Propitiate To appease or reconcile with an offended spirit, god, or person.

Provenance The origin, derivation, and history of something.

Reiterative Done or said repeatedly, again and again.

Repudiation Denial of a person, facts, or action; no longer considered valid.

Sarcophagi A stone coffin decorated with inscription, carvings, or sculptures, used in ancient Egypt, Rome, and Greece.

Sentinels Those who protectively watch over and stand guard.

Shaman An individual, especially in tribal cultures, who connects with spirits and the supernatural in order to heal people or influence events.

Tutelary Serving as a protector, guardian, or patron of a person or place.

Utterance A spoken phrase, word, or sound from a living creature.

Venerated Honoured to the point of being worshipped.

Vernacular Terms that are commonly used and understood by most people.

Vestiges Traces of something that is passing away or completely gonet.

Index

138, 148

see also spontaneous generation

Crete 9, 12, 27, 29, 32–33, 39, 42–43, 102, 120

cricket 8, 72, 85

crocodile 10, 43, 43, 82

crossbill 27

crow 27, 43–47, 44, 46, 57

cuckoldry 49

cuckoo 27, 47–49, 47, 48

Czechoslovakia 44, 131

D

dance(S) 9, 12, 20, 27, 29, 42–43, 62, 77, 88, 117, 122, 127, 127

death associations 19, 27, 28, 34, 36, 43–44, 45, 52, 54–55, 72, 80, 82, 83, 85, 88, 91, 95, 98, 106, 108, 131

death-watch beetle 83

deer 9

see also stag

deer women 127

deities, animal 10, 12, 19, 21, 31–32, 49–50, 64, 70, 71, 76, 91, 116, 117, 118, 125

deluge myths 26, 44, 64, 67

Denmark 71, 148

Devil *see* Satanic associations

devil's coach-horse beetle 82

divination *see* augury

dog 7, 9, 14, 15, 49–52, 51, 52, 81

dolphin 52–53, 53

domestication 6, 29–30, 31, 49, 53–54, 117–118, 127

donkey 14, 18

dove 12, 13, 14, 14, 25, 53–55, 94

dragon 141

dragonfly 85–86, 86

dung-beetle 82, 83

E

eagle 7, 8, 13, 14, 23, 25, 27, 55–58,

55, 56, 57, 62, 151

eagle stone 57

Easter eggs 59–60, 59, 74

Eden story 11, 11, 13, 114

eggs 8, 22, 58–60, 74, 97, 99

egret 41

Egypt 10–11, 22, 29, 31, 32, 34, 39, 43, 49–50, 55, 58, 60, 64, 66–67, 67, 70, 72, 82, 86, 88, 91, 95, 97, 101, 102, 106, 114, 118, 120, 140

elephant 11, 13, 60, 61, 82

England 14, 19, 20, 27, 35, 47, 48, 54, 55, 56, 59, 60, 66, 77–78, 80, 81, 82, 83, 86, 87, 91, 94, 96, 99, 101, 103, 105, 108, 109, 121, 124, 125, 131, 136, 138, 148, 152

Estonia 21, 49, 148

Ethiopia 82, 85, 88

Evil Eye, defence against 59, 60, 77, 99, 146

see also amulets; charms

evil, tokens of 9, 19, 29, 103–104, 114, 115, 117, 122, 124, 136, 137–138, 146

F

fairies 34, 77, 91, 127, 142

falcon 10, 60

familiars (spirits in animal shape) 9, 18, 35, 36, 65, 77, 124, 136

feathers 26, 34, 57, 58, 60–63, 99, 101

fertility 11, 28, 29, 30, 31, 32–33, 39, 42, 54, 55, 58, 69, 71, 74, 77, 91, 106, 122, 127, 129, 132, 148

see also sexuality

fiddle fish 66

Fiji 11, 139

Finland 21, 145

fire-bringers 41, 91, 107, 148, 151

fire-fly 86

fish 12, 13, 15, 63–66, 63

flamingo 41

flea 86

fly 87, 124

fox 17, 43, 86

France 21, 22, 35, 47, 58, 65, 69, 74, 82, 93, 94, 107, 116, 125, 131, 133, 145, 146, 148, 150, 151

Francis of Assisi, St 96, 107, 143

frog 66–68, 67, 73

G

Garuda 23, 23, 43, 56

Germany 19, 26, 28, 38, 46, 47, 58, 71, 74, 80, 82, 91, 93, 94, 95, 99, 107, 108, 121, 128, 133, 145, 146, 148

ghost lore 20, 74, 77–78, 105, 127

glow-worm 86, 87

goat 12, 13, 68–71, 68, 69

Golden Fleece 118

goldfinch 15

good and bad luck 6, 9, 27, 36, 38, 47, 48, 52, 53, 58, 60, 64, 65, 66, 68, 78, 80, 83, 86, 93, 94, 96, 98, 99, 104–105, 108, 121, 129, 131

see also amulets; charms; Evil Eye, defence against

goose 13, 17, 18, 25, 27, 28, 41, 62, 70, 71–72

grasshopper 72, 85

great northern diver 47

Greece/Greek mythology 11, 21, 25, 28, 29, 37, 41, 44, 52, 54, 56, 58, 59, 60, 74, 76, 82, 83, 85, 87, 95, 96, 98, 99, 101, 102, 106, 114, 115, 120, 126, 130, 132, 140, 142, 148, 151–152

see also Crete

Greenland 66, 112, 140

griffin 140–141

Author List

Contributors to *Man, Myth, and Magic: Animals and Animal Symbols in World Culture*

Rev. E. A. Armstrong is an authority on the folklore of birds and animals. Formerly Vicar of St. Mark's Cambridge; Armstrong is the author of *The Folklore of Birds; The Wren; Bird Display and Behaviour*, and others.

Jack Conrad is a Professor of Anthropology, Southwestern University, Memphis; author of *The Horn and the Sword; Museum of Man*, and others.

Nona Coxhead is an editor and the author of *The Relevance of Bliss: a Contemporary Exploration of Mystic Experience.*

Charles De Hoghton a former Political and Economic Planning researcher; co-author of *And Now the Future.*

Douglas Hill is the author of *Magic and Superstition; Return From the Dead; The Supernatural* (with Pat Williams); *The Opening of the Canadian West; Regency London*, and others.

Eric Maple is the author of *The Dark World of Witches; The Realm of Ghosts; The Domain of Devils; Magic, Medicine and Quackery; Superstition and the Superstitious.*

John Montgomery is a journalist and the author of numerous books, including *Your Dog, The Twenties, The Fifties*, and more.

Venetia Newall is a folklorist, traveler and lecturer; hon. secretary of the Folk-Lore Society; author of *An Egg at Easter.*

Eric J. Sharpe is a Senior Lecturer in Religious Studies, Lancaster and the author of *Not to Destroy but to Fulfill*, and more.

Bryan Wilson was a Professor of Semitic Languages, was a fellow of All Souls and Reader in Sociology at Oxford; as well as author of *Sects and Society; Religion in Secular Society*, and more.